50 Years of the
Chinese Community
in Singapore

World Scientific Series on Singapore's 50 Years of Nation-Building

---

Published

50 Years of Social Issues in Singapore
  edited by David Chan

Our Lives to Live: Putting a Woman's Face to Change in Singapore
  edited by Kanwaljit Soin and Margaret Thomas

50 Years of Singapore–Europe Relations: Celebrating Singapore's Connections
  with Europe
  edited by Yeo Lay Hwee and Barnard Turner

50 Years of Singapore and the United Nations
  edited by Tommy Koh, Li Lin Chang and Joanna Koh

50 Years of Environment: Singapore's Journey Towards Environmental Sustainability
  edited by Tan Yong Soon

50 Years of the Chinese Community in Singapore
  edited by Pang Cheng Lian

For more information about this series, go to http://www.worldscientific.com/page/sg50

World Scientific Series on
Singapore's 50 Years of Nation-Building

50 Years of the Chinese Community in Singapore

Editor

Pang Cheng Lian

World Scientific

NEW JERSEY · LONDON · SINGAPORE · BEIJING · SHANGHAI · HONG KONG · TAIPEI · CHENNAI · TOKYO

Published by

World Scientific Publishing Co. Pte. Ltd.

5 Toh Tuck Link, Singapore 596224

USA office: 27 Warren Street, Suite 401-402, Hackensack, NJ 07601

UK office: 57 Shelton Street, Covent Garden, London WC2H 9HE

Library of Congress Cataloging-in-Publication Data
50 years of the Chinese community in Singapore / edited by Pang Cheng Lian.
    pages cm. -- (World Scientific series on Singapore's 50 years of nation-building)
   ISBN 978-9814675406 -- ISBN 978-9814678780
   1. Chinese--Singapore. I. Pang, Cheng Lian, editor. II. Title: Fifty years of the Chinese community
in Singapore.
   DS610.25.C5A14 2016
   959.57'004951009045--dc23
                                                                        2015030123

British Library Cataloguing-in-Publication Data
A catalogue record for this book is available from the British Library.

In-house Editor: Dong Lixi

Typeset by Stallion Press
Email: enquiries@stallionpress.com

世界華商大會
WORLD CHINESE ENTREPRENEURS CONVENTION

In 1991 the Singapore Chinese Chamber of Commerce & Industry (SCCCI) organised a ground-breaking World Chinese Entrepreneurs Convention (WCEC) which attracted more than 800 Chinese businessmen from 30 countries and regions. Then Senior Minister Lee Kuan Yew was the guest of honour (seated in centre). Since then the WCEC has been organised biennially in various parts of the world. (By courtesy of SCCCI.)

To honour those entrepreneurs who have contributed to Singapore's growth during the past five decades, the SCCCI presented SG50 Outstanding Chinese Business Pioneers awards in February 2015. The 28 recipients received their awards from President Tony Tan at a gala dinner. (By courtesy of SCCCI.)

In December 1984 Minister Ong Teng Cheong gave the keynote address at a forum to discuss the future of clan organisations. Organised by nine clan associations, the forum led to the establishment of the Singapore Federation of Chinese Clan Associations (SFCCA) a year later. (By courtesy of SFCCA.)

SFCCA's 25th anniversary held in 2010 had Minister Mentor Lee Kuan Yew as guest of honour. He joined the SFCCA Council members to cut the birthday cake. That year the Federation saw a leadership change. Chua Thian Poh (on the right side of MM) succeeded Wee Cho Yaw (on the left side of MM) as President. (By courtesy of SFCCA.)

Led by then PM Goh Chok Thong, several ministers took to the stage to sing to raise funds for Chinese Development Assistance Council (CDAC) at its inaugural dinner on 20 September 1992. Standing to the right of PM Goh is Wee Cho Yaw, Chairman of the Fundraising Task Force. To the PM's left are Ministers Wong Kan Seng and Lee Yock Suan. (By courtesy of CDAC.)

In 2012 CDAC celebrated its 20th anniversary with its patron PM Lee Hsien Loong as guest of honour. On his right is Minister Lim Swee Say, Chairman of the Board of Directors; to his left is Wee Cho Yaw, Chairman of the Board of Trustees. The children are some of CDAC's beneficiaries (By courtesy of CDAC.)

This Chinese-styled structure was the Administration Building of the old Nanyang University (Nantah). It now houses the Chinese Heritage Centre (CHC) in the Nanyang Technological University. (By courtesy of CHC.)

The CHC was officially inaugurated by then Minister for Information and the Arts George Yeo in 1995. To the right of the Minister is the Chairman of CHC, Wee Cho Yaw, and on the Minister's left is celebrated calligrapher Pan Shou, who wrote the Chinese name of CHC (*Hua Yi Guan*) in the background. (By courtesy of CHC.)

The Chinese community has been a staunch supporter of educational causes. This picture shows the signing ceremony of Ngee Ann Kongsi's $15 million gift to the National University of Singapore's University Town Fund in 2010. The donation was to provide bursaries and scholarships as well as visiting professorships. Standing from left to right are Teo Chiang Long and Lim Kee Ming of Ngee Ann Kongsi and Professor Tan Chorh Chuan and Dr Tan Eng Chye of NUS. (By courtesy of NUS.)

Founded in 1895, Ee Hoe Hean started as a social club for rich Chinese businessmen. The Bukit Pasoh Road premises was reconstructed but retained its original façade. Re-opened in 2007, the building houses a "Pioneers' Memorial Hall" on its ground floor. (By courtesy of Ee Hoe Hean.)

Lau Pa Sat Kopi Yew celebrating the Chinese New Year on 25 January 2004. The man with tie facing the camera is Lok Chwee Hin, founder of the group. (By courtesy of Lok Chwee Hin)

In 1979 Singapore's Founding PM Lee Kuan Yew launched the Speak Mandarin campaign to get the Chinese community to use more Mandarin and less dialects. Today the campaign is aimed at reminding English speaking members of the Chinese community of the usefulness and beauty of Mandarin. (Ministry of Information and the Arts Collection, by courtesy of National Archives of Singapore).

A group of new immigrants visiting a celebration of the Hungry Ghosts festival (*Zhong Yuan Jie*). As part of its integration efforts, the SFCCA organises familiarisation tours to help new immigrants understand local customs and practices. (By courtesy of SFCCA.)

A group of Buddhist monks and devotees genuflecting at one of Singapore's leading monasteries, Kong Meng San Phor Kark See (KMSPKS), on Vesak Day in 2009. Buddhists make up 43% of the Chinese community. (By courtesy of KMSPKS.)

The 85-member strong Singapore Chinese Orchestra (SCO) performing under the baton of its Music Director, Yeh Tsung in 2002. Formed in 1992, the professional SCO was restructured as a company limited by guarantee in 1996. (By courtesy of SCO.)

Reflecting the strong friendship between the two countries, Chinese Vice President Xi Jinping made an official visit to Singapore in 2010, to mark the 20th anniversary of diplomatic ties. He is seen here addressing guests at a luncheon hosted by the SCCCI. (By courtesy of SCCCI.)

Preface

PHUA Kok Khoo

Chairman
World Scientific Publishing Company

The year 2015 marks the 50th year of Singapore's nationhood. Amidst the joyful celebration of this golden jubilee, is a wave of reflection and introspection. Fifty years may well be a mere drop in the river of history, but for a young republic like ours, it marks the entirety of our existence as a nation.

As the adage goes, one needs to understand the past to appreciate the present and to prepare for the future. It is indeed an opportune time for us to reflect on the experiences and the process by which our nation has managed to transform itself from a third world country to a first world economy within five short decades. To plan for the future it is essential for us to achieve a conclusive understanding about our own history.

With this in mind, World Scientific Publishing proudly presents a book series on Singapore's 50 years of nation-building to celebrate this jubilee year. This series covers all areas that are vital to an understanding of Singapore's development. It leads readers on a journey through the changes that Singapore has experienced in the half century of its existence. The series covers issues related to urban development, science, education, environmental protection and diplomatic relations, amongst others. The authors and editors of the series are all outstanding members of society who have made significant contributions to Singapore.

50 Years of the Chinese Community in Singapore is a part of this series. Also in the pipeline are books that focus on the growth and development of the Malay, Indian, and Eurasian communities during the five decades of nation–building. As a harmonious society that is multiracial and multicultural, Singapore has seen the fruits of economic success and prosperity that arise from the contributions of its Chinese, Malay, Indian, Eurasian and other communities.

This book records the contributions of diverse groups such as the Singapore Chinese Chamber of Commerce & Industry, the Singapore Federation of Chinese Clan Associations and the Chinese Development Assistance Council, as well as new immigrants' organisations. It also focuses on Chinese visual and performing arts, and Chinese religious traditions. These essays provide a basic understanding and insight of the roles played by the Chinese community in the first 50 years of nation–building.

Finally, I would like to thank Ms Pang Cheng Lian for her efforts in roping in the distinguished contributors to share their knowledge and passions in this celebratory book. Without her hard work, this book would not have been possible. I also thank the writers and all others who have contributed to this salute to Singapore's Chinese community.

Foreword 1

Thomas CHUA

President
Singapore Chinese Chamber of Commerce & Industry

"The history of the Singapore Chinese Chamber of Commerce is a reflection of the history of Singapore", so said our Founding Prime Minister Lee Kuan Yew in his congratulatory message to the SCCCI at its 60th anniversary in 1966.

This simple statement underscored the importance of the Chamber during a momentous period, as Singapore crossed the threshold of its first anniversary as an independent republic. The SCCCI is not only a business organisation that is intrinsically linked to Singapore's economy. It is also a private sector institution that personifies the entrepreneurial spirit of the Chinese community in contributing to Singapore's development. After Singapore achieved nationhood, the Chamber concentrated on building up a formidable business network to promote economic development, trade and investment, and expand Singapore's links with other countries.

In the past 50 years, the Chamber has pushed forward with initiatives to support Singapore's transformation into an industrial and global nation, by organising several prominent trade and industry fairs, and bringing members to explore overseas markets in Western and Eastern Europe, Australia, Africa, as well as many countries within Asia. Even before Singapore established diplomatic relations with China, Chamber presidents led numerous business missions to various provinces and cities in China.

Encouraged and supported by Founding Prime Minister Lee Kuan Yew, the Chamber organised the World Chinese Entrepreneurs Convention (WCEC) in 1991, a monumental effort which gathered ethnic Chinese entrepreneurs and business leaders around the world to discuss economic, social and cultural issues of mutual interest. Since then, the WCEC has gained international acclaim and become an established biennial convention.

While the Chamber still assumes a significant role in the social, educational and cultural milieu, its overriding mission is to serve the business community. On the domestic front, the Chamber continues to play a pivotal role in championing the interests of local Chinese enterprises, particularly the SMEs, helping them to adapt to the fast-changing business environment and the restructuring of the Singapore economy.

We are delighted that the Chamber's achievements and contributions have been included in this celebratory book on Singapore's Chinese community. We take pride that the SCCCI with its network of 4,000 corporate members and more than 150 trade association members covering 40,000 enterprises, has made its mark in the history of Singapore.

Moving forward, the Chamber will continue to complement our nation's economic development and progress with the times. We firmly believe that Singapore's future is the future of the SCCCI!

Foreword 2

CHUA Thian Poh

President
Singapore Federation of Chinese Clan Associations

In the past 50 years the Chinese community in Singapore has journeyed with the nation through some of its most tumultuous years, overcoming daunting difficulties and achieving phenomenal successes in the process.

Singapore has developed from an impoverished island to a modern first-world metropolis since gaining independence in 1965. This was achieved through the hard work and steadfast resolve of our pioneer generation. The Chinese community, together with the other communities, worked hand-in-hand towards the common goal of nation–building.

Clan associations and other social organisations played an instrumental role in alleviating critical gaps in healthcare, education and other welfare issues. This was especially so during the pre-independence days. After the nation gained independence, citizens were better taken care of by other civil and social groups spearheaded by the government. As a result, the original role of clan associations in catering to the social needs of the communities gradually diminished.

By the 1980s, as Singapore became increasingly Westernised and globalised, the fear that clan associations were becoming obsolete was very real. There was, therefore, the need to rethink, reposition and re-strategise, so that these associations remained relevant in society. A conference themed "More Active Roles for Clan Associations in the New Era" was held with representatives from 185 clan associations. This led to the inception of the Singapore Federation of Chinese Clan Associations (SFCCA) at the end of 1985 and the transformation of clan associations to meet new challenges.

As SFCCA celebrates its 30th anniversary this year, it continues to play a paramount role in preserving and promoting Chinese culture and, in the process, uniting the Chinese community in Singapore. In more recent times, SFCCA has been playing a leading role in promoting national integration, by welcoming new immigrant associations as associate members, and individuals as individual and council members.

In 2012, recognising that the soul of a community cannot be isolated from its culture, SFCCA advocated the establishment of the Singapore Chinese Cultural Centre (SCCC), an idea which garnered the support of the Government. When completed in 2016, the SCCC will be an excellent venue for local and overseas talents to showcase both traditional and modern arts, music, and literature. It is also intended as a platform to synergise and hopefully spark exciting new developments in the Chinese cultural landscape.

As Singapore celebrates SG50 this year, the publication of this book to document the Chinese community's contributions towards nation–building is indeed timely and of great significance. This book records the resilience, the gumption and the confidence exemplified by our forefathers as they toiled to build the nation we are proud of today. The book not only encapsulates the development of the Chinese community in Singapore, it is also a tribute to our pioneers who have dedicated their lives to the nation. The extraordinary vision and wisdom of our pioneers have laid an excellent foundation for a united, progressive and inclusive Singapore.

It is my hope that the values of loyalty, courage, commitment and conviction of the Chinese community towards our nation will continue to serve as an impetus and motivation for our future generations, and that the unique *Nanyang* culture and Singapore spirit will thrive for generations to come.

Introduction

PANG Cheng Lian

Singapore's success story is essentially a "people" story. Against all odds and amidst dire predictions, Singaporeans proved that a united and resourceful community could build a nation from scratch. This book is dedicated to one segment of these Singaporeans — the Chinese community. In particular, this collection of essays will focus on the Chinese-speaking members of the community whose many contributions are less familiar to those who have been brought up on a strict diet of the English language.

Singaporeans have good reason to celebrate the nation's golden jubilee with pride. In the short time of five decades the Republic has moved from Third World to First. Since 1965 its real GDP has risen by 40 times. It is universally acknowledged that this phenomenal success is attributable to Founding Prime Minister Mr Lee Kuan Yew and his pioneer team who had the vision and the determination to turn Separation into a blessing. No less important is the fact that its motley citizenry of 1.879 million, of whom many were first generation Singaporeans, rallied behind these leaders to meet the challenges faced by the new nation.

Five years later the population had swelled to 2.074 million. The first Census conducted by the new Republic in 1970 reported that out of this number 76.2% (1.579 million) was Chinese, 15% was Malay, 7% was Indian, 0.9% was European and 0.5% was Eurasian. The Census that year did not show languages spoken at home, which was captured in subsequent censuses. However, it did indicate literacy rate among the various races. It was reported that among Singaporeans of 10 years and above, the literacy rate for the Chinese-speaking segment was 58.9% while for the English language it was 39.9%. Though English was the official language of the administration, a legacy of the British rule, Chinese (dialects and Mandarin) was the dominant language in 1970.

In terms of language usage the young Republic was very much a Chinese country. One could survive, and even prosper, without knowing the English language, but one would be socially handicapped without knowledge of a smattering of Hokkien and other Chinese dialects, as well as Mandarin. Indeed, in those early years dialects were essential to win hearts and votes during general elections.

So we had this remarkable situation where the overwhelming majority of the governed was more at home in the Chinese language, but the ruling elite was largely from the English language stream. Of the 10 members of Singapore's first cabinet, only two (Ong Pang Boon and Jek Yuen Thong) came from the Chinese education stream. Three members were non-Chinese, Othman Wok (Malay), S Rajaratnam (Sri Lankan) and Eddie Barker (Eurasian). The remaining five — Lee Kuan Yew, Dr Toh Chin Chye, Dr Goh Keng Swee, Lim Kim San and Yong Nyuk Lin had studied in English schools.

In his book, *From Third World to First, The Singapore Story (1965–2000)*, Lee Kuan Yew made this observation of the Chinese- and English-educated Singaporeans. He wrote,

> When I acted as legal adviser for the Chinese middle school student leaders in the 1950s I was impressed by their vitality, dynamism, discipline and their social and political commitment. By contrast I was dismayed at the apathy, self-centredness and lack of self-confidence of the English educated students.

And it was the vigour and dynamism of the Chinese-speaking community that propelled the People's Action Party into successive electoral victories and transformed Singapore from an entrepot port to an export-oriented industrial nation in the post-Separation years.

Since then, Singapore's *lingua franca* has changed. According to the 2010 Census Report Singapore had a resident population (meaning citizens and permanent residents) of 3.8 million. Of this, 2.8 million (74.1%) are Chinese.

Hokkiens still formed the dominant group with 1.1 million, with the Teochews coming in a far second with 562,000. Cantonese were the next largest dialect group with 409,000, followed by the Hakkas with 233,000, the Hainanese with 178,000, the Foochow with 54,200 and Shanghainese with

22,053. The rest comprised the Hockchia and Henghua people of Fujian province.

Although the proportion of Singapore Chinese using dialects at home has been declining over the years, the usage of Mandarin at home rose from 45.1% to 47.7% between 2000 and 2010, attesting to the success of the Speak Mandarin Campaign launched in 1979. Dialects used at home, on the other hand, dropped from 30.7% in 2000 to 19.2% in 2010. This decline was offset by an 8.7% increase in the use of English at home. Usage rose from 23.9% to 32.6% during the decade. As English has become the *lingua franca* of the international community, it is unlikely that the ascendancy of this language will be reversed in Singapore.

Going forward, a more likely scenario is that a greater number of Singaporeans will use English as their first language and their respective mother tongues as their second language. As Singapore celebrates its first 50 years of nationhood, it is timely to take a closer look at the Chinese-speaking community which had been the backbone of the Republic in its founding years. Some of the older Chinese organisations (several clan associations and the Tanjong Rhu Club) have become historical footnotes. As the state of Singapore plugs into the global economy, its Chinese community will be further transformed.

This celebratory book is divided into four broad categories. The first section examines the major Chinese organisations and their contributions in the past five decades. These include the Singapore Chinese Chamber of Commerce & Industry, the Singapore Federation of Chinese Clan Associations, the Chinese Development Assistance Council, and the Chinese Heritage Centre. In addition, we look at the history and work of some of the social clubs and charitable organisations in the Chinese community.

In the second section the focus is on some topical issues that have engaged the Chinese community in Singapore's first 50 years. This collection of essays reviews the evolution of the Chinese language, the integration process of the new immigrants from China, and the influence of Chinese religions. All these subjects continue to arouse passionate debate within the local Chinese community.

The third section looks at the development of Chinese art forms in the Republic while the final section studies the interactions between Singapore's

Chinese community and China on the one hand, and with the regional Chinese communities on the other.

The essayists of this collection come from diverse backgrounds and professions. They have been invited to contribute because of their interest or involvement in the various organisations and topics and they were encouraged to express their passions freely.

Fiona Hu, who has been with the SCCCI for close to 30 years, kindly agreed to share her in-depth knowledge of this leading Chinese institution.

As I was much involved in the formation of the SFCCA (I had worked as Special Assistant to Mr Wee Cho Yaw, the founding Chairman of the organisation), I contributed the essay on this subject.

Gerald Singham, a lawyer by profession, promptly agreed to write about the CDAC because he has been its company secretary since its founding in 1992.

Lee Tang Ling was equally enthusiastic about writing on the Chinese Heritage Centre as she continues to have fond memories of her stint at the CHC and her involvement in the publication of *The Encyclopedia of the Chinese Overseas*.

Au Yue Pak, a retired senior journalist of *Lianhe Zaobao*, who used to cover the social activities of the Chinese community, has contributed an insightful report of past and present private clubs based on her first-hand experience.

Chew Kheng Chuan, who has spent a large part of his life raising funds for universities, has provided a succinct account of Chinese philanthropy in Singapore, a subject close to his heart.

Leong Weng Kam, who has been reporting and analysing events and issues of the Chinese community in *The Straits Times*, has written an easy read on a convoluted topic — the evolution of the Chinese language in the past five decades.

Another senior journalist who has contributed is Zhou Zhaocheng. A new immigrant who is now deeply involved in integration efforts, he was an obvious choice to write about the trials and tribulations of new immigrants from China.

The other writers who have kindly contributed essays are academics with well-established reputations in their respective areas of specialisation. These include Dr Leo Suryadinata (Chinese in Southeast Asia), Prof

Kenneth Dean (Buddhism), Dr Hue Guan Thye (Buddhism), Dr John Wong and Lye Liang Fook (both have done extensive research on China and Sino-Singapore relations).

For the collection of essays on the state of Singapore's arts scene, Choo Thiam Siew, the Director of the new Singapore Chinese Cultural Centre was approached. Through his good offices, we managed to get Dr Bridget Tracy Tan, Wong Joon Tai, Terence Ho and Edmond Wong to write about their passions — Chinese painting, Chinese calligraphy, Chinese orchestral music and Chinese dance respectively.

In conclusion I would like to express my deep appreciation to three leaders of the Chinese community. Thomas Chua, President of the SCCCI and Chua Thian Poh, President of the SFCCA, have graciously endorsed this publication as a salute to the Chinese community of Singapore. In truth, Singapore's success in its first 50 years owes much to their two organisations and members. Many thanks are also due to Liu Thai Ker, one of Singapore's pioneer urban planners, for providing the book cover. As Chief Executive Officer, first of the Housing and Development Board and subsequently of the Urban Renewal Authority, Thai Ker played a key role in the transformation of the Singapore landscape in the post-Separation years. Asked to portray a landmark closely associated with the Chinese community, he chose the Thian Hock Keng Temple. The result is an iconic Chinese community building drawn by a leading member of our pioneer generation.

Gazetted a national monument, Thian Hock Keng Temple has a special significance for the Chinese community. Because the Temple marked the waterfront then, it was often the first place visited by the early Chinese immigrants to give thanks for their safe journey. It was where the Singapore Hokkien Huay Kuan, a major clan association started. Today, the association continues to be involved in social, welfare, educational and cultural activities and its governing council comprises business and community leaders.

Thian Hock Keng Temple also serves as a useful reminder of what can be achieved by an immigrant community that is united in purpose and social commitment. The community has become a major segment of a prosperous nation. It is hoped that this book will provide a better understanding of the many facets and contributions of Singapore's Chinese community.

List of Contributors

PHUA Kok Khoo (潘国驹) obtained his PhD in Mathematical Physics from the University of Birmingham in 1970. He was awarded the Institute of Physics Singapore (IPS) President's Award by the IPS Council in 2006. He is a Fellow at the American Physical Society, the Founding Director of the Institute for Advanced Studies at Nanyang Technological University, an Adjunct Professor at the National University of Singapore, and Honorary Professor in many universities in China. He is also Chairman of the World Scientific Publishing Company, Chairman of the Tan Kah Kee Foundation, Vice-Chairman of the Tan Kah Kee International Society, and President of the Singapore China Friendship Association and Vice-President of Singapore China Business Association. Professor Phua's research interests are in theoretical high energy physics, science education and science policies. He has published many papers on scientific research in internationally refereed journals and comments on scientific research and higher education in the national newspapers *Lianhe Zaobao* and *The Straits Times*. For nearly 40 years, Professor Phua has dedicated himself to strengthening scientific research in Asia and promoting physics education, higher education and scholarly exchanges at the international level.

Thomas CHUA (蔡其生) is the President of the 57th and 58th Council of the Singapore Chinese Chamber of Commerce & Industry (2013–2017). Mr Chua graduated from Nanyang University with a Bachelor of Arts, majoring in Political Science. He joined Teckwah in 1979 and has been instrumental in transforming his family business into a public listed company. He is the Chairman and Managing Director of Teckwah. A recipient of the Pingat Bakti Masyarakat (Public Service Medal), Mr Chua was appointed a Nominated Member of Parliament (NMP) in September 2014 to voice the major concerns and issues of the business community. Mr Chua serves in many public and civic institutions in Singapore. He is a Director of Business China, serves on the Board of Trustees of the Chinese Development Assistance Council, and is Vice-Chairman of Singapore Kim Mui Hoey Kuan. Mr Chua is a member of the National Wages Council and a member of the Tripartite Panel on Community Engagement at Workplaces, Community Engagement Programme (CEP). He is a Vice Chairman of the Singapore Business Federation (SBF), a member of the National Productivity Council (NPC) and a member of Employer and Business Council (E&B) of the Advisory Council on Community Relationship in Defence (ACCORD).

CHUA Thian Poh (蔡天宝) is the founder of the Ho Bee Group. He is currently the Chairman and CEO of Ho Bee Land Limited, which is listed on the mainboard of the Singapore Exchange. Mr Chua serves on the boards of several other companies and community organisations. He is the President of the Singapore Federation of Chinese Clan Associations, Board Chairman of Business China, Honorary President of Singapore Chinese Chamber of Commerce & Industry, Chairman of Ren Ci Hospital, President of Singapore Hokkien Huay Kuan and Chairman of Bishan East Citizens' Consultative Committee. Mr Chua is also Chairman of the Board of Trustees of the Chinese Development Assistance Council. Mr Chua was conferred the Public Service Star (BBM) in 2004 and appointed Justice of the Peace in 2005. He was conferred the 2006 Businessman of the Year award. In 2012, Mr Chua was conferred The President's Award for Philanthropy (Individual). He was conferred the Distinguished Service Order (Darjah Utama Bakti Cemerlang) in 2014.

PANG Cheng Lian (冯清莲) has been involved in many of the organisations in the Chinese community, first as a journalist with the New Nation and subsequently as Special Assistant to Mr Wee Cho Yaw, Chairman and CEO of United Overseas Bank and widely acknowledged as a leader of the Chinese community. Her MA thesis on the People's Action Party was published by Oxford University Press in 1971. She helped edit many of the English books published by the SFCCA and wrote an authorised biography of Wee Cho Yaw which was published in 2014. A graduate of the University of Singapore, Ms Pang has served as Singapore's Ambassador to Italy and Switzerland (Non-Resident) as well as Chairman of the Films Appeals Committee.

Fiona HU Ai Lan (胡爱兰) holds the position of Senior Director (Communications and Publications) at the Singapore Chinese Chamber of Commerce & Industry, where she has been employed since 1988. Her portfolio includes corporate communications, media relations, writing and editing for the Chamber's various regular and commemorative publications, Chinese to English translation, and the planning and coordination work for special projects like the World Chinese Entrepreneurs Convention. She graduated from the University of Singapore with an Honours degree in English, and later went on to do her Master's Degree in English at the University of California at Los Angeles.

Gerald SINGHAM (沈结乐) is a partner in the law firm of Rodyk and Davidson LLP. He was the lawyer who drafted the constitutional documents when incorporating CDAC in 1992 and continues to act as legal counsel and company secretary to CDAC. In his spare time, Gerald is actively involved in community work, including serving as Vice-Chairman of the National Crime Prevention Council, a member of the Casino Regulatory Authority and a member of the National Council of Problem Gambling. He is also Vice-Chairman of OnePeople.sg. Gerald was awarded the Public Service Medal and the Public Service Star by the President of Singapore in acknowledgement of his community work.

LEE Tang Ling (李丹琳) a graduate from the Faculty of Arts and Social Sciences of the National University of Singapore, joined the Chinese Heritage Centre as the Centre's manager when it was set up in 1995. She provided editorial support for the compilation of *The Encyclopedia of the Chinese Overseas* as its Editorial Manager and Maps/Picture Researcher and initiated the Centre's Museum Student Docent Programme. Tang Ling is currently Corporate Communications Manager at Haw Par Corporation Limited.

CHEW Kheng Chuan (周庆全) is an independent consultant in philanthropy. He is Chairman of The Substation Limited, and a board member of the Intercultural Theatre Institute. He also serves as the Honorary Secretary to Nalanda Library Fund Limited. He has been acknowledged as one of the most successful fundraisers in Asia in the field of private philanthropy; a founding Director of the NUS Development Office and later Vice-President, Endowment & Institutional Development at NUS (2003–2008). He was the Chief University Advancement Officer at Nanyang Technological University from 2009–2012. He is co-author of *Chew Boon Lay: A Family Traces Its History*, on his great grandfather the immigrant pioneer. The first Singaporean to be admitted to Harvard College in 1978 where he graduated with a Bachelor's Degree (AB cum laude) in Social Studies in 1982, KC has built enduring ties with his alma mater, having served as Chairman of the Harvard Alumni Interviewing Committee in Singapore since 1983. In recognition of his longstanding service, he received the Hiram Hunn Memorial Schools & Scholarships Award from Harvard College in 2005.

AU Yue Pak (区如柏) is a graduate of Nanyang University's Chinese Language and Literature Department. She worked in the Chinese press for 28 years, first with *Sin Chew Jit Poh* and subsequently with *Lianhe Zaobao*. After her retirement, she continued writing as a freelancer. She has authored 14 Chinese books on a wide variety of subjects, including *The Glorious Years*《峥嵘岁月》and *Wonderful Journey*《逍遥游》. The former is a two-volume book on Singapore during the Japanese Occupation and the latter is a record of her many overseas travels. Mdm Au is a councillor of the Kwangtung Hui Kuan, where she teaches the Cantonese dialect. She is also a council member of Kong Chow Wui Koon.

LEONG Weng Kam (梁荣锦) is a senior writer with *The Straits Times*. He started his journalism career as a bilingual reporter with the newspaper in 1977. He has written on the Chinese-speaking community in Singapore for nearly four decades. He co-authored *Men In White: The Untold Story of Singapore's Ruling Political Party* (2009), and was a member of the editorial team for *Lee Kuan Yew — A Life In Pictures* (2013). He has a Bachelor of Arts degree in Chinese Language and Literature from Beijing Normal University, and Master of Arts degrees in Asia Pacific Studies and Contemporary

China from the University of Leeds and Nanyang Technological University respectively.

ZHOU Zhaocheng (周兆呈) obtained his PhD from Nanyang Technological University (NTU) and is the editor of zaobao.com and Crossroads with *Lianhe Zaobao,* Singapore Press Holdings' Chinese flagship paper. Besides his service in the community as Chairman of the Social Affairs Committee of the Singapore Federation of Chinese Clan Associations, and committee member of the Media and Community Working Group in the National Integration Council Singapore, Dr Zhou also holds some academic positions. He is Adjunct Associate Professor with the Nanyang Centre for Public Administration, NTU, and Adjunct Professor with the Institute of Arts and Humanities, Shanghai Jiaotong University. Dr Zhou is also President of the Singapore Society of Asian Studies. His publications include *Communication Strategy of Public Policy in Singapore; Language, Politics and Nationalization; Three Places across Two Shores: The Singapore Perspective,* amongst others.

HUE Guan Thye (許源泰) is a Research Fellow of the Max Planck Institute (MPI) for the Study of Religious and Ethnic Diversity, Göttingen, Germany. He obtained his Bachelor of Arts in Chinese Language and Literature from Peking University, China, and his MA and PhD in Chinese Studies from Nanyang Technological University, Singapore. A revised version of his PhD dissertation has been published《沿革与模式: 新加坡道教和佛教传播研究》[Evolution and Model: The Propagation of Taoism and Buddhism in Singapore] (2013). He is also the co-author of《新加坡汉传佛教发展概述》[A Study of the Development of Chinese Buddhism in Singapore] (2010). In the past few years, he has been working on a field project "Mapping Religious Sites of Singapore" under the direction of Professor Kenneth Dean. As part of this project, they performed a survey of more than 800 Chinese temples and clan associations in Singapore. Part of their collection of stone inscriptions from these temples and associations has been compiled as a historical reference book, entitled *Epigraphic Materials in Singapore: 1819–1911* and will be published with NUS Press in the near future. Dr Hue's research interests include the Philosophy of Buddhism, Chinese folk religion, Singapore Chinese temples, Chinese Culture, and the Chinese in Singapore and Malaysia.

Kenneth DEAN (丁荷生) is Professor and Head of the Department of Chinese Studies and a Senior Researcher at the Asia Research Institute of the National University of Singapore. He is Lee Chair and James McGill Professor Emeritus of McGill University. Professor Dean is the author of several books on Taoism and Chinese popular religion, including *Ritual Alliances of the Putian Plains: Vol. 1: Historical Introduction to the Return of the Gods, Vol. 2: A Survey of Village Temples and Ritual Activities* (with Zheng Zhenman, 2010); *Epigraphical Materials on the History of Religion in Fujian: The Quanzhou Region*, in three volumes (with Zheng Zhenman, 2014); *Lord of the Three in One: The Spread of a Cult in Southeast China* (1998); *Epigraphical Materials on the History of Religion in Fujian: The Xinghua Region* (with Zheng Zhenman, 1995); *Taoist Ritual and Popular Cults of Southeast China* (1993); and *First and Last Emperors: The Absolute State and the Body of the Despot* (with Brian Massumi, 1992). He directed *Bored in Heaven* (2010), an 80 minute documentary film on ritual celebrations around Chinese New Year in Putian, Fujian, China. His current research concerns transnational trust and temple networks linking Singapore Chinese temples to Southeast China and Southeast Asia. As part of this project, he is conducting a survey of 800 Chinese temples in Singapore. He plans to publish a collection of stone inscriptions from these temples with NUS Press, entitled *Chinese Epigraphy of Singapore: 1819–1911* (with Dr Hue Guan Thye).

CHOO Thiam Siew (朱添寿) is CEO of the Singapore Chinese Cultural Centre. Prior to this, he was President of Nanyang Academy of Fine Arts from 2003 to March 2014. In 1976, Mr Choo joined the then Parks and Recreation Department and was Deputy Commissioner till 1995, and later became the Deputy Chief Executive Officer of the National Parks Board. He was CEO of the National Arts Council from 1997 to 2003. Mr Choo has a passion for both Chinese and Western arts and culture, and he is active in the arts and cultural community. He published his first Chinese classical poetry collection in 2001.

Bridget Tracy TAN (陈莉玲) is Director for the Institute of Southeast Asian Arts and Art Galleries at the Nanyang Academy of Fine Arts. In March 2005, her book *Style and Imagination: Art in the Nanyang Academy* featuring highlights of the academy's collection and its regional significance was published.

To date, she has written books and essays on the work of Cultural Medallion artists, such as Chua Ek Kay, Lim Tze Peng, Ang Ah Tee, Chng Seok Tin, Han Sai Por, Thomas Yeo, Ng Eng Teng and Yip Cheong Fun, as well as pioneer and master artist, Cheong Soo Pieng. In 2011, Select Books published the debut *Women Artists in Singapore* book that she wrote, as commissioned by the National Heritage Board. From 1996 to January 2004, Bridget was a curator at the Singapore Art Museum. While at the museum she specialized in acquisitions and researching Second Generation Singapore artists. Bridget graduated with a Master of Arts, obtaining First Class Honours in Art History from the University of Glasgow in Scotland. She holds a Doctor of Philosophy from Chelsea College of Art, London, focusing in practice-led research as a curator and critical art historian in Southeast Asia.

WONG Joon Tai (王运开) is the founder of the Nanyang Calligraphy Centre in Singapore. Before his retirement, he worked in the Infocomm Technology field and received the Public Administration (Silver) Award on National Day in 2000. He now works full time on the promotion and teaching of Chinese calligraphy.

Terence HO (何伟山) is the Executive Director of the Singapore Chinese Orchestra (SCO). He was the first local arts company manager to be awarded the Singapore Tote Board Scholarship to attend "Strategic Management for Non-profit Leaders" in Harvard Business School. Terence won the first Prize of the erhu senior category in the 1985 National Music Competition and was then invited by the Singapore Youth Orchestra (SYO) to tour the UK as a soloist. Terence played the cello with the Conway Civic Orchestra during his college education in USA. He is also an active participant and speaker at many arts management conferences, lectures, workshops, orchestra management meetings and arts markets overseas. He has presented papers and attended conferences in numerous countries including USA, UK, China, New Zealand, Australia, Canada, Hungary, Hong Kong, Taiwan, Japan and Korea. Terence has served in the following committees: Chairman, NAFA Music Curriculum Advisory Committee; Chairman, NAFA Arts Management Curriculum Advisory Committee; National Arts Council Seed and Major

Grant Assessment Panel; National Arts Council Arts Scholarship Assessment Panel; Advisor, Singapore Chin Kang Huay Kuan Youth Division.

Edmond WONG (黄鼎翔) is the CSR Director of Kim Choo Holdings Pte Ltd. He is also the Chairman for the Community Arts & Culture Club, and Family Life Champion at the Tampines West Community Club. Having graduated with two Bachelor degrees in Computer Science and Political Science, Edmond is also a keen observer and contributor to the art scene in Singapore. In his continuous efforts to promote the Peranakan culture through community engagements with local arts practitioners, he is recognised as an active champion for the arts and cultural scene in Singapore. Edmond is also known for his efforts in conservation works in Singapore, particularly in bids to conserve the workshop of the late Cultural Medallion artiste Ng Eng Teng.

John WONG (黄朝翰) is currently Professorial Fellow and Academic Advisor to the East Asian Institute (EAI) of the National University of Singapore. He was formerly Research Director of EAI and Director of the Institute of East Asian Political Economy (IEAPE). He obtained his PhD from the University of London in 1966. He taught Economics at the University of Hong Kong from 1966 to 1970 and at the National University of Singapore from 1971 to 1990. He also taught at Florida State University briefly as a Fulbright Visiting Professor. He has held visiting appointments with Harvard's Fairbank Centre, Yale's Economic Growth Centre, Oxford's St. Antony College, and Stanford University's Economics Department. In 1996, he held the Chair of ASEAN Studies at the University of Toronto. He has written/edited 34 books and published over 500 articles and papers on China and other East Asian economies, including ASEAN. In addition, he has written over 90 policy-related reports on China's development for the Singapore government. He has served and is still on the editorial boards of many learned journals on Asian studies and economic development. He has done consultancy work for the Singapore government and many international organisations, including UNESCAP, ADB, UNIDO, APO and ADI.

LYE Liang Fook (黎良福) is Assistant Director and Research Fellow at the East Asian Institute, National University of Singapore. His research interests cover China's central–local relations, political legitimacy, print media, China–ASEAN relations and China–Singapore relations. He was part of a team that completed a study on the Suzhou Industrial Park, a flagship project between China and Singapore. He has also conducted research into the Sino-Singapore Tianjin Eco-city project, the second flagship project between China and Singapore. He attended the Hanban programme for distinguished scholars in China Studies in 2009. His publications have appeared in Routledge, International Relations of the Asia Pacific, Journal of Chinese Political Science, Eastern Universities Press, Institute of Southeast Asian Studies (ISEAS) Publishing, Konrad Adenauer Stiftung Publishing, World Scientific Publishing and China: An International Journal. Besides his work in academia, he manages the Singapore Secretariat of the Network of East Asian Think Tanks (NEAT) and the Network of ASEAN-China Think Tanks (NACT), two Track II bodies that aim to foster ASEAN + 3 cooperation and ASEAN + 1 cooperation respectively.

Leo SURYADINATA (廖建裕), PhD, is Visiting Senior Fellow at the Institute of Southeast Asian Affairs (ISEAS) and Adjunct Professor at the S. Rajaratnam School of International Studies, Nanyang Technological University. He was formerly Director of the Chinese Heritage Centre (CHC) and Professor in the Department of Political Science, National University of Singapore.

Contents

Section 1
Chinese Organisations

Chapter 1

Singapore Chinese Chamber of Commerce & Industry

Inextricably Linked to Singapore's Economic Miracle

Fiona HU Ai Lan

In 1906, when the Chinese business community founded the "General Chinese Trade Affairs Association" (新加坡中华商务总会) the original name of the Singapore Chinese Chamber of Commerce & Industry (SCCCI) (新加坡中华总商会), the intention was to serve as a self-help group for the Chinese community. Today, after the passage of more than 100 years, the Chamber is the apex Chinese business chamber in Singapore, and plays an important role not only in the areas of commerce and industry and overseas networking, but also in culture, education and community development.

The Chamber's history is inextricably linked to Singapore's national and economic development. When Singapore was under British rule, the Chamber devoted much time on providing welfare for the Chinese community. It helped to establish schools, resolved conflicts within the Chinese community, raised funds to aid disaster relief, and even supported China's revolution and anti-Japanese war efforts. During Singapore's pursuit of self-government, the Chamber relentlessly fought to attain citizenship rights for Chinese residents, and the use of Chinese in the Legislative Assembly.

After Singapore achieved nationhood, the Chamber concentrated on building up a business network to promote economic development, trade and investment, and expand Singapore's links with other countries. In the areas of culture and education, the Chamber continued to work very closely with other clan associations and schools. In fact, many of the

Chamber's leaders occupied important positions in the civic organisations involved in many aspects of cultural and community work. The Singapore Chinese Chamber of Commerce Foundation was also set up in 1966 to provide financial assistance to charitable causes, support welfare projects, and disburse scholarships to local university undergraduates regardless of race or religion.

Whether it was in securing citizenship rights, supporting the founding of Nanyang University (南洋大学), fuelling economic development, nurturing local enterprises, or establishing a global Chinese business network through the World Chinese Entrepreneurs Convention (WCEC), the SCCCI's spirit of endeavour has always echoed Singapore's nation-building aspirations.

As Singapore celebrates its 50th year of nation-building, the Chamber continues to re-invent and remake its roles to adapt to the ever-changing environment. The changing geopolitical landscape, the wave of globalisation, and awesome breakthroughs in science and technology, have all driven us beyond the peripheries of Singapore's small island economy. SCCCI's challenge is how to upgrade and stay competitive globally in its next chapter of growth.

The next sections will highlight some of the milestones and contributions of the Chamber over the last 50 years.

Post-1965

Awakening of Social and Community Consciousness — The Memorial to the Civilian Victims of the Japanese Occupation

The Memorial to the Civilian Victims of the Japanese Occupation (The Civilian War Memorial) (日本占领时期死难人民纪念碑) at Beach Road was officially opened on 15 February 1967, the 25th anniversary of the Japanese Occupation. Few may remember that the idea of building this memorial was set into action by the SCCCI. In early 1962, large numbers of the remains of civilian victims of the Japanese Occupation were unearthed in many parts of Singapore, namely Siglap, Changi and Bukit Timah. Survivors of the Japanese Occupation felt that it would be appropriate to gather the remains and provide them with a proper resting place.

The Chinese Chamber took on the grave challenge and set up a Remains Disposal Committee in February 1962. On 13 March 1963, then Prime Minister Lee Kuan Yew (李光耀) set aside 4½ acres of land in Beach Road for a memorial cum park for the civilian victims. A week later the Chinese Chamber set up a Memorial Building Fund Committee to get this project off the ground.

Acting on the suggestion of the Prime Minister, the Chamber convened a mass meeting in April involving representatives from 600 organisations of all races, which raised a sum of $100,000 on the spot and another $30,000 thereafter. A competition for the design of the memorial was launched, with participation opened to all. After a week-long exhibition of the submitted designs at Victoria Memorial Hall, the winning design was awarded to Messrs Swan and Maclaren.

The Chinese Chamber contributed $150,000, about half of the estimated cost of $300,000, and set up a Memorial Working Committee in May 1965 with government participation to supervise the construction work. The Chamber was represented by then President Soon Peng Yam (孙炳炎), who was appointed Chairman of the Working Committee, Vice-Presidents Lim Kee Ming (林继民) and C H Tong (汤景贤), and Chew Teng How (周镇豪), Chairman of the General Affairs Committee.

The Swan and Maclaren design comprised a memorial with a height of 200 feet formed by four tapering columns symbolising the major ethnic groups of Singapore. Soon Peng Yam personally drove down the first pile on 4 March 1966.

The memorial was finally completed in January 1967 and the opening ceremony was held a month later. The simple but solemn ceremony was attended by 1,000 people, comprising members of the diplomatic corps, business community, the Chinese Chamber and families of the victims. Then Prime Minister Lee Kuan Yew unveiled the plaque and laid a wreath on behalf of the government and the people. After the speeches of PM Lee and Soon Peng Yam, religious rites were conducted by officials of the Inter-Religious Organisation (新加坡宗教联谊会). The ceremony concluded with a three-minute silence in remembrance of the civilian victims of the Japanese Occupation.

Though the memorial was handed over to the government for management and maintenance, the Chamber faithfully holds a War Memorial

Service at the site on the 15th day of February every year. It is also one of the events marking Singapore's Total Defence Day.

The Civilian War Memorial was gazetted as a National Monument on 15 August 2013, for its socio-historical merit and importance to the community.

Breaking the Monopoly of the Shipping Conferences

In the early years of Singapore's independence, the Chinese Chamber took up the cudgels to fight for fairer shipping rates to help the local trading community. It succeeded in breaking the dominant shipping monopolies after a long hard tussle.

It all started in 1964, when the Straits/New York Conference (SNYCON) announced a rate revision, which would have caused Singapore and Malaysia to raise the fees for rubber exports from US$47 to US$52.25 per ton. With the rubber industry in dire straits then, the increment would impose a huge burden on the shippers. In an unprecedented move, Tan Eng Joo (陈永裕), then President of the Rubber Association of Singapore, together with Tan Keong Choon (陈共存) (then a Chamber Council member) led the rubber industry in resisting the hikes by marshalling the support of the local chapters of the rubber trade association in the Malayan Peninsula to opt out of SNYCON. This successfully forced SNYCON to withdraw its proposed hike. By the same action, the Far Eastern Freight Conference (FEFC), which commanded 95% of the Far East-Europe seaborne trade in the 1960s, was forced to abandon a planned rate increase.

The issue of steep conference freight rates resurfaced in 1967. At the Chamber's installation ceremony on 15 March, incoming Vice-President Wee Cho Yaw (黄祖耀) urged the government to take appropriate measures to control freight rates in order to boost Singapore's entrepot trade. This set in motion a long struggle by the Chinese Chamber to break free from the stranglehold of the conference monopolies, with a special Shipping and Entrepot Trade Study Sub-Committee set up to study the problem.

On 20 May a meeting was convened, bringing together 160 representatives from 62 trade and industrial organisations, and the Malay, Indian and International chambers of commerce. All who attended, amongst them rubber and pineapple packers, garment manufacturers, pepper and sago traders, voiced their grievances against the unfair monopoly system of the conference, and rallied behind the Chinese Chamber's battle to fight for free competition in shipping rates.

The Chinese Chamber's strategy consisted of four measures. Firstly, it sought to work closely with the Chinese business leaders in Malaysia. A six-member delegation was sent to a meeting hosted by the Association of Chinese Chambers of Commerce of Malaysia (ACCCM) (马来西亚中华商会联合会) in September 1967, focusing on ways to collectively break away from the shipping conferences' monopolies. A working committee comprising 18 members was set up to look into possible strategies. In 1968, 122 rubber dealers, packers and shippers (who were the main clients of the shipping conferences and the most vociferous in the campaign against the conference system) terminated their contracts with the FEFC.

Secondly, the Chinese Chamber also sought to engage both the Singapore and Malaysian governments. The Shipping Freight Working Committee (SFWC) led by Soon Peng Yam briefed Finance Minister Goh Keng Swee (吴庆瑞) on the plight of the shippers, and Dr Goh agreed to take the matter up with the FEFC. Although the government empathised with the SFWC's cause, it did not accede to the committee's request to outlaw the conference system, but it did render its assistance by setting up a special Shipping Freight Unit in 1972 to study shipping and freight rates.

The third measure adopted by the Chinese Chamber was to mobilise resources within Singapore. In October 1968, the SCCCI started a Booking Centre to help exporters arrange for new cargo ships. As the government had rejected calls by SFWC to set up a shippers' council as a new government entity, the SFWC decided to form a national shippers' council as a non-governmental organisation. The Singapore National Shippers' Council (SNSC) (新加坡全国配货人理事会) was officially set up in September 1972, with Tan Eng Joo and Tan Keong Choon appointed Chairman and Vice-Chairman respectively, as an organisation responsible for the welfare of the local shippers.

The fourth and last measure was to enlist the support of non-conference members from overseas. The Chamber's Booking Centre managed to secure ships operated by independent carriers from East Germany, Russia, Italy, Bulgaria and Japan. While the non-conference lines were unable to match the conference carriers in terms of schedule and speed, their rates were substantially lower. At the same time, the Chinese Chamber solicited the help of shippers from China. In October 1971, the Chamber organised a trade delegation to China, headed by then President Wee Cho Yaw. Among other objectives, the delegation sought China's help to break the stranglehold of the shipping conferences. The Chinese agreed to assist and in December 1971, Vice President Tan Keong Choon visited Beijing to work out the technical details. The result was that from February 1972, cargo vessels from China called on Singapore regularly to ship goods to the major ports of Europe and China. Between the months of February and December, China sent 38 cargo ships to Singapore, averaging three ships a month. The number of non-conference carriers increased from 11 to 16. Although it failed to cripple the freight monopolies in the short term, the SCCCI's relentless efforts successfully prevented the shipping conference from increasing its freight charges inequitably.

1984

Lending a Helping Hand to Industry — Singapore Chinese Chamber Institute of Business (SCCIOB)

The SCCCI has always been a forerunner in responding to the needs of industry. (In 1979, the Chamber added "Industry" to its name to reflect the growing importance of the manufacturing sector in Singapore and within the Chamber itself.) To complement the government's manpower training policy, the SCCCI set up a Training Centre (培训中心) in 1984 to help member companies improve their productivity and management skills, as well as encourage local enterprises to adopt IT. This initiative received the resounding support of all members.

In the first year of the Centre's operations, more than 3,000 people were trained in language, business management and computer knowledge, with 80% of the trainees coming from Small and Medium Sized Enterprises (SMEs). Starting with a Micro Computer Centre and conducting many practical Mandarin courses in the early years, the Training Centre progressively expanded its facilities and course offerings. A Language and Computer Centre with the latest equipment and teaching facilities was opened in 1989. In 1990, the year Singapore established diplomatic ties with China, the Training Centre began conducting training courses for senior Chinese officials. To better fulfil the Chinese Chamber's mission of promoting

Singapore's commerce and industry development and economic prosperity, the Training Centre was restructured in 1996 and transformed into a full-fledged training institute. It was renamed as the Singapore Chinese Chamber Institute of Business (SCCIOB) (新加坡中华总商会管理学院).

This repositioning was a strategic move to propel SCCIOB into its next chapter of growth. The revamped Institute launched several new courses, among which were a "Gateway to Mandarin" course specifically designed for foreigners keen on developing Chinese listening and conversational skills, the Professional Diploma in Tourism and a Professional Certificate for tour guides conducted in Mandarin, and Chinese Workplace Literacy courses. By 2008 and 2009, the SCCIOB had developed other highly acclaimed signature programmes like the Certificate in China Business Practices in conjunction with Tsinghua University, WSQ Service Excellence Framework and WSQ Advanced Certificate in Training and Assessment. Leveraging on SCCIOB's reputation as an acclaimed language training provider, the Public Service Commission (PSC) engaged the institute to conduct a special preparatory course in Chinese language and culture for PSC scholars prior to their departure for study stints in China.

Since the 1990s, the SCCIOB has been instrumental in furthering Singapore-China business relations through its customised programmes for Chinese government officials and senior management personnel of China's state-owned enterprises. It is one of the approved overseas training institutions of the People's Republic of China State Administration of Foreign Experts Affairs (SAFEA), and the immersion programmes it conducts include short courses in public administration, banking, enterprise management, and urban planning in the Singapore context. SCCIOB also partners International Enterprise Singapore to develop the "International Business Fellowship Executive Programme" to equip local enterprises and SMEs with a better understanding of China's business environment.

Even as it continued to capitalise on its core strengths in language and business studies, SCCIOB has steadily established new partnerships to enter into new areas of excellence. It has:

* developed courses like "Practical English for Community Integration" to help new immigrants integrate into the community;
* conducted courses on attaining international quality standards and safety in partnership with the British Standards Institution;

* developed the landmark "Aspiring Productivity Excellence — Certified In-Company Productivity Manager Programme (APEX-CIPM), jointly launched with the Singapore Institute of Manufacturing Technology; and
* launched the Personal Data Protection Act course to help businesses comply with the Act.

In August 2014, SCCIOB celebrated its 30th anniversary. Moving ahead, its targets are, firstly, to consolidate its leading edge in the teaching of the Chinese language, especially in the niche areas of business Mandarin and Chinese business culture, to help local businesses tap on the opportunities of China's rapid economic transformation. Secondly, SCCIOB aspires to help entrepreneurs and management personnel change their mindsets, embrace modern technology and improve their work processes.

1985–1990

These were important years as the Chamber strengthened ties with the international market.

Cementing Ties with China

Historically, the Chinese Chamber has always had strong business linkages with China. These were attributed in a large part to the strong kinship ties between Singapore businessmen and their clansmen in mainland China. In the 1970s and 1980s, the Chinese Chamber initiated and led a number of important business delegations to major cities in China, including one led by Lim Kee Ming and Tan Keong Choon to Suzhou, Wuxi and Nanjing in 1984. President Linn In Hua (林荫华) took the lead to arrange for joint business missions with the Singapore Malay Chamber of Commerce (新加坡马来商会) to explore business deals in Beijing, Qinhuangdao and Ningxia Hui Autonomous Region in 1988.

As the Chinese Chamber was highly regarded by the Chinese government, it was visited by numerous business delegations (some led by influential Chinese leaders). Hu Ping (胡平), China's Minister of Commerce, visited the Chamber in 1989; Zhu Rongji (朱镕基), then Mayor of Shanghai, led an 11-member delegation and spoke at a seminar on "Investment Opportunities in Pudong New Area" in June 1990; Madam

Wu Yi (吴仪), then China's Minister for Foreign Trade and Economic Cooperation, led a 60-member delegation to meet with Chamber leaders in May 1993.

The Trade and Industry Fairs organised by SCCCI in 1985 and 1989 paved the way for a significant Chinese presence as they attracted the participation of many companies from all over China. In the first Trade and Industry Fair held in July 1985, 550 companies from Australia, Japan, Taiwan, Hong Kong, Malaysia, Germany and France, took part. A total of 14 overseas trade delegations from countries like Hungary and Japan attended the Fair.

Building upon the success of the 1985 event, the Trade and Industry Fair held in 1989 was even more successful, recording a total of 100,000 local and international visitors. The Fair attracted exhibitors from 349 companies spanning 13 countries and regions.

Besides the prominent China pavilion that was set up to showcase the country's consumer products and machinery and equipment, made-in-China fashion designs and fabrics were featured in fashion shows which brought in top models from Beijing and Tianjin to present a collection of 110 outfits by the China National Textiles Import and Export Corporation.

1987–1990

Playing an Active Role in the ASEAN-Chambers of Commerce and Industry (CCI)

In 1967, the governments of Indonesia, Malaysia, the Philippines, Singapore and Thailand formed the Association of Southeast Asian Nations (ASEAN) to promote regional economic cooperation. To complement the public sector efforts, the national business chambers of the five countries created the ASEAN-CCI (亚细安工商总会).

Keen to show the world that the private sector was as enthusiastic as the governments in promoting intra-ASEAN trade and investments, ASEAN-CCI held six-monthly meetings in the national capitals by rotation. Its presidency moved from one country to another in alphabetical order biennially. In fact, it was the urgent need for Singapore to take over the chair of ASEAN-CCI in 1979 that accelerated the formation of the Singapore Federation of Chambers of Commerce and Industry (SFCCI) (新加坡工商会联合会) in 1978.

It consisted of five members — the three local ethnic Chambers (the Chinese, the Malay and Indian Chambers), the Singapore Manufacturers' Association (SMA) (新加坡厂商公会) and the Singapore International Chamber of Commerce (新加坡国际商会). Before SFCCI was set up, these four chambers and the SMA had been participating in regional meetings through a joint standing committee. But with the imminent move of the ASEAN-CCI presidency to Singapore, there was a need for a more formalised structure.

As Wee Cho Yaw was then President of the SCCCI, he ended up taking the lead role in the new business body. Announcing that registration of the SFCCI had been approved in March 1978, Wee explained that the SFCCI intended to facilitate the involvement of the private sector in national, regional and international affairs. SFCCI was officially inaugurated by then Finance Minister Hon Sui Sen (韩瑞生) in May 1978.

In accordance with the ASEAN-CCI constitution, Singapore was then next in line to take over the chair from the Philippines. On 16 December 1979, at the 4th Conference of the ASEAN-CCI, SFCCI's President Wee Cho Yaw was unanimously elected President of the ASEAN-CCI.

Over the next two years, Wee travelled extensively to preside over ASEAN-CCI meetings. They were busy years for the ASEAN-CCI as the business grouping was asked to match the enhanced pace of regional cooperation at the governmental level. Besides its biannual meetings, the ASEAN-CCI also held regular dialogues and set up business councils with private sector organisations of the US, Japan, and Australia.

The Chinese Chamber was particularly involved in the ASEAN-Japan Economic Council, ASEAN-US Business Council and ASEAN-Australia Business Council, as the head of the Singapore chapter for these councils. In the late 1980s and throughout the 1990s, when Tan Eng Joo was Chamber President, he and his Vice-Presidents Freddy Lam Fong Loi (蓝宏赉) and Teo Chiang Long (张昌隆), and council member Ng Kok Lip (黄国立), were extremely active on the ASEAN-CCI circuit, especially at the business council meetings in these countries, to champion the interests of ASEAN in general and Singapore in particular.

In 2002, the SFCCI was replaced by the Singapore Business Federation (SBF) (新加坡工商联合总会), set up under legislation requiring all Singapore registered companies with a paid-up share capital of $500,000 and above to be its members.

1991

Extending the Global Network — World Chinese Entrepreneurs Convention (WCEC)

Finding new markets for its members and extending Singapore's global reach have been major preoccupations of the SCCCI. While China remained one of the most important trade and investment countries, the Chamber made concerted attempts to penetrate other markets around the world. Starting from the late 1980s, President Linn In Hua and his Vice-President Tan Eng Joo were a formidable pair in exploratory missions to Eastern Europe (Hungary and Yugoslavia), Mauritius, Reunion Island, as well as Rotterdam and Bremen.

The biennial World Chinese Entrepreneurs Convention (WCEC) (世界华商大会), now recognised as an influential business, social and cultural networking forum for the global Chinese community, was conceptualised and founded by the SCCCI in 1991 in line with this determination to extend Singapore's global business network. Thus far, the WCEC has been successfully organised in major cities around the world, including Singapore, Hong Kong, Bangkok, Vancouver, Melbourne, Nanjing, Kuala Lumpur, Seoul, Kobe, Osaka, Manila and Chengdu.

The WCEC evolved out of an idea conceived by Chamber President Linn In Hua. Convinced that this was a concept worth pursuing, a committee was set up to consider the feasibility of holding a World Chinatown Conference. The Committee concluded that a Chinatown conference was not the best platform for the world's Chinese communities.

The Committee decided to do an in-depth study of Chinese business communities around the world. One salient characteristic stood out. While deep-rooted cultural differences exist among ethnic Chinese depending on their nationality or land of adoption, Chinese entrepreneurs have excelled in business and built business empires, wherever they have settled and called home. Despite their humble beginnings many have demonstrated the true spirit of entrepreneurship.

There were then some 25 million ethnic Chinese outside China, Taiwan and Hong Kong. But up till then, there was no concerted effort to bring ethnic Chinese entrepreneurs from these disparate communities together. Although meetings and gatherings of Chinese traders had been held by some organisations over the years, they lacked a strong economic orientation and did not seek primarily to strengthen business linkages. More than ever, the SCCCI became convinced that it was imperative to maximise the latent strengths of the Chinese business community.

It decided to shoulder the responsibility of creating a global platform for business networking among the ethnic Chinese. It would be a convention enabling Chinese entrepreneurs and technocrats to network and discuss issues of mutual economic and socio-cultural concern. It was decided that this eminent gathering should be named the World Chinese Entrepreneurs Convention.

Right from the start, the Chamber approached Singapore's founding Prime Minister Lee Kuan Yew about this initiative of holding the inaugural WCEC in Singapore. SM Lee (then Singapore's Senior Minister) gave his wholehearted support to the Chamber's leaders who had initiated this idea and also agreed to be the Guest of Honour and deliver the keynote address at the opening ceremony in August 1991.

Groundwork then began in earnest. Integral to this process was the building of a database of potential participants — locating the various Chinese Chambers of Commerce and Chinese business associations around the world, and identifying prominent business personalities who did not belong to any Chinese business grouping. With the endorsement of SM Lee, the Chamber benefited from the very strong involvement of key government agencies like the Economic Development Board, Trade Development Board and Singapore Tourist Promotion Board, which found this to be a bold and meaningful initiative. Advisors from the local academic institutions were recruited to help draw up the programme. Marketing missions to key enclaves of Chinese business groupings were dispatched to promote the Convention, gather support and participation. The entire Council and secretariat of the SCCCI were mobilised into action.

This Convention presented an opportunity for integration of the Chinese business communities around the world and was a concerted attempt by the SCCCI to promote global trade and investment. Prominent Chinese business leaders, entrepreneurs and scholars were invited to participate in the panel discussions. They included Rong Yiren (荣毅仁), then Chairman of China International Trust and Investment Corporation (CITIC) (中国国际信托投资公司) and the All-China Federation of Industry and Commerce (中华全国工商业联合会) and former Vice-President of the PRC; Chancellor Chang-Lin Tien (田长霖) of the University of California at Berkeley, and John Kao (高健), a prominent Chinese American who built a teaching career at Harvard University, as well as achieved success as a film producer and business pioneer.

The inaugural convention in Singapore, held on 10–12 August 1991 under the leadership of President Tan Eng Joo, drew participation from some 800 delegates from 75 cities in 30 countries and regions. It was declared open by SM Lee Kuan Yew who delivered the keynote address. On the last day of the first WCEC, George Yeo, then Minister for Information & the Arts and Second Minister for Foreign Affairs, gave a keynote speech on "Asian Civilisation in the Pacific Century". Owing to its overwhelming success, an immediate decision was made to set up a Founder Members Board consisting of SCCCI, the Chinese General Chamber of Commerce (CGCC) of Hong Kong (香港中华总商会) and the Thai-Chinese Chamber of Commerce (TCCC) (泰国中华总商会). It was further agreed that the WCEC would be held once in every two years, with CGCC hosting the second WCEC in Hong Kong in 1993 and the TCCC the third WCEC in 1995 in Bangkok. The subsequent hosts for the WCEC would also be decided by the Founder Members Board.

SM Lee continued to have a strong presence in the WCEC throughout the years. He gave the keynote address at the 2nd WCEC in Hong Kong in 1993, and showed his support by contributing messages via specially recorded videos during the 4th WCEC in Vancouver in 1997 and the 5th WCEC in Melbourne two years later, in 1999.

At a meeting in October 1999, the Founder Members Board decided to establish the WCEC Secretariat and appointed the SCCCI to host the Secretariat for a six-year term. CGCC took over the Secretariat in 2005 and it was passed to TCCC in 2011.

Twenty years after its inception, SCCCI secured the honour of hosting the 11th WCEC in October 2011. This Convention saw the participation of 4,624 delegates from 125 cities in 34 countries and regions. Founding Prime Minister Lee Kuan Yew (who had just stepped down from the Cabinet as Minister Mentor), was the Guest of Honour at the gala dinner on October 7 during which he held a dialogue with participants and shared valuable insights on issues such as the role of Chinese entrepreneurs and China's challenges.

1998

Building a Vibrant SME Sector in Singapore

There are 180,000 SMEs which make up 99% of the corporations in Singapore. They contribute to nearly half of Singapore's GDP and employ 70% of the workforce. The Chamber places great importance on growing a resilient SME sector and has put in many programmes to pursue this objective.

SMEs Conference, Infocomm Commerce Conference and SME Expo

Both the Annual SMEs Conference (中小型企业大会) and the Infocomm Commerce Conference (资信商业大会) were conceived to serve the needs of the SMEs.

The Annual SMEs Conference had its origin in 1998 and attracted a total number of 200 participants. It catered for the Mandarin-speaking business community and its theme was "Total Business Planning: The Key to Competitiveness".

The Infocomm Commerce Conference was first organised in 1997 to impress upon SMEs the incipient growth and importance of the Internet. Its theme was NET PROFITS — Doing Business on the Internet. It brought together over 300 participants.

Over the years, attendance at both conferences has grown — reaching 1,000, and later to more than 2,000 participants. In order to accommodate the rising interest the Infocomm Commerce Conference (ICC) has been held at Suntec Singapore since 2001, whilst the SMEs Conference began to be organised at Suntec Singapore from 2004.

Starting from 2012, the Chamber made a strategic move to bring both the Annual SMEs Conference and the ICC together as back-to-back events, riding on the synergy of both events to optimise resources and maximise impact. In 2013, the exhibition component which brought together vendors offering practical and affordable solutions to the SMEs was rebranded as the SME Expo (中小型企业博览会). It now shares centrestage with these two flagship events. It has become the place for SMEs to identify suitable solutions to aid their business growth, increase their productivity level, and look for innovations in work processes.

SME Centre@SCCCI

Since 2006, the Chamber has been providing holistic business advisory and capability development services for the benefit of local SMEs, aspiring entrepreneurs and micro-enterprises. Formerly known as the Enterprise Development Centre@SCCCI (EDC@SCCCI), it assumed a new identity as SME Centre@SCCCI in April 2013, signifying a major step forward in providing even more targeted assistance to SMEs through a wide range of value-added services. These include broad-based business advisory, productivity and capability development, and government incentives and grant consultation.

Since then, the SME Centre@SCCCI has expanded into the heartlands of Singapore, setting up satellite offices at Toa Payoh and Ang Mo Kio to engage the micro-enterprises and provide requisite consultancy services to help them grow and transform.

SIRC@SCCCI

The SME Infocomm Resource Centre@SCCCI (SIRC@SCCCI) was officially launched in August 2008 with the support of the Infocomm Development Authority of Singapore (IDA) to help SMEs address all their technology needs. The primary objective is to provide SMEs with an avenue to gain awareness on the benefits of adopting infocomm technology to improve business productivity and profitability.

Through the efforts of the SIRC@SCCCI, SMEs have gained access to hands-on learning sessions conducted by industry champions, participated in site visits to explore relevant solutions, and introduced to enterprise-wide applications and industry-specific solutions for their business.

2001

Remembering Singapore's Role in the History of China — Sun Yat Sen Nanyang Memorial Hall

Tucked away in Tai Gin Road, off Balestier Road, is a two-storey colonial bungalow, formerly known as Wan Qing Yuan (晚晴园), or Sun Yat Sen Villa, which is not only connected to the Chamber but also played a significant role in Dr Sun Yat Sen's revolutionary activities in Nanyang. In 1906, rubber magnate and the villa's owner Teo Eng Hock (张永福) offered to let Dr Sun stay there on several occasions. The villa became the Southeast Asian headquarters of Dr Sun's revolutionary movement against the Qing dynasty.

Shortly after Singapore gained independence, the Sun Yat Sen Villa underwent a small refurbishment. Memorabilia of the civilians who perished at the villa during the Japanese Occupation, together with Dr Sun's artefacts and pictures were displayed for public viewing. In 1994, the villa was gazetted as a national monument.

A turning point came with the visit of BG George Yeo (杨荣文), then Minister for Information and the Arts, who felt that the villa was an important part of history, for the 1911 Revolution headed by Dr Sun not only changed China but also affected the rest of the world.

In 1996, the villa was renamed Sun Yat Sen Nanyang Memorial Hall (孙中山南洋纪念馆). The Chamber formed a subsidiary company, Sun Yat Sen Nanyang Memorial Hall Co Ltd in 1997, led by Kwek Leng Joo (郭令裕) to oversee its restoration, sponsored by the Lee Foundation (李氏基金). The cultural and historical research team was chaired by Foong Choon Hon (冯仲汉), who possessed invaluable contacts with the Sun Yat Sen Memorial Halls in China, Hong Kong and Taiwan.

This renovation and extension of the villa which cost over $8 million, was completed on 12 November 2001. On the occasion of the 135th birthday of Dr Sun, the refurbished Sun Yat Sen Nanyang Memorial Hall was officially opened by then Senior Minister Lee Kuan Yew.

In his speech, Senior Minister referred to Sun Yat Sen as one of the greatest Asian leaders of the 20th century:

> Most Singaporeans, especially the young, are not aware of the history of this building which was not gazetted as a national monument until 1994. The Singapore Chinese Chamber of Commerce & Industry has taken great pains to restore the building and to make it meaningful. This restored and enlarged villa joins the ranks of the other 43 national monuments which reflect our multiracial and multi-religious society.

Kwek Leng Joo, who was then Chairman of the Sun Yat Sen Nanyang Memorial Hall Co Ltd, emphasised that the newly restored Memorial Hall had an important role in Singapore's national education as well as in facilitating cultural exchanges. By capturing the highlights of Dr Sun's revolutionary vision and mission, the Memorial Hall was a chronicle of Singapore's role in changing China's destiny.

In 2009, the Sun Yat Sen Nanyang Memorial Hall entered another new chapter when the Chamber signed a Memorandum of Understanding with the National Heritage Board (NHB) (国家文物局). From then on, the Memorial Hall became a Community Heritage Institution under the management of the NHB. The Chamber, through the Board of the Sun Yat Sen Nanyang Memorial Hall Co Ltd continues to play a key role in the strategic planning and direction for the Memorial Hall, to ensure it meets its mission as a community heritage institution with its emphasis on national education.

Under the new management, the Memorial Hall once again went through extensive renovation works. It was re-opened to the public on 9 October 2011 with new galleries which highlight Singapore's role as a base for the 1911 Revolution and explore the impact and influences of the 1911 Chinese revolution on the Singapore Chinese community.

2006

The First 100 Years — Grand Centennial Celebrations

2006 marked not only a major milestone in the Chamber's history; it was also the starting point of a new journey for the next 100 years. It was a year of celebrations, during which SCCCI launched a number of outstanding business, cultural, education and community events.

The Chamber's centennial celebrations were anchored on the theme of "跨世纪　越四海", which literally means "Towards Global Connectivity". The 100th Anniversary Organising Committee, headed by Vice-President Chia Ban Seng (谢万森), said the suite of centennial activities would honour the achievements of the Chamber and its leaders, bringing to light the rich tapestry of its historical heritage, as well as valued thoughts and experiences amassed over a century.

On the first day of the Lunar New Year, then Senior Minister Goh Chok Tong (吴作栋) graced the unveiling ceremony for the 100th Anniversary logo. In February, the Chamber and *Lianhe Zaobao* jointly presented "A Dream Journey to Tang Dynasty", a musical depicting the dream-like poetry, music and dance of the Tang Dynasty.

To mark the centennial, the Singapore Botanic Gardens specially cultivated a breed of orchid for the Chamber, and the orchid-naming ceremony for Dendrobium Singapore Chinese Chamber of Commerce & Industry was officiated by then President S R Nathan on 22 April. Another first for the Chamber was the special stamp series issued by Singapore Post to commemorate the 100-year journey of the Chamber. These featured the Chamber's building which was officially opened in 1964, the Nanyang University administration building, the Civilian War Memorial in Beach Road, the Sun Yat Sen Nanyang Memorial Hall, the logo of the inaugural World Chinese Entrepreneurs Convention in Singapore, and the special Chamber orchid hybrid. It was the first time Singapore Post had issued stamps on behalf of a local business organisation.

In July a concert featuring renowned Chinese soprano Huang Hong Ying (黄红英) was held at the Esplanade and in August a charity golf tournament was held to raise funds for the Singapore Cord Blood Bank. A month later the Chamber jointly organised "A Symposium on Southeast Asian Culture in an Era of Globalisation" with the Chinese Heritage Centre, with speakers from local and overseas academia.

Business-related events for the centennial included the inaugural Trade Association Congress held on 24 June, bringing together 600 delegates representing 89 trade association members. The theme of the day-long discussions was "The Challenge and Role of Trade Associations in the New Economy".

The centennial celebrations culminated in two major events on 22 October; the Asian Chinese Entrepreneurs Summit held in the morning, followed by a Gala Dinner that evening. Both events were attended by more than 1,200 members, guests, speakers from the region and business partners. Prime Minister Lee Hsien Loong (李显龙) was the guest of honour and officiated the unveiling of the Chamber's new logo. The logo represented the Chamber's new vision and its resolve to continually re-invent itself in an ever-changing environment.

In his address to the guests at the Gala Dinner, Chamber President Chua Thian Poh (蔡天宝) said:

Our centennial celebrations represent an important milestone in the history of our Chamber. Even as we reflect on our past, we look forward to our common aspirations and a promising future ahead. Manifold changes in the global economic order and the continuous restructuring of the regional economy have presented unprecedented business opportunities and untold challenges. As we are thrust headlong into a new economic era, we have resolved to channel all our energies, in unison, to uncover business leads, champion business interests, and lead local enterprises to globalise and promote the Singapore brand in the overseas marketplace.

A fitting tribute to the centennial came in the form of *Elements of Enterprise*, a publication launched in February 2007, which unfolds the story of the Chamber based on the Five Elements in traditional Chinese philosophy — water, earth, fire, wood and gold.

2007

A Trailblazing Networking Platform — Business China

Business China (通商中国) is an entity harnessing the strengths of the public and private sectors to enhance Singapore-China relations. Centering on the opportunities generated by China's burgeoning economic development, Business China aims to establish widespread acceptance and appreciation of the Chinese language and culture among young Singaporeans.

The initial idea for establishing this non-profit organisation was mooted by then Minister Mentor Lee Kuan Yew, who suggested, during an interview for SCCCI's centennial publication *Elements of Enterprise*, that the Chamber could set up a Mandarin-speaking networking platform for some 5,000 Singaporeans currently doing business in China. Taking this idea seriously, the Chamber took immediate steps to form a Task Force responsible for formulating the fundamental objectives and mandate of Business China.

Facility with language and an appreciation of culture and other socio-economic conditions are indispensable tools for business and cultural interactions. After numerous rounds of discussions involving the Task Force and key members of the community, it was unanimously agreed that through the use of Mandarin, Business China would be able to develop a strong economic and cultural bridge linking Singapore and China. At the same time, Business China would organise activities aimed at impressing upon younger Singaporeans the importance of Chinese as a living language of practical value.

Minister Mentor Lee Kuan Yew was the first Patron of Business China, and Deputy Prime Minister Wong Kan Seng (黄根成) and other ministers were brought in to serve as advisers and members of the Board of Directors. The Board also consists of eminent personalities from statutory boards, business entities, the media and academia, whose presence will steer the development of Business China.

After an intense year of preparations, Business China was officially launched by SCCCI on 19 November 2007 at the Cultural Centre of the National University of Singapore (新加坡国立大学). China's Premier Wen Jiabao (温家宝), who was on an official visit to Singapore, was invited to deliver a keynote speech. The engaging Premier pointed out that China's history bore testimony to the paramount importance of an open-door policy. He said, "Only an open and inclusive nation can become strong and prosperous, while a nation that shuts its doors to the world is bound to fall behind."

Referring to relations between Singapore and China, Premier Wen said that mutual opening up and inclusiveness had led to rapid growth in cooperation between both countries, and he cited the phenomenal growth in bilateral trade, the training of more than 9,000 Chinese officials in Singapore in the past decade, and the 19-fold increase in bilateral visits between 1990 and 2006. Premier Wen added that the opportune establishment of Business China by the SCCCI would provide "a new platform for conducting cultural and business exchanges between the two countries".

Addressing some 1,300 guests at the official launch of Business China, Minister Mentor Lee said that Singaporeans needed three capabilities to do business in China:

> fluency in the Chinese language, knowledge of China's traditional culture and an understanding of the ongoing changes in the social, economic and political conditions of a society with changing lifestyle that is transiting from an agricultural to an industrial economy.

Minister Mentor Lee expressed the hope that Business China would be able to nurture more Chinese Singaporeans to attain a proper grasp of the

Chinese language and understanding of Chinese culture. The objective of Business China was to develop a core of bilingual and bi-cultural Singaporeans with the ability to strike up an immediate rapport with the Chinese and thereby facilitate their business activities in China.

2010

Establishing an Overseas Presence — SCCCI's Shanghai Office

Another significant initiative was the establishment of SCCCI's Shanghai Representative Office in 2010, the Chamber's first overseas presence. The principal objective was to strengthen the linkages with Chinese government officials and the private sector, and to help the Chamber's corporate and trade association members venture into the China market and integrate better into China's business environment.

In 2013, the SCCCI joined hands with International Enterprise Singapore (新加坡国际企业发展局) to upgrade the Shanghai Representative Office into the IE-SCCCI Singapore Enterprise Centre (ISSEC).

This was a strategic move to effectively leverage on the shared resources of the government and private sector to facilitate SMEs' access into the China market. The one-stop centre is dedicated to help SMEs venture into China and provides a full suite of services.

Since its launch, ISSEC has helped many SMEs to gain a foothold and expand their outreach in the China market. Leveraging on the Chamber and IE Singapore's existing network in China, it has helped SMEs with the marketing and distribution of their products, reviewing their corporate strategies to achieve greater efficiencies and matching them with suitable partners to grow their business.

Besides being a contact point and base for Singapore businesses in China, ISSEC also seeks to attract Chinese enterprises to Singapore. The Chamber will work with the government-linked companies and large corporations to encourage SMEs to enter the China market as a group so as to tap on the existing Singapore flagship projects established in China.

2014

Recognition for the Chamber's Role in Sino-Singapore Relations — Business China Enterprise Award

Over the years, the Chamber has been an important platform for many of China's leaders to engage and interact with Singapore's business community. It has welcomed business delegations led by political leaders like Zhu Rongji, then Mayor of Shanghai, in June 1990; Madam Wu Yi, then China's Minister for Foreign Trade and Economic Cooperation, led a 60-member delegation to the Chamber in May 1993.

In July 2007, the Chamber presented Wu Yi, then China's Vice-Premier, with an "Excellence in Leadership Award" for her outstanding contributions in promoting economic cooperation between Singapore and China, particularly in the strategic areas of human resources development, health and the environment, technology and private enterprise.

In November 2007, the Chamber hosted a dinner for Premier Wen Jiabao. In the following years the Chamber organised a dinner in November 2009 for then China's President Hu Jintao (胡锦涛) during his first state visit to Singapore. On 15 November 2010, the Chamber organised a luncheon in honour of Xi Jinping (习近平), then China's Vice-President, to commemorate the 20th anniversary of Singapore's diplomatic ties with China.

In recognition of its multifaceted contributions towards developing trade, business and relational contacts between Singapore and China, SCCCI was presented with a Business China Enterprise Award on 18 November 2014.

Deputy Prime Minister Teo Chee Hean (张志贤), guest of honour at the awards presentation ceremony, commended the Chamber on its singular dedication to building linkages with China. DPM Teo said that prior to our pre-Independence days,

> linkages with China were set up through business groups like the Singapore Chinese Chamber of Commerce & Industry, the winner of this year's Business China Enterprise Award. Today, the SCCCI continues to help Singapore businesses by tapping its extensive networks in China.

In particular, DPM Teo singled out the IE-SCCCI Singapore Enterprise Centre in Shanghai and lauded its role in helping local SMEs develop essential market contacts, competencies and knowledge in China.

SCCCI President Thomas Chua (蔡其生), in his acceptance speech, expressed his appreciation to all who had supported the Chamber in achieving this milestone.

> Owing to everyone's selfless contributions, the Chamber has been able to galvanise the strength of the business community, and contribute back to the nation and to the community... only with the unwavering support of our political leaders, government agencies, business organisations, and individuals from the fields of business, culture and education, could our Chamber carry out such an important role in our links with China.

Mr Chua declared that "receiving this Business China Enterprise Award truly encourages us to strive even harder at furthering the business and trade cooperation between Singapore and China".

2015

Exemplars of Society, Pillars of the Nation — SG50 Outstanding Chinese Business Pioneers Awards

On the night of 6 February 2015, 28 Chinese business pioneers were presented with the SG50 Outstanding Chinese Business Pioneers Awards to acknowledge their exceptional achievements and entrepreneurial spirit, their demonstrable contributions to the Singapore economy, as well as their firm belief in giving back to the society — by pledging their support to education, culture, the arts, healthcare and community projects, and their involvement in the government's policy-making process.

Addressing the 720 dinner guests, SCCCI President Thomas Chua said:

> The Chamber has initiated these awards to promote and pay tribute to the Chinese entrepreneurial spirit, uphold the pursuit of excellence and the virtues of giving back to society, sharing the fruits of

prosperity with the community. We hope that the young generation can learn from them.

In the early years of Singapore's independence, most business sectors were in their early stage of development. When Singapore was forced into independence, these Chinese business pioneers chose to remain here and be a part of our nation's destiny. I believe our younger generation could never imagine just how difficult the early years of nation-building were, nor envisage the challenges during those turbulent periods. Within just half a century, Singapore has transformed from a small trading post with no resources and an uncertain future into a thriving metropolis. Singapore could only have achieved such economic prosperity owing to the hard work and perseverance of the pioneer generation.

The most notable of all is that these entrepreneurs were not only preoccupied with the success of their business. They also devoted time, energy and resources into society, culture, education and charitable projects, and they continue to be active in community organisations; they lead the way in industry development, working hard to promote Chinese culture and personally putting into practice traditional values, and helping the less privileged among us.

The business sectors represented by the 28 individuals included many of the trades and industries in Singapore. These include finance, trade, real estate, energy, manufacturing, chemicals, shipping, port operations, the legal profession, cinema operations, tourism, garments, food, architecture, urban planning, transport and logistics, heavy machinery, environmental engineering, manufacturing of electrical equipment and healthcare, amongst others.

The most senior of the recipients was 99-year old Tao Shing Pee (陶欣伯), Chairman of the Shing Kwan Group. He was one of the three recipients in their 90s. There were eight recipients in their 80s, seven in their 70s, and 10 belonged to the 60s age group. Among the 28 recipients were two ladies, Gan See Khem (颜诗琴) and Dorothy Chan (黄淑娇).

They received the awards from President Dr Tony Tan Keng Yam (陈庆炎), and in the presence of Minister Heng Swee Keat (王瑞杰) in his capacity as Chairman of the SG50 Steering Committee.

Speaking at the Awards Ceremony, President Tony Tan made a resounding tribute to the Chinese business pioneers. He said:

Despite the challenges and uncertainties surrounding Singapore's future then, many of our Business Pioneers decided to build their lives here. They left their former homes in China, Malaysia, Indonesia, and even Hong Kong and Taiwan to start their businesses from scratch in Singapore. As the Singapore economy evolved and progressed, these Business Pioneers seized opportunities and adapted to the environment. Our Pioneers believed in Singapore's future and remained rooted here.

President Tony Tan concluded his speech by saying that

our Pioneers have left us a rich legacy by working together as a community, taking care of the less fortunate, and succeeding in spite of their adverse conditions. I therefore urge the next generation of entrepreneurs and business representatives in SCCCI to continue the good work of your predecessors. I am confident that with the fortitude our Pioneers have shown us, we can rise to meet the challenges ahead of us. Together, let us build on our achievements and strong partnerships to bring Singapore and Singaporean businesses to new heights over the next fifty years.

In a short video screened at the awards ceremony, PM Lee Hsien Loong acknowledged the contributions of this group of Chinese business pioneers:

Recipients of the Chinese business pioneers awards have made important contributions to Singapore's economic development. Not only are they accomplished, they also actively give back to society with their time and resources. They are the pillars of our nation and role models for our society.

The SG50 Outstanding Chinese Business Pioneers Awards was a landmark event initiated by the SCCCI in celebration of Singapore's 50th year of independence and was co-organised with *Lianhe Zaobao* and *The Business Times*.

Tracing the Chamber's Contributions to Singapore's Development — SCCCI-SG50 Special Exhibition

Another key SG50 project of the Chinese Chamber was an exhibition staged at the Singapore Flyer from July to September 2015. The Special Exhibition featured a 20-minute immersive multi-media show depicting the many milestones the Chamber has achieved in the nation-building journey followed by a pictorial exhibition of the significant contributions of the Chamber.

It was named "47 Hill Street" not only because this is the premises of the SCCCI but it is also a heritage building that has witnessed many important episodes in the history of Singapore, both before and after Singapore's independence.

The multi-media show and the photographic exhibition showed the leading role played by the SCCCI in championing the rights of the Chinese community when Singapore was under British rule, the many social and welfare services provided by the Chamber and its leaders, and the support given to the fund-raising efforts for Nanyang University. Visitors were also reminded that when the young Republic founded the National Defence Force, the SCCCI was in the forefront of the fund-raising efforts.

More importantly the exhibition highlighted the Chinese entrepreneurial spirit of pursuing excellence, the philanthropic spirit of giving back to society and sharing the fruits of prosperity. These were the qualities that propelled the pioneers of the Chinese community and leaders of the Chinese Chamber. It is hoped that their stories will be a source of inspiration to future generations of Singaporeans.

Chapter 2

Singapore Federation of Chinese Clan Associations
Revitalising Clan Associations

PANG Cheng Lian

The Genesis

A ministerial tour of Tanjong Pagar concluding with a dialogue at a community centre — this was the genesis of the Singapore Federation of Chinese Clan Associations (SFCCA) (新加坡宗乡会馆联合总会). Since its inauguration dinner held on 27 January 1986 this umbrella body of clan associations (*huiguan* in Mandarin) has played a major role in the promotion of the Chinese language, and Chinese heritage and culture in Singapore.

It all began on a Sunday (15 April 1984) when then Minister without Portfolio, Mr Ong Teng Cheong (王鼎昌); began his tour with a stop at the Singapore Chin Kang Huay Kuan (新加坡晋江会馆) in Bukit Pasoh Road. Founded in 1918 by fellow clansmen hailing from Quanzhou, Fujian, the Huay Kuan was then led by a 35-year old businessman, Chua Gim Siong (蔡锦淞) who was intent on revitalising his association.

Ong Teng Cheong's visit to the area ended with a lively exchange of views at the Tanjong Pagar community centre. The Chin Kang Huay Kuan President took the opportunity to talk about the important role played by clan associations in the past, and more importantly, their future contributions in the new socio-political environment. Clan associations, the earnest young man pointed out, could and should be galvanised into a pro-active communal force in Singapore.

Chua Gim Siong was voicing a concern uppermost in the minds of many Chinese community leaders — how to ensure that clan associations continued to play useful roles in the fast-changing Singapore landscape.

These uniquely Chinese organisations based on kinship ties had operated long before Singapore became an independent Republic. Records indicate that the Tsao Clan association (曹氏总会) formed by Tsao clansmen from the Taishan district in Guangdong province was operating as early as 1819, the year Sir Stamford Raffles arrived in Singapore.

As more immigrants from different parts of China found their way to the thriving port, the number of clan associations mushroomed. The associations were formed by people originating from the same district (Chin Kang Huay Kuan), or the same province (Hokkien Huay Kuan (福建会馆) or Hainan Hwee Kuan (海南会馆)), or by people with the same surname (Fong Clan General Association (冯氏总会) or Nanyang Huang Shi Chung Huay (南洋黄氏总会)). Others were formed by people having the same surname and coming from the same Chinese province or district such as Hainan Tan Clan Association (海南陈氏公会) and Singapore Cantonese Wong Clan Association (新加坡广东黄氏宗亲会).

These original Chinese self-help groups were the life-lines of the many early Chinese immigrants who arrived here without friends and money. Largely ignored by the British colonial government, these *sin keh* ("new guests" in the Hokkien dialect), turned to their fellow clansmen for support and assistance. From helping to secure employment to providing basic accommodation, the *huiguan* managed temples and cemeteries and, later, schools for the children as the migrant community took root. The Singapore Hokkien Huay Kuan, among the biggest and oldest, even issued marriage certificates as part of its functions.

Ironically, from 1965, the clan associations found their welfare role progressively diminished in the new Republic. As each successive People's Action Party (PAP) government extended coverage of social amenities for Singaporeans, the associations' "welfare role" shrank. Citizens could get their requests met via the "meet-the-people" sessions with Members of Parliament or directly from government agencies. Reliance on fellow clansmen to resolve welfare issues was replaced by dependence on government departments.

Education, especially the provision of Chinese medium schools, which had distinguished the bigger clan associations during the British colonial era, largely became part of the government domain after 1978 when all schools were converted into "national" schools. English became the main medium of instruction with "mother tongues" (Mandarin, Malay and Tamil) taught as a second language. (In 1979 SAP [Special Assistance Plan] schools were introduced which taught Chinese as a first language, side by side with English).

Although some *huiguan* continue to provide financial support for the schools founded by them, many have reduced their support for education to the provision of bursaries and scholarships for children of members and even non-members.

Even more worrying to the elders of the clan associations was the challenge of recruiting new members into their fold. Younger Singaporeans were not only dropping their dialects as the Speak Mandarin campaigns took hold; born and bred in Singapore, they had less affinity to the "home" villages and provinces represented by the geography based clans. Rejuvenation of the *huiguan* became a major issue.

The problem was exacerbated by the perception that the old clan associations had lost their relevance in modern Singapore. A plethora of civic, charitable and sports organisations had sprouted up in a vibrant and thriving Singapore, vying for the attention and support of the younger citizens.

Equally worrying to the older members of the clan associations was the growing influence of Western ideas and social mores in the community. The new Republic of Singapore had launched a two-pronged approach towards economic growth immediately after Separation — an export-oriented industrialisation programme and creation of a financial centre. Both required the new nation to open its doors to the West, for Western investors and Western technology.

The twin engines of economic growth propelled Singapore to become Asia's "boom" country. The many multinational companies and banks expanded the expatriate community. By the mid-1980s, there was growing concern among the older Chinese community leaders over the "Westernisation" of Singapore. In particular, many worried about the loss of their Chinese heritage among the younger population.

When Chua Gim Siong raised the issue of the future roles of clan associations at the dialogue session at the close of Minister Ong Teng Cheong's visit to the Tanjong Pagar constituency, therefore, he was voicing a major concern of the Chinese community. While there was recognition and acceptance of the future dominance of the English language and Western ideas, members of the Chinese community hoped that the Chinese language and Chinese traditional virtues would continue to have important roles in the country.

The Minister was empathetic. Chng Jit Koon（庄日昆）, then Minister of State for Community Development was asked to follow up and he held several meetings with Chua Gim Siong and other clan leaders to discuss the subject.

Asked to recall the events in 2014 Chng Jit Koon told this writer,

> There was general agreement that clan associations had contributed greatly in the past, and should continue to play a vital role in the community. But it was also recognised that the socio-political environment had changed considerably, and the *huiguan* would have to find new functions and new activities to stay relevant.

The deliberations with the clan representatives culminated with a lunch hosted by Chng and attended by Minister Ong and the leaders of several clan associations. It was decided that a major seminar would be organised to map out the future directions of the *huiguan*. Minister Ong agreed to speak at the proposed seminar.

Nine clan associations [Singapore Hokkien Huay Kuan (新加坡福建会馆), Singapore Teochew Poit Ip Huay Kuan（新加坡潮州八邑会馆）, Singapore Nanyang Khek Community Guild（新加坡南洋客属总会）, Singapore Kwangtung Hui Kuan (新加坡广东会馆), Singapore Hainan Hwee Kuan（新加坡海南会馆）, Singapore Sam Kiang Huay Kwan（新加坡三江会馆）, Singapore Chin Kang Huay Kuan（新加坡晋江会馆）, Singapore Hui Ann Association (新加坡惠安公会) and Singapore Nanyang Fang Shee Association (新加坡南洋方氏总会)] and representatives of the Chinese press formed an organising committee for the seminar. The Chairman of the Hokkien Huay Kuan, Wee Cho Yaw (黄祖耀) was appointed the Committee Chairman.

Wee Cho Yaw, who was then Chairman and Chief Executive Officer of the United Overseas Bank (大华银行), was already a respected community leader. He was the Honorary President of the Singapore Chinese Chamber of Commerce & Industry (新加坡中华总商会), having served as its president between 1969–1973, and 1977–1979. He had been the founding President of the Singapore Federation of the Chambers of Commerce & Industry in 1978 and had served on the boards of several government bodies.

The one-day forum held on 2 December 1984 was attended by 665 representatives from 185 clan associations and 37 representatives from Chinese cultural groups. The theme was appropriately entitled "How Singapore's clan associations can play a more useful role in the new era".

In his opening address, Minister Ong Teng Cheong made five suggestions. To meet the challenges of modern Singapore, he urged the associations to review and update their constitutions, to rejuvenate by attracting younger members, to introduce new activities that resonate with the new interests of the young, to complement the welfare services of government agencies and to collaborate with other grassroots organisations for greater effectiveness.

The Chairman of the seminar's organising committee, Wee Cho Yaw was more blunt. Unless clan associations found new roles in the new era, he warned, they faced oblivion.

The forum concluded with 10 recommendations, which included all the suggestions made by the guest of honour. In addition, the forum called on *huiguan* to promote the Chinese language and Chinese culture and to increase and improve their relations and cooperation with one another. It also called on the government to assist those clan associations which wanted to rent or buy their own premises. Most important of all, the seminar proposed the setting up of a central body to facilitate collaboration among the associations.

With the Hokkiens being the dominant dialect group in the country, and the Hokkien Huay Kuan being among the oldest and biggest clan associations, its chairman was tasked with the challenge of establishing the umbrella body. Wee Cho Yaw and his team took a year to draw up the objectives and structure of the SFCCA.

In an interview with this writer in September 2014, Wee Cho Yaw revealed the thinking behind the SFCCA framework.

Right from the start our intention was to have a voluntary association of like-minded *huiguan* that wanted to pool their resources to continue to make positive contributions to the community and the nation. SFCCA wasn't about merging the weaker clans with stronger ones. What we wanted was to get the bigger associations help the smaller ones to revitalise themselves through new programmes and new activities.

Mr Wee added that there was general agreement on the need to focus on preserving the rich Chinese heritage by promoting the Chinese language, Chinese values and traditions. With the growing influx of Western ideas and culture, the clan associations saw themselves as the bastions of Asian values. The SFCCA would spearhead and support their efforts in meeting this challenge.

But the new activities and programmes required funding and support. Some associations were financially sound because they were receiving rentals from their properties acquired years ago. Many of the smaller associations, however, relied largely on the donations of their more wealthy members. As the number of these financiers dwindled with the passage of time, many of the small *huiguan* were inactive through lack of funds.

If there was to be a national effort to revive the *huiguan* and enhance their role in promoting Chinese traditions and values, the bigger associations would have to lend a helping hand. The founders of SFCCA worked out a two-fold solution.

Recognising that the seven so-called *da (major) huiguan* representing the largest dialect groups (Hokkien Huay Kuan, Teochew Poit Ip Huay Kuan, the Kwangtung Hui Kuan, the Khek Community Guild, the Hainan Hwee Kuan, the Foochow Association and Sam Kiang Huay Kwan) would have to take the lead because of their stronger resources, their special position was enshrined in the SFCCA constitution. The heads of these associations were automatically members of the 15-member governing Council of the Federation. The constitution further provided that the president of the new body would have to be chosen from among these seven representatives. (The Appendix provides details of these seven founding *huiguan*.)

Wee Cho Yaw was unanimously elected as pro-tem Chairman and Teo Soo Chuan (张泗川), head of the Teochew Poit Ip Huay Kuan was named the Vice-Chairman. The other pro-tem committee members were: Cheong Weng (张荣) (Kwangtung Hui Kuan), Chok Chai Mun (卓济民) (Khek Community Guild), Chwee Meng Chong (水铭漳) (Sam Kiang Huay Kwan), Wee Tin Teck (王先德) (Hainan Hwee Kuan) and Ling Lee Hua (林理化) (Foochow Association). Besides these representing the seven "big" associations, the pro-tem committee included Chua Gim Siong (Chin Kang Huay Kuan) and Teo Liang Chye (张良材) (Teochew Poit Ip Huay Kuan).

To encourage public donations to fund the new activities of the Federation and its members, Wee Cho Yaw proposed the creation of a Clan

Foundation with the status of an Institution of Public Character (IPC). This would allow donors to enjoy tax exemptions for their donations to the Foundation. The Government accepted the need for such an arrangement and Hsu Tse Kwang (徐籍光), then Comptroller of Income Tax was requested to facilitate the registration of the IPC. Within six months of the registration of SFCCA, the Singapore Clan Foundation was registered with IPC status.

On 9 December 1985 the SFFCA was registered as a society. A month later, on January 27 an inauguration dinner attended by more than 1,000 *huiguan* and community leaders heralded the birth of the second major Chinese organisation in Singapore. While the older Chinese Chamber of Commerce & Industry's primary focus was business, the SFCCA's main activities would be in the cultural sphere. Still, discerning observers would have noted that the leaders of these two Chinese organisations were largely the same people. From the start the two bodies had a symbiotic relationship, with many common leaders and many collaborative efforts.

The man who had started the ball rolling, and who had been promoted to Deputy Prime Minister in 1985, Ong Teng Cheong formally launched the new organisation. Dwelling on the theme of unity through strength, the guest of honour told the audience that "united as one, the influence of the clans would be greater and they would achieve more."

SFCCA's President Wee Cho Yaw emphasised that the new Federation would enable the clan associations to cooperate and increase their activities. He announced that more than $400,000 had been raised to fund the activities of the new organisation and its members.

The Federation was founded on three basic objectives:

- To promote the understanding and appreciation of the Chinese language, culture and values.
- To assist clan associations to rejuvenate and cooperate for mutual benefit.
- To work closely with other civic organisations to ensure a stable and harmonious Singapore.

A 15-member Council comprising the heads of the seven founding clan associations, six elected members and two co-opted members formed the apex of the organisation. Below the Council was a Working Committee headed by the SFCCA's Secretary General and made up of representatives of other clan associations. Wee Cho Yaw was confirmed as Chairman while Teo Soo Chuan was confirmed as Deputy Chairman. Teo Liang Chye was appointed Secretary General and Cheong Weng became its first Treasurer.

SFCCA started with 65 members which increased to 104 in its first year, representing a third of the estimated 300 *huiguan* registered under the Societies Act at that time. To kick-start the new organisation, the Hokkien Huay Kuan provided free secretariat space and services in the Federation's first few years.

Promoting Understanding and Appreciation of Chinese Culture and Values

Recognising that the young Federation needed to communicate effectively with its members and the rest of the Chinese community, among its first initiatives was a Chinese quarterly magazine *Yuan* 原 (origin/source).

Reflecting on the idea behind *Yuan*, Chua Gim Siong who was the SFCCA's Secretary General from 1988 to 2005, said in an interview in 2014,

> We wanted to keep our members informed of what the Federation and our members were doing. More importantly, we wanted a channel to encourage discussion on Chinese culture and the Chinese language and to disseminate the rich heritage of clan associations in Singapore.

The editorial team (made up of volunteers from the *huiguan* and journalists from the Chinese press, including the editor of *Lianhe Zaobao* (联合早报) Loy Teck Juan (黎德源) led by Secretary General Chua took pains to highlight the activities of the Federation's members as well as the colourful history of the clan associations. As at beginning of 2015 Yuan is into its 113th issue and continues to focus on the social and cultural aspects of the Chinese community.

Because of financial constraints, the SFCCA has depended largely on volunteers. Madam Lim Boon Tan (林文丹), a Nanyang University graduate who was hired as Executive Secretary in 1987 and retired in 2014, pointed out the secretariat was a one-woman show until it relocated to its own building in Toa Payoh in 1997. But the SFCCA managed to organise about two dozen projects each year because of its corps of dedicated volunteers.

While the Council focussed on fund-raising and approved the annual projects and budget, the Working Committee made up of volunteers drawn mainly from the clan associations and cultural groups formed the think tank and worker bees of the fledgling organisation.

Helmed by the Federation's Secretary General, the Working Committee started with four main sub-committees — administration, research and publications, culture, and membership. The sub-committee heads and their deputies held monthly meetings to strategise and organise SFCCA's wide-ranging programmes. Discussions were often intense as the sub-committees argued for greater funding support for their respective projects.

Following the constitutional changes in 2012, the committees have been re-organised and increased to six — Members' Affairs, Social Affairs, Cultural, Research, Youth and Property. The chairmen of these six committees form the SFCCA's Executive Committee, which is chaired by the President and includes the two Vice Presidents, the Secretary General and his two deputies as well as the Treasurer.

Publications

Besides *Yuan*, the SFCCA has published a host of books on Chinese culture and clan associations. Among the first was a 146-page *History of the Chinese Clan Associations in Singapore* published in 1986 in collaboration with the National Archives, Oral History Department and Singapore News & Publications Ltd (SNPL). The bilingual pictorial was published in conjunction with an exhibition of clan associations and their contributions organised by the SFCCA.

Three years later, in 1989, the Federation brought out another landmark publication with a bilingual handbook *Chinese Customs and Festivals in Singapore*. As explained by SFCCA President Wee Cho Yaw in the foreword, "A major objective of the handbook is to explain the origins and more important, the meaning of Chinese festivals and customs."

Aimed at reminding young readers of their rich heritage, the stories behind eight major Chinese festivals were told in simple terms. The significance of the festivals and the rituals of births, marriages and funerals were explained in a Singapore context. The observance of *Qing Ming Jie*, for example is a reminder for Singaporeans to practise filial piety, while *Duan*

Wu Jie (the dragon boat/dumpling festival which commemorates the death of Qu Yuan) is cited as a celebration to honour patriots. The book was a runaway bestseller and its first print of 50,000 was sold within six months. The book went into its fourth print run in 1993.

Over the years the Federation has produced more than a dozen books on a broad range of subjects catering to the young and the senior citizens, and to academics as well as lay readers. In 2005 it published a ground-breaking two-volume bilingual history of 203 clan associations in Singapore, tracing their origins as well as updating their membership and activities. Entitled *History of Clan Associations in Singapore*, this informative book also lists 39 international clan associations which have links with Singapore *huiguan*. A glossary provides the schools, temples and cemeteries associated with the clan associations.

In celebration of Singapore's 50th anniversary and SFCCA's 30th birthday in 2015, the Federation is publishing a complete history of the Chinese in Singapore. Edited by Kua Bak Lim (柯木林), a Council member and Chairman of the Research Committee, this massive Chinese publication traces the growth and development of the Chinese community from the 14th century.

In 2012 the SFCCA launched a new magazine under the aegis of the National Integration Council. Appropriately entitled "Oneness" (*Hua Hui*), the publication is targeted at the new immigrants to help them settle down in their new country of adoption. Harking back to their historical role of providing help and succour to the *sin keh*, the SFCCA is encouraging its members to facilitate the integration of the new immigrants.

Cultural Performances

Right from the start, the SFCCA Council recognised that support for the cultural activities by *huiguan* was an effective way to help them attract younger members.

Perng Peck Seng (方百成), the first head of the Culture Sub-Committee who is now Deputy Secretary General of SFCCA explained in a 2014 interview,

> Starting singing, music and dance classes was one way to attract younger members into clan associations. But having started the classes, the associations needed to show off their students' achievements and the students also wanted a platform to demonstrate their new-found skills.

So among Peck Seng's first proposals to the SFCCA Council was the organisation of a concert showcasing the talents of the various *huiguan*. *Zhong Xiang Zhi Ye* (An Evening with the Clans) gave the smaller associations an opportunity to share the limelight with the bigger SFCCA members. To encourage younger Singaporeans' interest in the Chinese performing arts, the SFCCA's cultural sub-committee also organised several *Qing Chun Lang Hua (Waves of Youth)* concerts featuring performers of schools, universities and youth groups.

In line with its objective to promote Chinese culture, the SFCCA collaborated with the Chinese newspapers division of the Singapore Press Holdings (SPH) in 1987 to initiate the Singapore River Hongbao event. Many in the Chinese community were concerned with the loss of interest in their cultural heritage among the young. This loss of interest had extended to the most important Chinese festival, the Lunar New Year. It was hoped that the River Hongbao would revive this major event in the Chinese calendar.

In the first five years the event was led by the Chinese newspapers division of SPH, with supporting roles played by the SFCCA, SCCCI, People's Association and the Singapore Tourism Board. In 1992, the SFCCA took on the coordinating role with its President as Chairman of the organising committee.

Over the next 18 years the SFCCA and its Cultural Sub-Committee organised the annual celebration of the Chinese New Year based on the following principles:

1. Its programme and activities should cater to the young and old and be family-oriented, in line with the overarching message that the spring festival celebrates family unity and togetherness.
2. The site must have the ambience of spring since the lunar New Year is also known as the spring festival.
3. Besides being entertaining, the event should have an educational element, that is, to remind younger Singaporeans of their rich Chinese heritage.

The first Singapore River Hongbao was held along the walkways of the Singapore River near Parliament House. But the annual celebration had to move southwards progressively because of construction works in the area.

Since 2010 the organising committee of the annual event has been helmed by a Member of Parliament. However, the SFCCA continues to provide secretariat support and Perng Peck Seng continues to assist in the cultural shows.

Like the Chingay parade organised by the People's Association and the Chinatown lightup, the River Hongbao show is now an essential feature of Singapore's Chinese New Year festivities.

Chinese Language

The promotion of the Chinese language is embedded in the SFCCA constitution. While recognising that English has to be the dominant language in a multiacial Singapore plugged into the global economy, the Chinese community leaders believe the mother tongue is important for psychological ballast. To help raise the standard of Chinese in the country, the SFCCA has launched several initiatives.

In 1990 the Federation founded Zhong Xiang Kindergarten which was the first preschool to give greater weightage to the teaching of Chinese. It decided to allocate 70% of teaching time to the learning of Chinese. The emphasis on Chinese received favourable response. But as other pre-schools started offering more Chinese classes as well, SFCCA decided to close its kindergarten in 2003.

In an effort to encourage students to read more Chinese language books, the SFCCA established a Supplementary Reader Committee in 1993, tasked with vetting and approving Chinese publications suitable for young readers. Chaired by the Federation's Secretary General, Chua Ghim Siong and comprising educationists and publishers, the Committee's recommended supplementary reading materials were endorsed by the Ministry of Education. This endorsement helped to guide parents on the choice of Chinese supplementary books for their children.

In support of the government's efforts to nurture a corps of bilingual and bi-cultural young Singaporeans, the SFCCA provided scholarships to pre-university students, university undergraduates as well as graduates who chose to go overseas to further their Chinese studies. In 2004 it initiated a Chinese Language and Culture Fund.

At a joint SFCCA and SCCCI dinner to commemorate the appointment of Lee Hsien Loong as Singapore's third Prime Minister, the Federation's

President Wee Cho Yaw proposed the setting up of a $10-million fund to help finance community efforts to promote and raise the standard of Chinese in Singapore. The government responded with a pledge of a dollar-for-dollar matching grant. Within a few months more than $8 million was raised and a joint committee of representatives of SFCCA and SCCCI was set up to administer the Fund. As at end of 2014 the Fund has dispensed more than $9 million for a wide range of activities such as publications, China immersion trips for students, and seminars and forums.

Galvanising the Clan Associations

Article 4 of the SFCCA constitution which lists the objectives of the organisation has two references to clan associations. The SFCCA is "to lead the Chinese clan associations in Singapore" and "to establish an integrated network of Chinese clan associations in Singapore".

The new Federation, therefore, made it a point to meet up with its members to see how it could help them increase their membership and improve their organisational capabilities. Courses were conducted to upgrade the administrative abilities of the *huiguan* staff, and workshops were organised to advise on the maintenance and preservation of historical documents and artefacts. To assist the financially weak associations, the SFCCA President personally started a fund for activities organised by the smaller members of the Federation.

In the years following the establishment of the SFCCA there was a discernible burst of activities among the clan associations. While some focussed on cultural activities such as dance and Chinese orchestral classes, others preferred to delve into their history for publications of their past. Many started membership drives and established youth groups to lead their recruitment exercise.

In line with its leadership role, the SFCCA organised exhibitions to showcase the rich history of the various clan associations. To encourage its members to foster greater interaction, food fairs offering the traditional food of the different dialect groups were organised. The food carnival proved to be so popular that it was extended to include Malay and Indian food.

The 1990s saw an interesting phenomenon in the local *huiguan* scene, that is, a surge of world conventions of clan associations held in Singapore. According to a SFCCA report, between 1989 and 2003 Singapore's clan associations organised 38 global conventions involving their fellow clansmen. Many of these were mammoth events, attracting hundreds of overseas participants from the region and China. In 2012 a three-day World Fujian Fellowship Conference organised by the Singapore Hokkien Huay Kuan attracted more than 4,000 attendees.

Singapore's role as a centre of the Chinese overseas was further enhanced in 1995 with the publication of *The Encyclopaedia of Chinese Overseas* by the Chinese Heritage Centre (华裔馆) (CHC), established on the initiative of the SFCCA in 1992. The CHC story is related in another chapter. Suffices it to say here that the CHC, founded to study the story of the Chinese diaspora, was an extension of the SFCCA's efforts to enhance its members' international network in the global Chinese community.

Lending a Helping Hand to the Community

Helping the poor and the needy had been the raison d'état of Singapore's clan associations. The SFCCA has maintained this philanthropic tradition.

In 1992, the Federation joined hands with the Chinese Chamber to launch the Chinese Development Assistance Council (华社自助理事会) (CDAC). The Malays had established their self-help group Yayasan Mendaki in 1982 while discussions for the establishment of SINDA to assist the Indian community had begun in September 1990. (It was launched in August 1991.) In July 1991 Prime Minister Goh Chok Tong mooted the idea of a "Chinese Mendaki" to help the under-privileged in the Chinese community. The two leading Chinese organisations agreed with the Government's suggestion and appointed a committee to hammer out a framework for a supra Chinese self-help group.

CDAC was launched in 1992 and President Wee Cho Yaw of SFCCA was appointed Chairman of its Board of Trustees. The creation of CDAC and its programmes to improve the lives of the Chinese underclass are fully recounted by Gerald Singham in the following chapter.

What is pertinent to mention here is that the SFCCA was tasked by the CDAC to assist in the disbursement of funds urgently needed by the poor due to unforeseen calamities. As a start the SFCCA's Hardship Fund was provided with $2 million and the interest income from this was used to help those in dire straits. The Hardship Fund Committee was chaired by the Federation's secretary general.

Reflections at 20

In 2005 the SFCCA celebrated its 20th birthday with a series of activities that summarised its primary focus and successes over the past two decades.

Underscoring the Federation's determination to improve and upgrade the Chinese language, the first event which kicked off the year-long celebration was a "big walk" to raise funds for the newly launched Chinese Language and Culture Fund. The 2-kilometer walk attracted 4,000 participants from the Federation's members. It raised over $60,000.

Reflecting its interest in promoting Chinese cultural activities among the young, a forum on Youth and Culture was jointly organised with Chinese newspapers and radio and television stations. The forum featured well-known personalities from China, Taiwan and Hong Kong and generated lively discussions among the 600 attendees.

A review of the SFCCA's major achievements was published in an anniversary book. And to help the Federation charter its future course, a survey of its members was conducted. By then membership stood at 192.

The anniversary celebration culminated with a variety show put up by its members and a fundraising golf tournament, both held in November, as well as a gala dinner in December.

Changing of the Guards

In 2010 Wee Cho Yaw stepped down as President and was succeeded by Chua Thian Poh (蔡天宝), a prominent businessman who was then President of the SCCCI. Earlier that year Wee had stepped down as the President of the Singapore Hokkien Huay Kuan after 38 years.

Like many of the other clan associations, the Hokkien Huay Kuan constitution did not cap the term of its office bearers. Convinced that leadership renewal was essential for good corporate governance, as well as the future development of the organisation, Wee pushed to amend the constitution to limit the terms of office bearers. This was done at the 2004 *huiguan* annual general meeting. Henceforth, the president was restricted to serving three terms of two years each. As a consequence, Wee relinquished the *huiguan* presidency in 2010 after completing the six years.

Since the SFCCA constitution stipulates that its president must be the head of one of the seven big *huiguan*, Wee also stepped down as the Hokkien Huay Kuan's representative in the SFCCA and as the Federation's president. The newly elected president of the Hokkien Huay Kuan, Chua Thian Poh was elected as SFCCA's president.

A successful entrepreneur, Chua Thian Poh had emerged as an active community leader in the 1990s. The Chairman and CEO of Ho Bee Land, he had served as President of the SCCCI from 2005 to 2009 and was Deputy President of the Hokkien Huay Kuan from 1992. He is also Chairman of Singapore Business China and Renci Hospital.

Among the first projects of the new president was "porridge" lunches with all SFCCA members. These "no frills" lunches were useful feedback sessions to discuss new issues and problems faced by the Chinese community and the *huiguan* in the 21st century.

In the 25 years since the SFCCA's inauguration in 1986, Singapore's socio-economic landscape had changed considerably. For one, census reports showed that the country's population had grown from 3 million in 1990 to 5 million in 2010. The increase was largely due to the influx of foreign workers and new citizens and permanent residents. In particular, the two decades had witnessed a large increase of new immigrants from China, creating new integration challenges.

To ensure that the SFCCA adapted to the changed environment, President Chua and his team launched several new initiatives.

The Federation's constitution was amended in 2012 to expand the Council to 21 members, who are empowered to co-opt up to 10 others. Each term of office is three years and members have to be below 75 years of age. A new clause provided for the admission of "community groups" into the Federation with no voting rights. A Second Vice-President was added to the list of office bearers but the constitution only specifies that the President and one of the Vice Presidents would be elected from among the seven founding members.

Integration of the new Chinese immigrants has become a core activity. Just as the clan associations had been centres of support for immigrants in the early history of Singapore, the SFCCA took on the task of helping the 21st century immigrants integrate into the community. The organisations registered by the new immigrants were welcomed into the SFCCA fold and are encouraged to participate in its activities. Significantly, a "new" immigrant, Zhong Sheng Jian (钟声坚) was elected SFCCA's 2nd Vice-President in 2012.

In the same year discussions started on the creation of a new centre to enhance cultural interaction in the Chinese community. Supported by the Government, the proposed building would serve as a nerve centre for cultural organisations and their programmes. SFCCA would spearhead and manage the centre.

After two years of planning, the Singapore Chinese Cultural Centre (新加坡华族文化中心) (SCCC) got off the ground on 29 September 2014 with a ground breaking ceremony officiated by Prime Minister Lee Hsien Loong. Choo Thiam Siew, who has had a distinguished career in the National Parks Board, National Arts Council and Nanyang Academy of Fine Arts, is the chief executive officer of the new Centre, which is expected to be in operation by 2016.

Asked to talk about his new project in late 2014, Choo Thiam Siew was clear about his new challenge.

> Getting the structure up is probably the easier part of the equation. The greater challenge is to develop the Triple C into a beacon for local and overseas arts and cultural groups. The Centre must come "alive" with performances, exhibitions and dialogues so that the Chinese cultural scene will be further enriched.

SFCCA's President Chua Thian Poh, who has been a driving force behind the project, considers the Centre to be an important extension of the Federation's mission to promote Chinese culture in Singapore.

In an interview with this writer in February 2015, he explained,

> SFCCA was formed because we saw a need to rejuvenate clan associations. We needed to adopt new roles so that the associations can stay relevant, especially to younger Singaporeans. One effective way is to build upon our strength as the repository of our rich Chinese heritage.

But, in the mind of the SFCCA President, the Chinese heritage must also move with the times. Chua Thian Poh pointed out,

> In the last 50 years we have relied mainly on China and Taiwan as the primary sources of Chinese traditions and culture. In the next 50 years we need to evolve our own Singapore values, art forms and cultural expressions.

Appendix: SFCCA's Seven Founding Members

Although the Chinese language has a common script, the pronunciation of the common characters varies widely across the various dialects. Thus it has been commented that it is sometimes easier for a Hokkien or a Cantonese to understand a non-Chinese than a fellow Chinese from Shanghai.

Arising from the difficulties in communication, the early Chinese immigrants tended to congregate in enclaves based on dialects. Telok Ayer was generally dominated by the Hokkiens, while the Teochews concentrated in the Clarke Quay area. Kreta Ayer had more Cantonese residents while the Middle Road/Beach Road vicinity was mainly populated by the Hainanese.

And when the penniless and largely uneducated new immigrants needed assistance, they naturally looked for clansmen speaking their dialects. So the clan associations based on provinces and people speaking the same dialect attracted larger numbers of members. By virtue of their larger membership base, longer history and wider influence, seven of these became known as the seven *da huiguan* (大会馆).

All the seven major clan associations have histories dating well before the birth of the Republic of Singapore. All of them have played important roles in providing schools, temples, cemeteries and welfare services for their clansmen.

Singapore Hokkien Huay Kuan (SHHK)

Tracing its origin to the Thian Hock Keng Temple in Telok Ayer Street, this major clan association started operations in 1840, but was only officially registered as the Singapore Hokkien Kuan under the Company Act in 1937. In 1977 the *huiguan* registered The Hokkien Foundation (福建基金) as a non-profit company limited by guarantee to operate as its charitable arm.

A staunch supporter of education and schools, the SHHK made history when it donated 525 acres of its land in Jurong to establish Nanyang University in 1953. The first Chinese university founded outside China, Nanyang University merged with the Singapore University in 1980. In 1991 Nanyang Technological University was established on the campus.

Although schools now come under the Ministry of Education, the *huiguan* continues to aid five primary schools (Ai Tong, Chongfu, Kong Hwa, Nan Chiau and Tao Nan) and one secondary school (Nan Chiau

High). Except for Chongfu and Nan Chiau Primary, the others are Special Assistance Plan (SAP) schools which teach both English and Chinese as first languages.

In line with its objective of promoting Chinese performing arts, SHHK has been running a very successful Arts and Cultural Troupe since 1986, which conducts a range of activities catering to young children as well as retirees. In 2014 it established the Singapore Hokkien Huay Kuan Kindergarten, with emphasis on the teaching of Chinese.

Besides the Thian Hock Keng Temple (天福宮), the clan association also oversees the operations of three other old temples, namely Leng San Teng (麟山亭), Kim Lan Beo (金兰庙) and Rochor Tua Pek Kong (梧槽大伯公庙).

As its name implies, all members have to be Hokkiens, and at the close of 2014, membership stood at 5,500. The *huiguan* also works closely with the other 29 smaller Hokkien speaking locality clan associations in Singapore.

Teochew Poit Ip Huay Kuan

Founded in 1929, the Poit Ip Huay Kuan comprises members from eight Teochew-speaking districts in Guangdong province. These are Chaoan, Chenghai, Chaoyang, Jieyang, Raoping, Puning, Huilai, and Nanao.

Led by businessman Lim Nee Soon (林义顺) the clan association was pro-active in helping the poor and supporting educational institutions. It worked closely with the other Teochew organisation, Ngee Ann Kongsi (义安公司), which had been formed a century earlier in 1845 to manage the Yueh Hai Ching Temple (粤海清庙) and to acquire cemeteries for the Teochew community.

While Ngee Ann Kongsi has focussed on providing financial assistance to educational institutions, the *huiguan* has concentrated on improving interaction among the Teochews and their clan associations. In the past few decades it has spent considerable resources on promoting Teochew culture and publications. In 1998 it set up a historical and cultural resource centre cum library to compile materials of Teochews all over the world.

The Poit Ip Huay Kuan has 64 corporate members (which are smaller Teochew *huiguan*) and 5,000 individual members.

Singapore Kwangtung Hui Kuan (SKHK)

Although more closely associated with the Cantonese speaking Singaporeans, the SKHK is not a dialect-based clan association. Registered in 1937 the SKHK comprised the administrative divisions of Guangdong province. Besides the Cantonese, the province (and SKHK) has Hakka (Kheh), Teochew and Hainanese speakers.

Direct membership is not large. As at the close of 2014 the association had almost 300 members of which 65 were other clan associations and nine were corporate members. Of the individual members more than half (119) are Cantonese, 47 are Teochews, 42 are Hakka and less than 10 are Hainanese.

Besides promoting Chinese cultural activities (classes on language and performance arts are conducted virtually every day of the week), the SKHK has played an active role in promoting global interaction of Guangdong clansmen. In 1997, in conjunction with its 60th anniversary celebration it invited fellow Guangdong clansmen from around the world. This led to a proposal to establish The World Guangdong Community Federation (世界广东同乡联谊大会), which held its first convention in Singapore in 2000.

The Nanyang Khek Community Guild (NKCG)

In contrast to the Kwangtung Hui Kuan, the Nanyang Khek Community Guild is based solely on Chinese of Khek/Hakka origin. Unlike the other dialect groups the Hakkas do not have their own province. Instead, they are dispersed in districts in Guangdong, Fujian and Jiangxi. The Chinese word for Hakka is *ke* (客guest), a reference to their migratory history.

There are about a dozen Hakka clan associations in Singapore, including the Ying Fo Fui Kun founded in 1822, ranking it among the oldest *huiguan* in the country. In 1929 Ying Fo Fui Kun got together with seven other Hakka associations to register the NKCG as the umbrella body for fellow clansmen.

Since its founding the NKCG has played an active role in promoting Hakka culture and the history of the community. Its choir has made a name for itself in *shan ge* (traditional folk songs) performances, and its resource centre has a rich collection of Hakka historical records and artefacts.

The association has about 2,500 individual members and 24 corporate members. It lists current Prime Minister Lee Hsien Loong as its honourary adviser.

Singapore Hainan Hwee Kuan

The Hainan Hwee Kuan was founded in 1854 as the Kiung Chow Hwee Kuan (*Qiong Zhou Hui Guan*). This was the old name of the island when it was governed as part of Guangdong. In 1994 the Chinese government created Hainan province, and the clan association decided to change its name to Hainan Hwee Kuan.

Just as the Singapore Hokkien Huay Kuan is closely associated with Thian Hock Keng Temple, the history of Hainan Hwee Kuan is closely intertwined with Tin Hou Kong Temple. Prior to World War II the two organisations operated as one entity. While the *huiguan* handled the social issues of members, the temple managed the fundraising and financial matters.

From the 1980s, the association strengthened its cultural and research sections by organising a wide range of classes for its members and publishing the literary works of its clansmen. Today it also runs the Kheng Chiu Loke Tin Kee Home for the aged.

The *huiguan* continues to maintain close ties with Hainan province. In 1995 it established a Hainan Provincial Educational Foundation (海南省教育基金) to help train talents in the Chinese province. Tours to Hainan are organised regularly and especially during the *Qing Ming Jie*.

The association has 5,000 members, including 50 corporate members.

Sam Kiang Huay Kwan

Formed in 1906, the Sam Kiang Huay Kwan started as a clan association for immigrants from Zhejiang, Jiangsu and Jiangxi. Its Mandarin name, *Sanjiang* refers to these three places in China. In 1945 the *huiguan* constitution was amended to include clansmen of the provinces along the Yangtse River, Yellow River and Heilongjiang as its members. Shanghainese is the dominant dialect of these members.

Although the *Sanjiang* community is relatively small, the Sam Kiang Huay Kuan maintains an ancestral hall that keeps up to 30,000 urns of ashes. It is the focal point for the members at *Qing Ming Jie* every year.

Since 1974, the association has been operating a Sam Kiang Charity Medical Centre (三江慈善医疗中心) which provides free medical services for all races.

To ensure the financial strength of the association, clan leaders decided in 1989 to redevelop its old building into residential units. Two-thirds of the development was sold and part of the proceeds were used to purchase a new building for the *huiguan*. The rest has been rented out to provide a steady stream of income to fund its activities.

The association has 500 individual and six corporate members.

Singapore Foochow Association

Registered in 1909, this *huiguan* serves the clansmen from 10 Fuzhou prefectures in the northern section of Fujian province. Sharing the same Foochow dialect, the early immigrants were mainly engaged in the services sector such as coffee shops or working as barbers and tailors. The association's building in Jalan Besar completed in 1977 was a joint venture between the *huiguan* and the Foochow Coffee Restaurant and Bar Merchants Association (新加坡福州咖啡酒餐商公会).

Despite the small size of this dialect group, the Singapore Foochow Association is an active member of the Chinese community. It has managed a school and a cemetery, both of which have been closed because of government land acquisition. Today it continues to support the promotion of the Chinese language by organising competitions and presenting awards for excellence in the language among students.

It has about 880 direct and 20 corporate members.

CHAPTER 3

The Chinese Development Assistance Council
An Enriching Journey with a Self-Help Group

Gerald SINGHAM

An Illustrious History

> CDAC was formed in 1992 to help children of the Chinese community do better in school. We wanted to motivate and help the weaker students. Education, after all, is the best way to improve the lives of Singaporeans, and give the next generation a brighter future... From Kan Seng's [Wong Kan Seng] report, we can say that CDAC has succeeded in its mission... CDAC's success, as well as that of the other community self-help groups, shows that the Government's community-based self-help approach has worked.
>
> Former Prime Minister Goh Chok Tong,
> CDAC 10th Anniversary Charity Dinner, 11 May 2002

The CDAC's mission is to help the poor and raise their living standards... In the last 15 years, the CDAC has done many things to help the needy improve their lives. Every year, the CDAC reaches out to nearly 50,000 students and workers from low-income households. Students attend CDAC tuition classes, and benefit from leadership and enrichment activities. Workers upgrade their skills through the CDAC Skills Development Programme, and those looking for work are matched with jobs. Needy families are given assistance, including bursaries and subsidised personal computers for their children's education … The CDAC can be proud of its many achievements over the last 15 years.

Prime Minister Lee Hsien Loong,
CDAC 15th Anniversary Appreciation Dinner, 22 May 2007

CDAC was founded in 1992 to help less fortunate Chinese families and academically weaker students. It ensured that as Singapore progressed, all members of [the] Chinese community benefitted. It provided a platform for the Chinese community to help its less fortunate members… Over 20 years, the CDAC has helped many, many people.

Prime Minister Lee Hsien Loong,
CDAC 20th Anniversary Celebrations, 6 May 2012

If the success of an institution may be gauged by the tributes that it receives over the course of its history, these glowing accolades from the top leaders of our nation would confirm the Chinese Development Assistance Council's (CDAC) (华社自助理事会) illustrious achievements over the past 22 years. These words of approbation also serve as a useful reminder of CDAC's continued mission of nurturing and developing the potential of the Chinese community to contribute to the continued success of multiracial Singapore.

Established on 22 May 1992 as a corporate entity, the CDAC was first mooted by then Prime Minister Goh Chok Tong (吴作栋) in July 1991 with the strong support and backing of the Singapore Chinese Chamber of Commerce & Industry (SCCCI) (新加坡中华总商会) and the Singapore Federation of Chinese Clan Associations (SFCCA) (新加坡宗乡会馆联合总会). The creation of the CDAC in fact followed the footsteps of the earlier established ethnic-based self-help groups — Yayasan Mendaki and the Singapore Indian Development Association (SINDA) in 1982 and 1991 respectively.

Due to its similarities with its first predecessor — Yayasan Mendaki, it was not surprising that the CDAC was often branded as the "Chinese Mendaki". This characterisation was not without foundation. As with Yayasan Mendaki, the CDAC was designed to assist the lower income group of the Chinese community. This was patently acknowledged by then Senior Minister Lee Kuan Yew (李光耀) when he said in October 1991:

We were right in our policies to focus on economic growth which has benefitted all groups. But the lower income groups aspire to keep up with the progress of the other groups and more can be done to help them improve their earning capacity. It was not wrong for the Government to help Mendaki, AMP [Association of Muslim Professionals] and all the other professional Malay groups to increase the education standards and earning capacity of the Malays. But it was wrong not to have given parallel attention to the larger number of lower income Chinese who faced similar problems.[1]

To identify the "problems" referred to by Senior Minister Lee Kuan Yew, a special research panel was established under Dr Ow Chin Hock (欧进福), an economics professor who was then Minister of State in the Ministry of Foreign Affairs. Established in December 1991, the panel was tasked with identifying "the Chinese lower-income households, to analyse their causes of under-achievement and to recommend a plan of action and programme to assist them".[2]

In its report released in November 1992, the panel identified about 350,000 Chinese or 84,990 households who would need CDAC's help, based on the educational and income statistics of the bottom 20% of the Chinese community.[3] This group comprised primarily families with a monthly income of $1,212 or less and whose breadwinners did not hold "O" level qualifications.[4] Of these, 122,700 were identified as students, 85,000 were working adults and 139,200 were economically inactive individuals. The panel further noted that about 87% of the students under the study came from homes where the household income was between $500 and $1,500.[5]

Just as earlier concerns associated with the socio-economic position of the Malay community led to the creation of Yayasan Mendaki, the report on the Chinese community affirmed the creation of a self-help institution for the Chinese community mirroring that of Yayasan Mendaki. The

---

[1] "How grassroots leaders can help mobilise S'poreans for Next Lap", *The Straits Times*, 5 October 1991.
[2] "CDAC will do study to see who needs help", *The Straits Times*, 10 November 1992.
[3] "PM to CDAC: Stick to self-help plans", *The Straits Times*, 9 November 1992.
[4] Ibid.
[5] "Pressure to earn extra money for the family", *The Straits Times*, 28 October 1992.

report recommended the setting up of tuition classes for students and skills training for adults, specifically targeted at assisting lower-income Chinese households achieve upward social mobility. These recommendations were incorporated into CDAC's outreach efforts and formed two of CDAC's core programmes.[6]

While the creation of self-help groups based on ethnicity was aimed at addressing serious socio-economic concerns within each community, it was not without initial controversy. Although the focus of these self-help groups was on improving the educational achievements within each community, the use of an ethnic-based self-help model raised concerns of heightening ethnic differences and its incompatibility with Singapore's multiracial ideals.[7] Doubts were also raised about the potentially huge financial largesse that would accompany the CDAC's formation given the larger Chinese population, much to the detriment of the other minority self-help groups.[8] These concerns gained serious gravity and were hotly debated in Parliament in 1992. They were however succinctly refuted and addressed in the speech made by the Parliamentary Secretary to the Minister for Information and the Arts, Encik Mohamad Maiden on 13 January 1992:

In this regard, self-help efforts such as those by bodies like Mendaki Foundation, SINDA or the Chinese Development Assistance Council (CDAC) must be seen as positive additional stimulus for us to reach for the common goals of all Singaporeans. Success for each citizen means benefits for every other citizen and for the country. Success for each community means benefits for every other community and for the nation. The spill over of one person's or one community's achievements normally can be enjoyed by all others around them. Therefore, we must encourage one another to succeed and not succumb to jealousy. When people of all ethnic backgrounds progress and get to enjoy the fruits of progress, political stability in the country and harmony in

---

[6]Being the CDAC Tuition Programme and the CDAC Skills Training Award Scheme.
[7]Lorraine Pe Symaco, *Education in South-east Asia.* (London & New York: Bloomsbury Academic, 2013), p. 265.
[8]Lily Zubaidah Rahim Ishak, *The Paradox of Ethnic-Based Self-Help Groups,* in Derek De Cunha, ed., *Debating Singapore: Reflective Essays.* (Singapore: Institute of Southeast Asian Studies, 1994), p. 46.

this multiracial environment will be enhanced. This is what we want in the long term.

At the same time, there were also initial reservations among the Chinese leaders of the need for a supranational organisation for the Chinese community. Among them, Wee Cho Yaw (黄祖耀) was concerned that the CDAC might emasculate the *huiguan* (会馆 clan associations) and other civic Chinese bodies, which were facing survival challenges as their traditional welfare services were taken over by government agencies.[9] His view was shared by Tan Eng Joo (陈永裕), the SCCCI President at that time.[10]

However, with the formation of SINDA, the two leading Chinese organisations realised that the absence of a Chinese self-help group would be viewed as a serious omission by the Chinese community.[11] Accordingly, the presidents of the SFCCA and SCCCI appointed a committee to work out the framework of a self-help group for the Chinese community.

While some scepticism of the ethnic-based self-help model remained, the representational structure of the various self-help groups was finally complete in 1994 when the Eurasian Association was formed. Indeed, the self-help groups have each come a long way in achieving their objectives. It is comforting to note that none of the sectarian fears has materialised and Singapore remains a tolerant multiracial society. More importantly, as with the other self-help groups, the CDAC has shown its fervent rootedness in uplifting the underprivileged within the Chinese community and catalysing their eventual contribution to the continued success of a multiracial Singapore. This has not occurred by chance but has transpired from the prudent and wise guiding principles adopted by the CDAC from the outset.

The Heart of CDAC: Education and Training

In staying true to its founding intentions and purpose, the CDAC's focus since its inception has been to uplift the Chinese community primarily through

---

[9] Pang Cheng Lian, *Wee Cho Yaw: Banker, Entrepreneur and Community Leader.* (Singapore: Straits Times Press, 2014), p. 160.

[10] Ibid.

[11] Ibid.

education and training instead of relying purely on cash handouts.[12] Then Prime Minister Goh Chok Tong (吴作栋) also made clear his preference that the CDAC focused on self-help programmes such as tuition classes and worker training or it would face the risk of becoming "a big Chinese Community Welfare Fund, raising all kinds of unhealthy 'give-away' expectations".[13] This advice was etched in the mind of founding member, Chua Gim Siong (蔡锦淞) (a businessman and Secretary General of the SFCCA then) who recalled in 2014 that:

> The establishment of CDAC was not to provide financial assistance to the lower income households. More importantly we wanted to help low wage earners to upgrade their skills and to improve productivity to be in line with the government's aim of constantly raising productivity levels. We believed that by improving training and educational opportunities to the children from these households we could help their next generation break out of their poverty cycle.[14]

With this principle in mind, the sense of community stewardship over the CDAC was amply illustrated by the determined drive for donations by the various Chinese community leaders at the outset including Wee Cho Yaw[15] who pledged $1 million towards the Endowment Fund.[16] By September 1992, the CDAC's Endowment Fund had collected $5.5 million in pledges and donations from Chinese associations, business guilds, community groups and individuals.[17] Although the Chinese community

---

[12] Sikko Visscher, *The Business of Politics and Ethnicity: A History of Singapore Chinese Chamber of Commerce & Industry.* (Singapore: NUS Press, 2007), p. 289.

[13] "PM to CDAC: Stick to self-help plans", *The Straits Times*, 9 November 1992.

[14] As communicated by Chua Gim Siong (Founding Member, 1992–2005) to the author.

[15] As the then SFCCA President, he was appointed Chairman of CDAC's fundraising committee, with another prominent banker and Honourary President of SCCCI, Lien Ying Chow as Deputy Chairman. Please see Pang Cheng Lian, *Wee Cho Yaw: Banker, Entrepreneur and Community Leader* (Singapore: Straits Times Press, 2014), p. 161.

[16] Pang Cheng Lian, *Wee Cho Yaw: Banker, Entrepreneur and Community Leader.* (Singapore: Straits Times Press, 2014), p. 161.

[17] "Chinese papers' collection tops $1.7 m", *The Straits Times*, 5 September 1992.

comprises various dialect groups (Hokkiens, Teochews, Cantonese, Hakkas, Hainanese, Hockchias, Foochows, Henghuas, Shanghainese, just to name a few), many of which were supporting their own clan associations, it banded together in support of the CDAC.

The fundraising drive culminated in a gala dinner to inaugurate the CDAC on 20 September 1992. Jointly organised by SFCCA and SCCCI, the event was attended by more than 2,000 luminaries in the Chinese community. Then Prime Minister Goh Chok Tong was the guest of honour and gamely led a group to sing on stage to raise money for the new self-help body. More than $3.7 million was raised at the dinner.[18]

In recent years, efforts at fundraising have enjoyed similar community support. In 2014 for example, it was apparent that the expansion of the CDAC's programmes and services required additional funds. New activities to help the less privileged had led to operating deficits. The CDAC's reliance on government's grants and funding support from the accumulated income of its Endowment Fund was unsustainable in the long run. In 2014 alone, the deficit had risen from $5.7 million to $6.4 million.[19] Consequently, the CDAC's Board of Directors decided to raise Chinese employees' monthly contributions through the Central Provident Fund to CDAC. In line with the pioneering spirity of self-help, the CDAC's Board of Trustees also decided to organise its second fundraising gala dinner. The event raised $17.8 million from donations of individuals, corporations, foundations and clan associations.[20] In support of the fundraising efforts for CDAC's Endowment Fund, the government committed to providing a matching grant capped at $2 million per year over the next five years.

The manner in which the Chinese community has rallied behind the CDAC in the past two decades in fact deserves great admiration. This successfully executed communal approach is also hearteningly captured in

---

[18] Pang Cheng Lian, *Wee Cho Yaw: Banker, Entrepreneur and Community Leader.* (Singapore: Straits Times Press, 2014), p. 162.

[19] "Chinese Development Assistance Council charity dinner raises $17.8 million for Endowment Fund", *The Straits Times*, 24 October 2014, accessed on 1 February 2015: http://www.straitstimes.com/news/singapore/more-singapore-stories/story/chinese-development-assistance-council-charity-dinner-ra.

[20] Ibid.

the CDAC song which encapsulates the "family spirit" of the CDAC and the Chinese community:

Reaching out a helping hand
Let's do what we can
When troubles fall we stand tall
When storms come we heed the call
Reach out a helping hand
Let's do what we can
With all our heart and soul
We make this family whole[21]

To me, the essence of the CDAC and its principled approach is well ingrained in the song. Akin to the function of our national anthem and pledge, it sets the underlying ethos of the CDAC which is now accepted by every member of the Chinese community and which has, quite clearly, served the CDAC well.

The principled approach adopted by the CDAC is not without reward. Over the years, the Student Education and Development Programme, Workers' Upgrading and Employment Programme and Family Workfare and Support Programme have transformed the lives of many and improved the livelihood of the underprivileged in the Chinese community. Much as I am hesitant to quote statistics for the very reason that it may not do justice to the numerous achievements of the CDAC, I shall present a few to capture the measurable contributions of the CDAC in uplifting the Chinese community, particularly in the area of education and skills development which had been a major concern of the research panel's report mentioned earlier.

From 1990 to 2013 for example, the percentage of Chinese students with at least five GCE "O" level passes rose from 73% to 86.5%.[22] Likewise, the percentage of Chinese students admitted to post-secondary education

---

[21] This is an extract of the full song, accessed on 29 December 2014: http://www.cdac.org.sg/about-us/cdac-song.
[22] Ministry of Education, 10-Year Trend of Educational Performance 2004–2013; Progress of Malay Muslim Community Since 1980 Report, Ministry of Social and Family Development.

institutions rose from 91.6% in 2003 to 97.3% in 2012.[23] More notably, the percentage of Chinese students passing their Primary School Leaving Examination (PSLE) stood at an impressive 99% in 2012.[24] These figures attest to the significant success achieved by the CDAC in pushing for academic progress of the Chinese community.

As of 31 December 2014, the CDAC offered more than 440,000 tuition places to needy students. The CDAC has also sponsored more than 91,000 awards for low-skill low-income workers to upgrade their skills, and helped 11,300 job seekers to find jobs. These numbers demonstrate the enormity of the CDAC's outreach and impact on the Chinese community.

Nevertheless, many of the CDAC's efforts in helping with employment issues, skills training and social services transcend measurable statistics and will likely remain under-recognised. Quantifying the achievements of those who have benefitted from CDAC's programmes in monetary or other quantitative terms would be difficult, if not impossible. Suffice it to say, few can deny the contributions made by the CDAC in uplifting the Chinese community, and fewer still can argue against its continued relevance and significance in growing and developing the poorer segment of the Chinese community in the years to come.

Indeed, as my cherished friend, Goh Chim Khim (吴振钦), the current CEO of CDAC, has reminded me, the self-help group continues to strive to remain relevant. As part of the CDAC Vision 2012, it has been decided that three key thrusts, namely, *Social Mobility, Enhancing Community Co-ownership* and an *Effective Integrator* will continue to guide the CDAC in line with its vision to create: *A cohesive and resilient community that strives for upward social mobility through self-help and mutual support*. With such a lucid vision, the CDAC will continue to be an invaluable asset to the Chinese community.

Laying a Lasting Framework

The association between my firm, Rodyk and Davidson LLP ("Rodyk") and CDAC began in earnest when Rodyk assisted the CDAC to incorporate as a company limited by guarantee on 22 May 1992 (see Photo 1). I was a young

---

[23] *Education Statistics Digest 2014*, Ministry of Education, p. 53.
[24] *Education Statistics Digest 2014*, Ministry of Education, p. 50.

FORM 8

THE COMPANIES ACT
(CHAPTER 50)
Section 19(4)

No. of Company

199202625K

CERTIFICATE OF INCORPORATION OF PUBLIC COMPANY

This is to certify that **CHINESE DEVELOPMENT ASSISTANCE COUNCIL** is incorporated under the Companies Act, Cap. 50, on and from 22 May 1992 and that the company is a public company limited by guarantee.

Given under my hand and seal on 22 May 1992.

SIA SUAT HWA, MDM
REGISTRAR OF COMPANIES AND BUSINESSES
SINGAPORE

ssh:cdac

Photo 1. The CDAC's certificate of incorporation.

lawyer in Rodyk in late 1991 when I received a call from Pang Cheng Lian (冯清莲), then Special Assistant to Wee Cho Yaw, President of SFCCA. She explained that she had been informed of my involvement with the formation of Yayasan Mendaki (I had advised on the legal constitution and incorporation of Yayasan Mendaki two years earlier). The SFCCA required legal advice on the incorporation of the CDAC and my instructions were to establish the Chinese self-help group as a company limited by guarantee with the following objectives:

i. To support, foster and promote the socio-economic, educational and skills development of the less successful of the Chinese community in Singapore.

ii. To promote the educational performance of the under-achievers in all fields and to participate, aid and assist in educational programmes and undertakings to raise their educational level.

iii. To formulate ways and means to help working adults to improve their skills and earning capacities.

iv. To create an environment in which traditional Chinese virtues such as community service, concern for the underprivileged, thrift and filial piety are valued and practised.

v. To assist by way of grants, donations, or otherwise such objects or endeavours in Singapore as the Board of Directors considers desirable in the interest of, or to promote the objects of, the CDAC.

vi. To undertake any of the foregoing objects in conjunction or in association with any other institution or organisation.

With these objects in mind, the CDAC was, upon incorporation, to comprise of individual members with a maximum of 100 members (which still remains the maximum number today). The first patron of the CDAC was then Prime Minister Goh Chok Tong who has since been succeeded by Prime Minister Lee Hsien Loong (李显龙). The CDAC's Board of Trustees was to comprise the Chairman of the Board of Directors, seven representatives each from SCCCI and SFCCA along with 10 other persons nominated by the patron.

Since its inception, the CDAC has been guided and helmed by many distinguished and eminent individuals of the Chinese community. The first Chairman of the Board of Trustees was prominent banker and President of the SFCCA, Wee Cho Yaw, who held the position until 2012 when the current incumbent, Chua Thian Poh (蔡天宝), a distinguished businessman who had succeeded Wee as SFCCA President, took over. Since its founding, the CDAC's Board of Directors has been chaired by a Government Minister. The first Chairman was Minister Wong Kan Seng (黄根成) who was succeeded by Minister Lim Swee Say (林瑞生), who in turn, was succeeded by Minister Gan Kim Yong (颜金勇).

Operationally, the CDAC has, from the start, been led by highly competent senior officers of the civil service. Chan Soo Sen (曾士生) who served as the first Executive Director, was then the Deputy Secretary of the Ministry of Home Affairs. When he left CDAC following his appointment as Parliamentary Secretary in the Prime Minister's Office and

Ministry of Community Development in 1997, he was succeeded by his deputy Sam Tan (陈振泉). In 2009, Sam Tan resigned when he was appointed Parliamentary Secretary in the Ministry of Trade and Industry and Ministry of Communication and the Arts. He was succeeded by Goh Chim Khim, who has been with CDAC since 1995. I would say, without hesitation, that these dedicated individuals, along with the many directors, staff and volunteers, both past and present, have led the CDAC capably over the years and should, for their immense contributions to the CDAC, stand as the pride of the Chinese community in Singapore.

In 2015, when I asked Chan Soo Sen to talk about his early years helming CDAC, he revealed that he had started the office with a total staff strength of four — himself, Sam Tan and two junior officers. Commenting on CDAC's challenges Chan Soo Sen said:

> My main challenge was to gain the community's acceptance of CDAC. We knew there were some quarters of the community which were upset over their monthly contributions to the CDAC Fund. Our priority was to convince these people that their contributions were being put to effective use for the betterment of their fellow citizens.

Convinced that education was the great leveller, CDAC's first projects were tuition centres for the young and skills training for the school leavers. As a start the new self-help group worked with 15 clan associations to open tuition centres in their premises. Because of subsidies from CDAC, the centres charged nominal fees, enabling the children of poorer families to attend. Fees for the very poor were waived.

At a personal level, I am deeply privileged to have been entrusted with the incorporation of the CDAC as well as holding, to this day, the role of its company secretary. Despite not being from the Chinese community and as a member of a minority race, I am honoured to have been called upon to contribute to this chapter documenting CDAC's journey. Indeed there are many fellow Singaporeans from other minority ethnic groups who have volunteered and supported the CDAC by serving in its many committees and activities. Such cross-ethnic partnership and solidarity can only happen in our uniquely multiracial and multi-religious Singapore. Even as each ethnic self-help group focuses on the development of its own community, they have collaborated in many programmes for the good of all communities.

As the largest self-help group, the CDAC's contributions towards our multi-ethnic, multi-religious diverse nation merits mention and I shall attempt to highlight a few of these notable contributions.

CDAC and Nation–Building

Other than its strategic geographical location, it is widely known (and often judiciously inculcated in the minds of Singaporeans) that Singapore lacks natural resources and its growth and success are largely dependent on external conditions, in particular, international trade. Singapore's success as a small independent nation can however be attributed to its only natural resource — its *people*. This strategic resource is however not without its challenges. History is replete with painful reminders that peaceful co-existence of ethnic groups and races cannot be taken for granted but has to be nurtured and cultivated at all times. Notwithstanding the last five decades of relative peace and harmony, Singapore has witnessed instances of inter-ethnic strife. Indeed, the period leading up to the independence of Singapore saw racial riots and political uncertainties driven by race politics.

When independence was achieved in 1965, it was apparent to the ruling People's Action Party (PAP) (人民行动党), that political stability was key to Singapore's success. Singapore's population was (and remains) highly pluralistic, comprising 75% Chinese, 13% Malays, 7% Indians and the remaining 5% comprising other races.[25] The PAP recognised that racial harmony was (and continues to be) a political necessity to ensure and maintain internal stability and a cohesive nation. These in turn were pre-requisites for economic development and growth. Unlike other countries which viewed the suppression or downplaying of racial identities as necessary to achieve racial harmony, Singapore took a calibrated effort at recognising and celebrating the unique racial and cultural differences of each of its ethnic communities while emphasising the need for tolerance and respect of each other's religion, language and culture. Understanding and embracing our cultural diversities forms the bedrock of Singapore's nation-building efforts.

---

[25] Chan Sek Keong, "Multiculturalism in Singapore — The Way to a Harmonious Society", SAcLJ, 25 (2013), p. 84.

Unsurprisingly, early initiatives of nation-building began with the promulgation of multiracial, multicultural and multi-religious policies. To give form to these policies, multilingual schools were established and students were accorded parity in admission, thus sending a clear message of equality, regardless of race or language. In 1966, in its endeavour to achieve a national identity whilst maintaining each ethnic group's cultural values, Singapore adopted a bilingual education system with English taught alongside Chinese, Tamil or Malay as the "mother tongue".[26] This bilingual system continues to be in effect and has ensured Singapore's position in the global economy as well as maintaining its unique kaleidoscope of diverse races and cultures. Likewise, each of the self-help groups is either actively involved in or leading the efforts to ensure the continued use and vibrancy of each of the mother tongue language among the younger generation.

Like its multiracial and multicultural policies, the economic success of Singapore today is due as much to the stringent adherence to meritocratic principles. The PAP has promulgated policies based on principles of meritocracy, which as Emeritus Senior Minister Goh Chok Tong once described, is a "value system by which advancement in society is based on an individual's ability, performance and achievement".[27] Accordingly, education policies were designed to create a level playing field to reward competence and diligence and eventually, facilitate social mobility for all Singaporeans.[28] The interplay between a multiracial society and meritocracy must be duly recognised, for it has served to ensure that self-help groups do not fall into an abyss of communal exclusiveness or worse, the stratification of society.

To meet the twin demands of ensuring Singapore's continued economic growth through meritocratic policies as well as developing a cohesive multicultural and multiracial society, ethnic self-help groups such as the CDAC were designed to embody both ideals. On the one hand, self-help groups have the objective of encouraging customised initiatives for disadvantaged

---

[26] "Going back to the basics of effective English-language teaching", *The Straits Times*, 9 November 2009, accessed on 23 December 2014: http://news.asiaone.com/News/Education/Story/A1Story20091109-178771.html.

[27] "Understanding meritocracy", *Today Online*, 25 June 2014, accessed on 23 December 2014: http://www.todayonline.com/singapore/understanding-meritocracy.

[28] Sikko Visscher, The Business of Politics and Ethnicity: A History of the Singapore Chinese Chamber of Commerce and Industry. (Singapore: NUS Press), 2007, p. 290.

segments within their respective communities. In the words of Prime Minister Lee Hsien Loong:

> Self-help groups keep the pioneering spirit of "mutual help" alive, enable every beneficiary to strive for a better future, and foster a society where everyone, including those who have benefitted, contributes.[29]

Photo 2. The CDAC logo.

On the other hand, self-help groups are driven by the concept of equal opportunity to advance an individual's ability, performance and achievement. Guided by the overarching policy of community effort and "leaving no Singaporean behind",[30] the CDAC therefore enthuses itself with the objectives of providing educational support and skills upgrading within the Chinese community. This is amply illustrated in its logo which is inspired by traditional Chinese calligraphy (see Photo 2). As explained in its website, the CDAC's logo is representative of the following:

- The graphic lines symbolise a person, reflecting CDAC's focus on people;
- The top portion of the lines symbolises the efforts and endeavours made by the parties being assisted for educational advancement, self-reliance and self-improvement; and

---

[29] "Spirit of giving back 'alive and well' in CDAC", *The Straits Times*, 25 October 2014, accessed on 23 December 2014: http://news.asiaone.com/news/singapore/spirit-giving-back-alive-and-well-cdac.

[30] Speech by Prime Minister Lee Hsien Loong at CDAC 20th Anniversary Celebrations, Prime Minister's Office, 22 May 2012, accessed on 23 December 2014: http://www.pmo.gov.sg/mediacentre/speech-prime-minister-lee-hsien-loong-cdac-20th-anniversary-celebrations-english.

- The lower portion of the lines symbolises the assistance and the support provided by the community, which appears as a strong and unyielding motivating force.[31]

Notwithstanding that it was specifically created to help the less privileged in the Chinese community, the CDAC has recognised that the Chinese community can only prosper in tandem with the rest of Singapore. As the largest segment of the nation, it also has the responsibility of helping the underprivileged of the other minority groups.

Consequently, CDAC has established many initiatives in fulfilment of its mission "to nurture and develop the potential of the Chinese community in contributing to the continued success of multiracial Singapore".[32] These include collaborative efforts with the other self-help groups, Yayasan Mendaki, SINDA and the Eurasian Association such as the Collaborative Tuition Programme (CTP).

Launched in 2002, the CTP, as noted by Senior Minister of State for Education and Law, Indranee Rajah, "embodies our national spirit of the different communities coming together as one united society".[33] Established with the objective of providing subsidised tuition programmes (offered by each self-help group) to students from all ethnic groups, the programme optimises resources and widens each self-help group's outreach abilities. The CTP also celebrates diversity by creating more opportunities for interaction and bonding among the ethnic groups through its various activities. To date, there are 69 collaborative centres island-wide providing needy students with a helping hand in their academic pursuits.[34]

CDAC has also contributed to the wider objective of the promotion of values associated with multiracialism and multiculturalism in Singapore.

---

[31] "About the Logo", CDAC website, accessed on 23 December 2014: http://www.cdac.org.sg/about-us/about-the-logo.

[32] "Mission", CDAC website, accessed on 23 December 2014: http://www.cdac.org.sg/about-us/mission.

[33] "Self-help groups give awards to top tuition students", accessed on 23 December 2014: http://news.asiaone.com/news/edvantage/self-help-groups-give-awards-top-tuition-students.

[34] Ibid.

One notable example is the establishment of the Joint Social Service Centre (JSSC) in 1997. The idea of JSSC was first mooted by then Prime Minister Goh Chok Tong who envisioned a joint body organising and contributing to community development in Singapore. He had then encouraged the various self-help groups, namely, CDAC, Yayasan Mendaki, AMP, SINDA and the Eurasian Association to jointly set up the JSSC. In 2007, the JSSC was repositioned and given a new identity, OnePeople.sg. Today, OnePeople.sg continues to play an important role in promoting inter-racial harmony and social cohesion by organising joint activities for all races.[35]

As a whole, the CDAC has greatly contributed to nation-building efforts in Singapore and its notable contributions have been widely acknowledged by our leaders:

> While concentrating on its charter and mission of helping the needy in the Chinese community, CDAC has not forgotten the larger objective of promoting racial harmony and social cohesion in our multiracial Singapore. CDAC and the other self-help groups (SHGs) — Mendaki, SINDA, Eurasian Association and AMP have been jointly organising activities to enhance interaction among members of the various ethnic groups.[36]
>
> Wong Kan Seng
> Former Minister of Home Affairs and Chairman of CDAC,
> CDAC 10th Anniversary Charity Dinner
> 11 May 2002

> CDAC has provided valued assistance to students from lower income families, to help them improve themselves and gain confidence, helping children from lower income families do their best in education... The community self-help groups like the CDAC, Mendaki, SINDA and the Eurasian Association, are key partners in this effort. They are

---

[35]"Our History", OnePeople.Sg website, accessed on 23 December 2014: http://www.onepeople.sg/about-us/our-history.

[36]Speech by Minister Wong Kan Seng at the CDAC 10th Anniversary Charity Dinner, 11 May 2002, accessed on 23 December 2014: http://www.nas.gov.sg/archivesonline/speeches/view-html?filename=2002051105.htm.

key partners in keeping Singapore a place where everyone aspires to do well, and avoiding a society which becomes divided.[37]

Tharman Shanmugaratnam
Deputy Prime Minister and Minister of Finance
CDAC Student Education and Enrichment Day (SEED) and
Awards Presentation Ceremony
12 August 2007

It is clear that by recognising the unique circumstances and concerns of the Chinese community, the CDAC has greatly assisted the growth and development of the community through its customised initiatives whilst ensuring that the benefits of such growth and development transcends racial division at the national level, thus contributing towards Singapore's success as a multiracial republic. Through its multiracial-focused policies, the CDAC, as well as the other self-help groups, continues to help build a more gracious and inclusive society, thus ensuring that every Singaporean, regardless of race or ethnic background, benefits from the economic progress of the nation.

Concluding Notes: A Cherished Relationship

As a long-time supporter, friend and adviser to the CDAC, I am proud to have been a part of the very inception of this important institution. It has given me great pleasure to witness its various successes over the past two decades. As seen from the statistics presented, many individuals within the Chinese community have benefitted from the programmes and initiatives spearheaded by the CDAC and I am confident that many more will.

At this opportune milestone of our nation's 50th independence anniversary, I look back at the CDAC with many fond memories and count myself extremely privileged to be in the company of the successive CDAC board members, staff, volunteers and advisors, many of whom have become my

---

[37] Speech by Minister Tharman Shanmugaratnam at the CDAC SEED and Awards Presentation Ceremony, 12 August 2007, accessed on 23 December 2014: http://www.moe.gov.sg/media/speeches/2007/sp20070812_print.htm.

very close friends. It has indeed been an enriching journey. In the wise words of the great Chinese philosopher, Lao Tzu, *the journey of a thousand miles begins with a single step*. Undoubtedly, it has been a most rewarding and fulfilling journey since the first step of the CDAC 23 years ago and I am confident it will have many more fulfilling years to come.

CHAPTER 4

The Chinese Heritage Centre
Putting Singapore on the Diaspora Map

LEE Tang Ling

Telling the Story of a People

"A Landmark Achievement" (*New Straits Times*, 17 February 1999)

"A Worldview of the Chinese Diaspora Discourse" (Translated from *Hong Kong Commercial Daily*, 22 November 1998)[1]

"Tracing the Evolution of the Chinese Diaspora" (Translated from *Lianhe Zaobao*, 18 October 1998)[2]

"It's Their Own Story, on Their Own Terms" (*The Sunday Times*, 1 November 1998)

"Patching Gaps in the Fabric of Their History" (*The Sunday Times*, 7 June 1998)

Launched by the Chinese Heritage Centre (CHC) (华裔馆) on 26 October 1998, *The Encyclopedia of the Chinese Overseas* (the *Encyclopedia* hereafter) — the first of its kind to study the Chinese diaspora of some

---

[1] "从世界视野论述海外华人 (A Worldview of the Chinese Diaspora Discourse)" — 海外华人百科全书 (The Encyclopedia of the Chinese Overseas),《香港商报 (*Hong Kong Commercial Daily*)》, 22 November 1998.

[2] "追本溯源看华人移民演变 (Tracing the Evolution of the Chinese Diaspora)",《联合早报 (*Lianhe Zaobao*)》, 18 October 1998.

30 million people of Chinese descent at the time[3] garnered critical acclaim in the local and international media, as well as in academia, and put the CHC and Singapore on the map as the centre for the study of Chinese overseas.

> Singapore has a unique place in the Chinese diaspora.
> Nowhere else, outside the People's Republic of China and Taiwan, do Chinese form the majority of the citizenry of a nation-state and hold the majority of positions at the highest levels of government.

So began the chapter on the Chinese in Singapore in the *Encyclopedia*. Despite the large Chinese population, the commonly held view of Singapore as a "Chinese society", however, does not correspond to reality. Given its substantial non-Chinese population compared to China and Taiwan, "Singapore is multi-ethnic and 'plural' to a degree not shared by these other societies". English, with its neutral position, is the language of interface for all ethnic groups, making Singapore a largely English-speaking society and "the most 'Westernised' country in Asia".[4]

At the launch of the *Encyclopedia*, the Guest of Honour, then Prime Minister Goh Chok Tong (吴作栋), told the audience,

> As Singaporean Chinese are comfortable in both English and Chinese, and are familiar with both Western and Eastern cultures, they are able to plug into the economies of both the West and the East and serve as a bridge or interface between them. This has enhanced Singapore's position as a global city where East and West live and work comfortably together. The publication of the *Encyclopedia* by the Centre is a scholarly contribution to the literature on the "Chinese Diaspora". There is already a revival of interest among Chinese-origin people all over the world in their roots, culture and values. The *Encyclopedia* … will enhance this interest … the CHC can help Singapore develop into an important centre of Sinic studies in the Pacific Rim.[5]

---

[3] Lynn Pan, ed., *The Encyclopedia of the Chinese Overseas.* (Singapore: Archipelago Press & Landmark Books, 1998), p. 58.
[4] Kwok Kian Woon, "Singapore", in Lynn Pan, ed., *The Encyclopedia of the Chinese Overseas.* (Singapore: Archipelago Press & Landmark Books, 1998), p. 200 and p. 216.
[5] Speech by Prime Minister Goh Chok Tong at the launch of *The Encyclopedia of the Chinese Overseas* at the CHC, NTU, on 26 October 1998, National Archives of Singapore.

PM Goh called the publication of the *Encyclopedia* "a commendable and pioneering effort" that would lead to "a better understanding of the ethnic Chinese communities outside China".[6] CHC Chairman Wee Cho Yaw (黄祖耀) also expressed his confidence that

> this first *Encyclopedia* of the overseas Chinese will help the world to better understand the trials and tribulations of Chinese emigrants and, more importantly, their dedication and contributions to their adopted countries.[7]

Founded in 1995, the CHC completed its first major project — *The Encyclopedia of the Chinese Overseas* in three years. Unprecedented in academia and the publishing industry, the Centre achieved the goal of publishing three editions of the *Encyclopedia* simultaneously: an English edition with an initial print run of 7,500 copies that was distributed locally and regionally; a first order of 10,000 copies placed by the Harvard University Press and 1,500 copies by Curzon Press were marketed in the US and Europe respectively; a simplified Chinese edition for the Singapore and China markets and a traditional Chinese edition for the Hong Kong and Taiwan readers, both published in Hong Kong with a first print run of 2,000 copies each.[8]

In his foreword for the *Encyclopedia*, CHC Chairman Wee outlined his aspiration for the Centre to be a repository of materials on overseas Chinese settled across the globe — an information bank that would expand through its own efforts and through cooperation with research institutes throughout the world. While he recognised that the book was only the first step on a long journey for the Centre, he was also confident of the Centre's steady progress as the world's premier centre for the study of Chinese overseas.

Clear in his vision from the start, Wee had persuaded his overseas associates and friends to join the CHC's inaugural Board of Governors, thereby giving the Centre an international standing. The 16-member board featured luminaries from various fields: Professor Tommy Koh (许通美),

[6] Ibid.
[7] Pang Cheng Lian, *Wee Cho Yaw: Banker, Entrepreneur and Community Leader.* (Singapore: Straits Times Press, 2014), p. 168.
[8] "It's their own story, on their own terms", *The Sunday Times*, 1 November 1998.

Singapore's Ambassador-at-Large who served as CHC's Vice-Chairman; Sir Li Ka Shing (李嘉诚), Chairman of Cheung Kong Holdings (长江集团); Chatri Sophonpanich (陈有汉), Executive Chairman of Bangkok Bank (盘谷银行); Dr Jeffrey Koo (辜濂松), Chairman and CEO of Chinatrust Commercial Bank (中国信托商业银行); Dr Mochtar Riady (李文正), Chairman of Lippo Bank (力宝银行); Tun Dato' Seri Dr Lim Chong Eu (林苍佑), former Chief Minister of Penang; Washington Sycip (薛华成), Founding Chairman of the SGV Group; Simon Lee Sui Hee (李瑞喜), Chairman of Equigold N. L.; Professor Wang Gungwu (王赓武), Vice-Chancellor of The University of Hong Kong (香港大学); Professor Lim Pin (林彬), Vice-Chancellor of the National University of Singapore (NUS) (新加坡国立大学); Dr Cham Tao Soon (詹道存), President of the Nanyang Technological University (NTU) (南洋理工大学); Professor Tu Wei-Ming (杜维明), Professor of Chinese History and Philosophy at Harvard University; Lee Seng Wee (李成伟), Chairman and CEO of OCBC (华侨银行); Dr Liu Thai Ker (刘太格), Director of RSP Architects Planners and Engineers (雅思柏设计事务所); and Kwek Leng Joo (郭令裕), Managing Director of City Developments (城市发展集团).[9]

"The next important question was", Wee said in an interview with the *Straits Times*, "who to invite as editor to make this (the *Encyclopedia*) a success. We wanted a renowned writer and Lynn Pan was our top choice." Lynn Pan(潘翎) assumed directorship at the CHC in 1995 and was given the challenge of producing an encyclopedia of overseas Chinese within three years.[10]

Born in Shanghai, Lynn Pan studied at the universities of London and Cambridge, England, and had worked as a social scientist, journalist, historian and writer in London, Geneva, Helsinki and Hong Kong. Awarded the 1992 Martin Luther King Memorial Prize for her book, *Sons of the Yellow Emperor*, which had rekindled among Chinese all over the world a renewed interest in their heritage and family histories, Lynn Pan was in agreement with Chairman Wee on making the book user-friendly. "Unless people read and the book gets a very wide circulation", she told the *Straits Times*, "it is not going to make that much impact". She re-wrote substantial parts of the

---

[9] Lynn Pan, ed., *The Encyclopedia of the Chinese Overseas* (Singapore: Archipelago Press & Landmark Books, 1998), front matter.

[10] "Best growth is done one step at a time", *The Straits Times*, 23 October 1998.

Encyclopedia to ensure that the narratives were interwoven. The engaging text in this 400-page tome was further enhanced by excellent illustrations, from tables, figures, maps, art to evocative images of the lives of Chinese overseas then and now.[11]

Over 50 of the world's most eminent scholars and writers based in Asia, North America, Europe, Australia and Africa contributed to the *Encyclopedia*. Local historian Choi Kwai Keong (崔贵强), who specialises in the study of Chinese society in Singapore and Malaysia, was roped in by Lynn Pan to do the translation of the essays submitted in English for the Chinese edition. An effectively bilingual young graduate, Lim Bee Leng (林美玲), from NUS was specially recruited as a research assistant. The *Encyclopedia*'s distinguished panel of advisors comprised Professor Wang Gungwu, an eminent historian of China and a pioneering authority in the study of the Chinese diaspora; Philip A. Kuhn, a prominent sinologist and the Francis Lee Higginson Professor of History and Professor of East Asian Language and Civilisation at Harvard; J. A. C. Mackie, Professor of Chinese History and Philosophy, Australian National University; Tu Wei-Ming, Professor at Harvard and the world's leading Confucian scholar; Wang Ling-Chi (王灵智), Professor of Ethnic Studies at the University of California, Berkeley; Friedrich Wu (邬宏远), Vice-President and Head of Economic Research, Development Bank of Singapore; and Zhou Nanjing (周南京), Professor of Afro-Asian Studies, Beijing University.[12]

The Chinese diaspora, as defined in the *Encyclopedia*, is an

interplay of diverse histories and traditions. It has inherited Chinese experiences, but it has also been modified and enriched by transplantation to other continents and civilizations.

The *Encyclopedia* covers the most important aspects of these experiences and provides a panoramic and comparative view across past and present overseas Chinese communities worldwide. Not an A to Z book with short entries, the volume is topically and geographically organised with thematic sections on origins, migration, institutions, ties to China

---

[11] "Time is ripe for taking stock: Tracking the diaspora", *The Straits Times*, 1 November 1998.
[12] Lynn Pan, ed., *The Encyclopedia of the Chinese Overseas*, front matter.

and inter-ethnic relations, as well as country-by-country analyses of 37 individual Chinese communities in all continents of the world.[13]

The *Times Literary Supplement* observed that "the contributors are all authorities in their field, yet the editors have achieved a lively and accessible style throughout".[14] *CHOICE* published by the Harvard University Press commented that the *Encyclopedia* "represents the first attempt in the English-speaking world to provide a comprehensive survey of this unique subject" and called it "a pioneering work", noting that "throughout the volume, the material is both balanced and accurate".[15] The *Far Eastern Economic Review* identified the "tying together of the Overseas Chinese experience into a single volume" as "the *Encyclopedia*'s great strength", adding that

> the editor [had] stamped her easy-going and anecdote-rich style across the *Encyclopedia*, generating one of the most readable and accessible accounts of the Overseas Chinese published to date.[16]

At the CHC's 10th Anniversary Dinner held on 22 July 2005, Guest of Honour, then Minister Mentor Lee Kuan Yew (李光耀) mentioned in his speech that the *Encyclopedia* "has been well received and has inspired efforts to produce similar Encyclopedias of other diasporas".[17] In his address to the guests at the dinner, Professor Tommy Koh, the Centre's second Chairman, thanked Lynn Pan for her contributions to the Centre noting that the *Encyclopedia* "has been universally praised and has helped to put the Centre on the intellectual map of the world".[18]

---

[13] Lynn Pan, ed., *The Encyclopedia of the Chinese Overseas*, description on the inner cover.

[14] Delia Davin, "Settlers and Sojourners", *Times Literary Supplement*, 1 October 1999.

[15] W.S. Wong, "Book Review: The Encyclopedia of the Chinese Overseas", *CHOICE*, Vol. 37, No. 2 (October 1999).

[16] Michael Backman, "Tracking the Chinese Diaspora", *Far Eastern Economic Review*, 18 February 1999.

[17] Speech by Minister Mentor Lee Kuan Yew at the CHC's 10th Anniversary Fundraising Dinner on 22 July 2005, National Archives of Singapore.

[18] Speech by CHC Chairman Professor Tommy Koh at the CHC's 10th Anniversary Fundraising Dinner on 22 July 2005, *CHC Bulletin*, Issue 5, (June–July 2005), pp. 19–20.

When asked about her thoughts in 2014 on the project looking back, Lynn reminisced,

> Sixteen years on, I think I can say without boasting that the *Encyclopedia* has stood the test of time. There are not many things you do in life where you can be assured of long-term value; I think this work will still be read and consulted long after I'm gone.

The Story Behind CHC

In 1991, the Nanyang Technological University (NTU) (南洋理工大学) had just opened in the old Jurong campus of Nanyang University (Nantah) (南洋大学) and there was a proposal to put up a museum of technology in the former Nantah Administration Building. A remarkable example of Chinese architecture, this red brick building with its distinctive green tile roof had been a significant landmark during the Nantah days. BG George Yeo (杨荣文), then Minister of Information and the Arts and Second Minister for Foreign Affairs, thought the building would be more suited to house a museum of the Chinese diaspora.

The idea appealed to Wee Cho Yaw, a banker and community leader, as well as President of the Singapore Federation of Chinese Clan Associations (SFCCA) (新加坡宗乡会馆联合总会). He recognised at once that the migration of the Chinese to various parts of the world was a story worth telling and that Singapore is uniquely placed to recount their experiences. More importantly, the former Chairman of Nanyang University saw the proposal as a way to revive the extraordinary Nantah spirit.

Under the direction of Wee, SFCCA set up a preparatory committee to look into the scope and costs of the proposed museum. After a year of survey and deliberations, the 10-member committee chaired by Professor Tommy Koh, then Chairman of the National Arts Council (新加坡国家艺术理事会) as well as the Institute of Policy Studies (新加坡政策研究院), recommended to the SFCCA president in November 1993 a modification of the original concept.

Instead of a large-scale museum and a database of overseas Chinese that would require at least $60 million, it was decided that the focus should be on research and the publication of a ground-breaking encyclopedia of overseas

Chinese. An exhibition of the Chinese diaspora and a research library would form part of this initiative named the Chinese Heritage Centre.

The revised plans for the CHC required a budget of $25 million. Minister George Yeo had managed to secure government support with an endowment fund of $5 million. Taking the lead, Wee Cho Yaw, the founding Chairman of the CHC, pledged $1 million to the fund. Through his personal network, he raised $8 million from individuals and companies in Singapore as well as overseas, including million dollar pledges from Liem Sioe Liong (林绍良) of Indonesia, Sir Li Ka Shing (李嘉诚) of Hong Kong, as well as the Singapore Hokkien Huay Kuan (新加坡福建会馆) and the Ngee Ann Kongsi (义安公司).[19]

The result was *The Encyclopedia of the Chinese Overseas* launched by the CHC in 1998. Its publication reflected the growing interest of international scholarship in diasporic communities and the worldwide upsurge in ethnic awareness.

The 1990s was a period of cultural renaissance for Singapore. Worldwide, there was a revival of interest in heritage, not just among Chinese people in different parts of the world, but among other ethnic groups as well. The National Heritage Board summarised the cultural scene then in its *Renaissance City Plan III*:

> In the late 1980s, there was a growing realisation in Singapore that heritage and culture were crucial in acting as a counter-balance to the economic growth. A concerted push for museum development was mooted by the Advisory Council on Culture and the Arts (ACCA) in 1989. This laid the foundation for the initial capital investments in heritage infrastructure and the burst of cultural activities, which enlivened Singapore in the 1990s.[20]

Lim Siam Kim (林长鑫), former CEO of the National Heritage Board (国家文物局), who was in charge of drafting the National Heritage

---

[19] The information provided in the first four paragraphs of the section "The Story behind the CHC" is from: Pang Cheng Lian, *Wee Cho Yaw: Banker, Entrepreneur and Community Leader*, (Singapore: Straits Times Press, 2014), pp. 164–168.

[20] "National Identity and the Singaporean Heart and Soul", *Renaissance City Plan III — Heritage Development Plan*, (Singapore: National Heritage Board, 2008), pp. 5–6.

Board Act in 1993, said in an interview with Singapore's Oral History Centre (新加坡口述历史中心) that the government decided it would assist the communities, namely the Chinese, Malays, Eurasians and Indians, which constitute the racial composition of Singapore, to set up their own heritage centres to promote their respective heritage. The setting up of CHC was a step taken in this broader direction.[21] In *The Scripting of a National History: Singapore and Its Past,* the impulse to differentiate Singapore from mainland China through building on its heritage as well as the strengthening of ongoing Chinese diasporic economic networks at that time were identified as the factors that brought about "a shift in Singapore's identification of its Chineseness with the overseas Chinese".[22]

In his speech at the launch of the *Encyclopedia,* PM Goh pointed out that, while the Singaporean Chinese have generally retained Chinese cultural norms, customs, linguistic characteristics and traditional values, there are important differences that distinguish them from Chinese elsewhere. Singaporeans, for example, speak Mandarin with a mixture of English and Malay words. As he elaborated:

> In Singapore, the different racial communities have been moulded into a nation by their shared experiences before and after independence. Over the years, we have all accumulated common experiences and stakes which now form part of our collective history, psyche and value system. Each of these communities makes its own contributions to the well-being of Singapore without losing its respective cultural and intellectual heritage as Singaporean Chinese, Singaporean Malays, Singaporean Indians or Singaporean Eurasians.[23]

From sojourners to citizens, "Chineseness" among the Chinese in Singapore has evolved. The *Encyclopedia,* the Exhibition and the outreach programme

---

[21] "The Civil Service — A Retrospection", Oral History Interview with Lim Siam Kim, National Archives of Singapore, 17 May 2002, accession number 002587.

[22] Hong Lysa and Huang Jianli, *The Scripting of a National History: Singapore and Its Past,* (Singapore: NUS Press, 2008), p. 229.

[23] Speech by Prime Minister Goh Chok Tong at the launch of *The Encyclopedia of the Chinese Overseas* at the CHC, NTU, on 26 October 1998, National Archives of Singapore.

at CHC triggered some soul searching about one's identity in this fast-changing, globalising world.

Professor Wang Gungwu has observed that as overseas Chinese settle wherever they have made their homes, they get curious about what their ancestors have done, what contributions their parents have made to their society, and how they can continue to contribute and how they can identify with their society. He believes that a sense of history is the key to identity and the sense of belonging. "You can only understand yourself today by looking back and knowing the past," he told the *Sunday Times*. "Then you appreciate your own civilisation and culture — its strengths and limitations, and get a sense of pride and a feeling of progress."[24]

In his speech as the Guest of Honour at the opening of CHC on 17 May 1995, BG George Yeo, then Minister for Health and Minister for Information and the Arts, explained,

> It is symbolically appropriate that CHC should be established here in the old Nantah Administration Block. In a sense, the history of Nantah reflects the history of the Chinese people outside China this century. The Nantah spirit is an admirable one because it expressed the determination of a people not to lose its sense of self... This Nantah spirit is a deep source of inner strength and deep inspiration to all Singaporeans. It is this spirit which will enable us to survive in adversity and enable us to bounce back even if we are temporarily defeated.[25]

Minister Yeo's mention of the Nantah spirit must have touched a chord among the guests at the opening, many of whom were alumni of the old Nanyang University, the first and only Chinese-medium institution of higher learning outside China which was, during its existence from 1956 to 1980, a beacon of hope for the supporters of Chinese language education and culture in Southeast Asia.

The context of the times was discussed in the section on the "Chinese-educated" from the Singapore chapter in *The Encyclopedia of the Chinese*

---

[24] "Overseas Chinese: Patching gaps in the fabric of their history", *The Sunday Times*, 7 June 1998.
[25] Speech by BG George Yeo, Minister for Health and Minister for Information and the Arts at the opening of the Chinese Heritage Centre on 17 May 1995, National Archives of Singapore.

Overseas. Between 1959 to 1978, the enrolment in Chinese-stream primary schools in Singapore fell from nearly 46% to about 11% of the total primary school enrolment. In 1975, Nanyang University adopted English as the medium of instruction and in 1980, it closed its doors when it was legislated to merge with NUS.[26]

At the Centre's opening, Minister George Yeo unveiled the calligraphy, *Hua Yi Guan* (the Chinese name of the Centre), specially done by Pan Shou (潘受). A renowned poet and calligrapher, Pan Shou had also been greatly involved in the early years of Nantah as Secretary General of the University. The opening of CHC at the old Nantah building was a nostalgic moment for many of the Nantah alumni present.

The Exhibition

To complement the launch of the *Encyclopedia*, an exhibition entitled *From Segregation to Integration: The Story of the Chinese Overseas* was held at the CHC using photographs and materials gathered in the course of producing the *Encyclopedia*. What better way to engage the public than with a miniature encyclopedia of the Chinese overseas that one could walk through and experience? Despite being located at a remote corner of Singapore in Jurong, the Exhibition attracted some 2,000 visitors in the first three months of its opening. Visitor numbers continued to increase as student groups and overseas scholars were drawn to the Exhibition following good reviews in the media.

Founding Director Lynn Pan conceptualised and wrote out the storyline for the Exhibition that focused on Chinatowns and its people in different parts of the world. Weaving together the past and present, the Exhibition explored what life in a Chinatown was like through three interlinked themes: the evolution of Chinatowns from "ghettos" and isolated spaces where the Chinese community was segregated from the mainstream society to multicultural spaces for all, the businesses — the lifeline of Chinatowns and a showcase of a people's ingenuity in supporting the needs of their self-contained and independent enclaves, and the culture of Chinatowns and how the Chinese banded together in clan and

---

[26] Kwok Kian Woon, "Singapore", in Lynn Pan, ed., *The Encyclopedia of the Chinese Overseas* (Singapore: Archipelago Press & Landmark Books, 1998), pp. 214–215.

district associations modelled after those in China and how they replicated a home away from home complete with Chinese newspapers and Chinese schools.

Mok Wei Wei (莫玮玮), a leading architect in Singapore and Managing Director of W Architects, was so inspired by the project he offered his service gratis. Although the exhibition space was only 560 square metres, Mok managed to feature some 400 images within the limited area. Ingenious in his use of space, he was able to bring out the themes and the layers of meanings through winding corridors, evoking a sense of an unending narrative that continued to unfold at the turn of each corner. He explained to *Lianhe Zaobao* that it was challenging to create an exhibition on a topic as complex and geographically broad as the Chinese diasporic experience. The task was made more difficult because the exhibit materials comprised mainly photographs and pictures with few artefacts. To recreate the story in multiple dimensions, he made use of space to fit the flow of the narrative. The corridors in the section on segregation were designed to be narrow and the lights dim to highlight the poor and crowded living conditions then, while rows of "shophouses" were set on both sides of the section on businesses with hollering and noise of shopkeepers selling their wares added in the background to bring out the buzz in Chinatowns.

"The way of life of the Chinese overseas continues to evolve," said Mok to *Lianhe Zaobao*, "it is not only about the past, but also about the present as well. To express this spirit in an abstract manner, I adopted clean modern lines for the design of this Exhibition."[27]

To promote awareness and interest in the study of Chinese overseas, the Centre started an outreach programme to recruit students from NTU as student guides for the Centre's exhibition. After going through training sessions by the Centre's researchers, the student guides conducted free tours of the Exhibition for the public. A typical visit to the Centre started with a guided tour of the Exhibition followed by the viewing of a film on Chinese overseas at the auditorium.

---

[27] "华裔馆展出历史图片和文物 — 主题:《落地生根 — 海外华人的变迁》(Chinese Heritage Centre exhibits historical memorabilia with theme: Putting down roots — Changes in the journeys of the Chinese overseas", 《联合早报 (*Lianhe Zaobao*)》, 25 October 1998.

Written feedback from visitors indicated an emotive response to the Exhibition. A student from a local secondary school wrote,

A person's past, the heritage, helps define oneself — it will always be a part of one's identity. If one doesn't realise one's roots and understand the ancestral past, it is as if a part of oneself is missing.

Another visitor commented,

It touches my heart to know that our forefathers worked so hard to set up Chinese schools, organise lion dances and other activities, just so that we, their children, will not lose the opportunity of knowing our Chinese culture.

Perhaps an exchange student from New York said it best,

The fact that the Chinese survive and thrive in countries all over the world makes me proud of my roots… What I gained from my experience at the Exhibition was not only a closer affiliation with my Chinese roots. It was also a lesson learnt about the resilience, tenacity, and courage of human spirit in its drive towards survival.

Advancing Knowledge and Understanding of the Chinese Overseas

Upon completion of the *Encyclopedia*, founding Director Lynn Pan left the Centre to pursue her writing interest. Professor Kee Pookong (纪宝坤), a specialist on Chinese migration, assumed directorship of the Centre. CHC Chairman Wee Cho Yaw, who always believed in leadership renewal, also stepped down and was succeeded by Professor Tommy Koh.

Under succeeding chairmen and directors, the CHC broadened and deepened its research collaboration with institutions worldwide, and seized opportunities to scale new heights: Professor Tommy Koh (Chairman, 2000–2005) and Professor Su Guaning (徐冠林), President of NTU (Chairman, 2006–2011); Professor Kee Pookong (Director, 1999–2002), Professor Ng Chin Keong (吴振强) (Director, 2002–2005), Professor Leo

Suryadinata (廖建裕) (Director, 2006–2013) and Professor Zhou Min (周敏) (Director, 2013–present).

Research and Publications

Following the publication of the *Encyclopedia* in 1998, the CHC embarked on numerous initiatives over the next decade. The research momentum continued to grow as the Centre collaborated with research partners worldwide in making valuable contributions to the global interest to study the Chinese diaspora. The CHC was in the vanguard of this new wave of research with the completion of two other flagship projects: an academic journal founded by the CHC under the auspices of the International Society for the Studies of Chinese Overseas (ISSCO) (世界海外华人研究学会) in 2005 and a biographical dictionary in 2012, both published in English to enhance visibility and global impact of research. Other notable publications by the CHC include:[28]

- *CHC Bulletin* (2003): a news bulletin on Chinese overseas published twice a year.
- Conference publications: *Genealogies and Chinese Overseas Migration* (2002) and *Chinese Diaspora Since Admiral Zhenghe with Special Reference to Maritime Asia* (2007) — a unique tri-lingual publication series featuring selected papers in English, Chinese and Bahasa Indonesia/Malay from the conference "Maritime Asia and the Chinese Overseas", organised to mark the 600th anniversary of *Zhenghe*'s maiden voyage to Southeast Asia and beyond.
- Monographs: *A Pictorial History of Nantah* (2000), *Chinese Newspapers in Southeast Asia* (2002), *A Historical Survey of Chinese-School Textbooks in Singapore, Malaysia and Indonesia* (2005), *Chinatowns in a Globalizing Southeast Asia* (2009).
- Archival projects: *The Hok Tek Chi Loke Yah Teng Series* (2005) — an effort to preserve 180 years of records of this Singapore's Chinese association founded in 1824.

---

[28]"About Us — History and Milestones" and "Our Publications — *CHC Bulletin*", CHC website, accessed on 1 September 2014: http://chc.ntu.edu.sg/.

- Collaborative publications: *Tongmenghui, Sun Yat Sen and The Chinese in Southeast Asia: A revisit* (2006) — jointly published by the CHC and Sun Yat Sen Nanyang Memorial Hall to celebrate the centenary of the establishment of the Singapore branch of the *Zhongguo Tongmenghui* (Revolutionary League of China) and *Sun Yat-Sen, Nanyang and the 1911 Revolution* (2011) jointly published by the CHC and the Institute of Southeast Asian Studies in commemoration of the 100th anniversary of the 1911 revolution.
- More editions of *The Encyclopedia of the Chinese Overseas* — the French edition (2000) reaching readers in France and other Francophone countries that have been significant areas of Chinese migrant settlement; a Japanese edition (2012); an updated English second edition (2006) published in paperback to reach a wider audience.

In the editors' note of the inaugural issue of the *Journal of Chinese Overseas* (JCO), Professor Ng Chin Keong, third CHC Director, and JCO's co-editor Professor Tan Chee Beng (陈志明) of the Chinese University of Hong Kong explained its significance to academia:

> The study of Chinese overseas has been growing in importance since World War II. With Chinese in almost all the countries in the world, their presence as well as their global networks and contribution to local societies have been the focus of interest of scholars, politicians, business people, and lay people. To date there are scholars and students of Chinese overseas all over the world. Their writings are mainly published in books and a diverse range of journals in social studies. However, there is not one internationally refereed journal that is professionally devoted to the study of Chinese overseas. The *Journal of Chinese Overseas* aims to fill this gap by providing an interdisciplinary forum for the promotion of research and writing on Chinese overseas.

Launched in May 2005, the JCO is CHC's second major project. The Singapore University Press was its publisher from 2005 to 2008, followed by Brill since 2009. Published in English for the CHC under the auspices of ISSCO, this cross-disciplinary and highly respected journal carries research articles, reports, and book reviews on Chinese overseas throughout the world and the communities from which they trace their origins. Moving across regions and disciplines, the JCO, published twice a year in May and November, examines "Chineseness" in its many diverse settings and contributes to transnational studies, as well as the study of Chinese communities in specific national contexts. JCO's editorial board is drawn from multidisciplinary fields as diverse as history, anthropology, sociology, geography, cultural studies, and political science. Contributors hail from the University of California, Harvard University, Centre National de la Recherché Scientifique (CNRS) in Paris, Chinese University of Hong Kong, Xiamen University, University of Pretoria and many other renowned research centres.[29]

> A Who's Who list of prominent Southeast Asians of Chinese descent has been compiled for the first time in a book that gives an insight into the lives and achievements of the men and women who have helped to shape the region,

reported the *Straits Times* (海峡时报) on the launch of the Centre's third flagship project — *Southeast Asian Personalities of Chinese Descent: A Biographical Dictionary* on 1 November 2012.[30]

The two-volume academic work published in collaboration with the Institute of Southeast Asian Studies Press, features 608 influential figures of Chinese descent, both past and present, from 10 countries in Southeast Asia where it is estimated some 75% of the ethnic Chinese outside China live. In the Introduction, Professor Leo Suryadinata, CHC's fourth director and chief editor of the *Dictionary*, explained that in drawing up the framework to transmit his ideas to 177 co-authors, he and his country editors had to grapple with challenging issues such as the definition of "ethnic Chinese" or "person of Chinese descent" in a diverse region where Southeast Asian Chinese have lived for centuries and may not share the same cultural identity. The final list of personalities was selected "because they are significant, prominent and have made a major impact, either positive or negative, in Southeast Asia," and either self-identify as Chinese or acknowledge their Chinese ancestry.[31]

---

[29] "Our Publications — Journal of Chinese Overseas", CHC website, accessed on 1 September 2014: http://chc.ntu.edu.sg/OurPublications/Pages/JournalofChineseOverseas.aspx.

[30] "New book features 608 people who shaped the region", *The Straits Times*, 2 November 2012.

[31] Leo Suryadinata, ed., *Southeast Asian Personalities of Chinese Descent — A Biographical Dictionary*. (Singapore: ISEAS Publishing, 2012), Introduction.

Taking six years to complete, the Dictionary is organised into 11 categories: Community Leaders, Businessmen/Businesswomen, Politicians, Professionals, Artists, Mass Media Leaders, Writers, Sportsmen/Sportswomen, Educators/Promoters of Education, Religious Leaders/Promoters of Religion and Others. Singapore has the most entries, followed by Indonesia and Malaysia. Among those included are political leaders Lee Kuan Yew, Goh Chok Tong and Lee Hsien Loong (李显龙), entertainer Dick Lee (李迪文), and Olympian Tan Howe Liang (陈浩亮) from Singapore, businessmen Liem Sioe Liong and banker Mochtar Riady (李文正) from Indonesia, as well Malayan Communist Party leader Chin Peng (陈平) and badminton champion Lee Chong Wei (李宗伟) from Malaysia.

The *Bangkok Post* (曼谷邮报) called the *Dictionary* "a veritable encyclopedia of Sinophilia" and noted that Thailand's 33 entries, while dominated by businessmen, also included

> community, media and religious leaders whose names are less well known but whose influence transcended the networks of Chinese and helped shape modern Thailand...

> and the inclusion of a gambling lord, Hong Taechawanit (郑志勇), offers context and colour to the *Dictionary*.[32]

In his keynote speech at the launch, Professor Wang Gungwu who chaired the *Dictionary*'s International Advisory Panel commented,

> This biographical dictionary is the first of its kind in several ways. It covers all kinds of activities and every country in Southeast Asia. And it goes beyond the older brief entries to try and flesh out personal attributes and distinctive contributions... Story after story, we see them [Chinese overseas] overcome their doubts and fears, achieve their goals and make their contributions to the communities they chose to identify with... Together these stories can build a clearer picture of what the people of Chinese descent have been able to contribute to the region.[33]

---

[32] "A group that went forth and prospered around the world", *The Bangkok Post*, 28 April 2013.
[33] Keynote Speech by Professor Wang Gungwu, Chairman of the East Asian Institute, NUS, and Member of the CHC's Board of Governors, at the launch of *Southeast Asian*

"Chinese More or Less" Exhibition

To celebrate the CHC's 10th Anniversary in 2005, the CHC Council decided to change the Centre's main exhibition — *From Segregation to Integration: The Story of the Chinese Overseas.* Founding Director Lynn Pan and architect Mok Wei Wei joined hands once again to conceptualise and design a new exhibition that explores the theme of "Chineseness" and Chinese identity.

Launched on 22 July 2005, *Chinese More or Less* examines Chinese in different parts of the world and across generations, delving into what it has meant to be defined as Chinese by oneself, by other Chinese, and by people other than Chinese. Through studio portraits, historical photos, caricatures and movie stills gathered from institutions, celebrities, scholars and families all over the world, a visitor is led to ponder questions such as "How Chinese am I?", "In what sense am I Chinese?" and "What does it mean to be Chinese?" and, in the process, may discover his or her Chinese identity.

In his speech at the opening ceremony, then Minister for Foreign Affairs BG George Yeo, suggested that the overseas Chinese identity is an evolving one influenced by the political and cultural developments in China as well as one's social adaptation within the adopted community. This discussion on identity had taken on immediacy with the re-emergence of China that had led to renewed pride among ethnic Chinese worldwide. Minister Yeo added,

> In Singapore, we hold fast to our position that while we are culturally Chinese, we are politically Singaporean… [This bi-cultural identity] makes life more complicated, but it also defines what it means to be what we are.[34]

At the Centre's 10th Anniversary fundraising dinner, then Minister Mentor Lee Kuan Yew gave his take on "Chineseness" and stressed the importance to stay relevant in the China of the future,

Personalities of Chinese Descent — A Biographical Dictionary at the National Library, on 1 November 2012, *CHC Bulletin*, Issue 19, (October 2013), pp. 1–5.
[34] Speech by BG George Yeo, Minister for Foreign Affairs, at the opening of the Exhibition *Chinese More or Less* at the CHC, NTU, on 22 July 2005, National Archives of Singapore.

As the world shrinks with globalisation, cultures and value systems are interacting, intermingling and synthesising... Chinese everywhere have to cope with powerful influences that affect their sense of being Chinese... To help these groups to be more conscious of what is happening to other groups in the world is one of the central purposes of CHC. It will help the widely dispersed Chinese overseas to identify and define themselves relative to their host communities and to the Chinese in China.

He urged the Centre to collaborate with institutions elsewhere that are similarly interested in this evolving saga.[35]

Today, the CHC hosts two main exhibitions, *Chinese More or Less* — the aforementioned exhibition on overseas Chinese identity and *Nantah Pictorial Exhibition,* comprising a collection of memorabilia and over 130 archival photographs taken from *A Pictorial History of Nantah* (published by CHC) that captures the spirit behind the founding of Nanyang University. Additionally, the Centre stages temporary and travelling exhibitions with different themes such as *Grooming Future Generations through Education: Chinese-School Textbooks in Singapore, Malaysia and Indonesia before 1965* (2003) that affords a rare glimpse of what the Chinese-educated were taught during the period; *Chinatowns in a Globalizing Southeast Asia* (2009) showcasing contemporary photographs that explores the human side of Chinatowns in 10 cities in the region[36] and *From Danmaxi to Xinjiapo: Ceramics and the Chinese in Singapore* (2013) with a display of some 400 archaeological finds, suggesting Chinese were in Singapore 500 years before Sir Stamford Raffles[37]

A New Chapter — Integration with NTU

Since its inception, the CHC had been closely associated with NTU. Dr Cham Tao Soon, then NTU's President, was a member of the Centre's first

---

[35] Speech by Minister Mentor Lee Kuan Yew at the CHC's 10th Anniversary Fundraising Dinner on 22 July 2005, National Archives of Singapore.

[36] "Exhibition" and "Our Publications — *CHC Bulletin*", CHC website, accessed on 1 September 2014, http://chc.ntu.edu.sg.

[37] "Exhibits show Chinese were in Singapore 500 years before Raffles", *The Straits Times,* 16 October 2013.

Board of Governors and the former Nanyang University Administration Block occupied by CHC was under a lease granted by the NTU Council at a token rent. The historic building was gazetted a national monument in 1998. Among the Centre's Board members, there was talk that it would make more administrative sense for CHC to be an integral part of NTU.

Professor Tommy Koh, the Centre's second Chairman, thought about it as far back as the early 2000s. In his speech as the Guest-of-Honour at the launch of the Centre's *Southeast Asian Personalities of Chinese Descent: A Biographical Dictionary*, Professor Koh recalled,

> When I was chairman of the board, I thought deeply about the future of CHC. I came to the conclusion that the best future for the Centre is to integrate with NTU and to become an autonomous entity within NTU... I shared my idea with him [Professor Su Guaning] and persuaded him to succeed me as the new chairman to bring about this integration.[38]

At the Centre's Annual General Meeting and the meeting of the Board of Governors held on 13 June 2006, a new Board of Governors was elected into office. After four years of dedicated service as the Centre's Chairman, Professor Tommy Koh was designated Honorary Chairman and Professor Su Guaning, President of NTU, was elected as the new Chairman of the Centre.

In 2009, CHC initiated discussions with NTU on integration to achieve synergy that would benefit both parties. In the case of CHC, it would be able to ride on the University's good reputation (NTU ranked 10th in Asia in the 2014 TIMES Higher Education World University Rankings[39]) and would be eligible for competitive research funding to support the Centre's research. Being part of NTU would also help CHC attract academic talents and raise funds.

---

[38] Speech by Professor Tommy Koh, Ambassador-At-Large, Ministry of Foreign Affairs, at the launch of *Southeast Asian Personalities of Chinese Descent — A Biographical Dictionary* at the National Library, on 1 November 2012, *CHC Bulletin*, Issue 19, (October 2013), pp. 6–7.

[39] "Corporate Information", NTU website, accessed on 26 October 2014: http://www.ntu.edu.sg/AboutNTU/CorporateInfo/Pages/universityrankings.aspx.

For NTU, incorporating CHC — a leading research centre on Chinese overseas known for its highly cited publications and other academic achievements and resources — would help the University develop special-ised programmes relating to the Chinese overseas. It would also buttress its "New Silk Road" initiative, one of the Five Peaks of Excellence identified in NTU's strategic blueprint and a metaphor for the unceasing flow of ideas and knowledge between Asia and the West that will help shape the course of the 21st Century.[40]

On 1 November 2011, CHC was reconstituted as a self-funded, autono-mous institute of NTU.[41]

Living up to its aspiration to be the intellectual hub for the study of Chinese overseas, CHC has organised numerous international and regional conferences and seminars, as well as public lectures, some of which included:

- "Chinese Community Organisations and Globalisations: Comparative International Perspectives" (2001) — an international conference that offered a rare opportunity for scholars and leaders of Chinese clan associa-tions to exchange views and understand one another in an increasingly globalised world.[42]
- "Contemporary Culture and Chinese Heritage in a Globalizing World" (2003) — a public lecture series co-organised by CHC and the Faculty of Arts and Social Sciences of NUS that examined how contacts with a wider world impact Chinese culture, be it in architecture, fine arts, law, science and technology, and medicine, and how Chinese culture influences environments outside China.[43]
- "*Tongmenhui*, Sun Yat Sen and the Chinese in Southeast Asia: A Revisit" (2006) — a bilingual international seminar co-organised with Sun Yat Sen Nanyang Memorial Hall to mark the 100th anniversary of the formation of *Tongmenhui* in Singapore and highlighting the significance of the role played by Singapore in the modernisation of China, featuring Dr Lien Chan, Honourary Chairman of the Kuomintang, as the keynote speaker

---

[40] "NTU unveils five-year strategic blueprint", NTU News Hub, 16 November 2010.
[41] *CHC Bulletin*, Issue 18, (October 2012), p. 28.
[42] "Staying Chinese in the global village", *The Straits Times*, 10 March 2001.
[43] *CHC Bulletin*, Issue 3, (June 2004), pp. 44–45.

and attended by leading experts on *Tongmenhui* and Sun Yat Sen from China, Taiwan and the Southeast Asian region.[44]

With Professor Su, then NTU President, assuming chairmanship of CHC's Board of Governors in 2006, CHC and NTU began working even more closely than before in various projects. Perhaps most noteworthy was the Centre's hosting of the 7th *ISSCO Conference* jointly with NTU from 7 to 9 May 2010 which attracted some 200 scholars from more than 20 countries and territories to Singapore.

The ISSCO Conference takes place once every three years and has been jointly convened by ISSCO and a higher education institution such as the University of California, Berkeley, USA, Hong Kong University, Peking University, China, and others. The 2010 ISSCO Conference was the first time that this largest gathering of overseas Chinese scholars was held in Singapore.

Professor Leo Suryadinata, then CHC Director and President of ISSCO, told *The Straits Times* that more than 200 papers — 120 in English and 90 in Chinese — were presented on the Conference theme: "*Migration, Indigenization and Exchange: Chinese Overseas from Global Perspectives*". These included studies on lesser-known Chinese communities in Africa, India, Latin America and Eastern Europe. Conference Secretary and Director of NTU's Centre for Chinese Language and Culture, Professor Lee Guan Kin (李元瑾), added that six papers relating to the former Nanyang University, including one on its founder Tan Lark Sye (陈六使), were presented by Singapore scholars.[45]

In his welcome speech at the 2010 ISSCO Conference, NTU President Su Guaning explained how the study of the Chinese overseas was closely linked to the history of NTU itself,

NTU's roots go back to 1955, when the first Chinese-language university outside of China, Nanyang University or Nantah, was set up with contributions from people of all walks of life in the Chinese community in Southeast Asia. In fact, it was at Nantah that courses on Chinese overseas and Southeast Asian studies were first taught. During that

---

[44] *CHC Bulletin*, Issues 7–8, (May & November 2006), pp. 28–29.
[45] "Conference on Chinese diaspora held in Singapore", *The Straits Times*, 7 May 2010.

period, Southeast Asian studies were better known as Nanyang Studies or *Nanyang yanjiu* and became one of the important differentiating characteristics of Nantah... Today, the study of the Chinese diaspora continues in our School of Humanities and Social Sciences as part of the Chinese Studies programme, complemented by CHC... which is also housed in the historic Nanyang University Administration Building.

Professor Su told the meeting that the Conference marked an important milestone for NTU and the CHC

> as we increase our engagement and exposure to international develop-ments in the field through collaborations with our regional and inter-national partners... By leveraging our respective strengths... we can all contribute to the continued expansion of knowledge about the Chinese diaspora around the world.[46]

With the integration of the CHC into NTU, the Wang Gungwu Library's catalogue was also integrated with the NTU Library system.

An eminent historian of China and a pioneering authority in the study of the Chinese diaspora, Professor Wang Gungwu is an author of numerous books and research papers. He has been a member of CHC's Board of Governors since its inception and chairs the East Asian Institute, the Institute of Southeast Asian Studies and the Lee Kuan Yew School of Public Policy in Singapore. He was the founding President of ISSCO and in 2009 the University of Cambridge conferred an Honorary Doctorate of Letters on Professor Wang in recognition of his contribution to scholarship on China and the Chinese.

In 2003, Professor Wang donated 20,000 volumes from his personal col-lection to the Centre's library, which was thus named the Wang Gungwu Library in recognition of his scholarship and significant contribution to the field of Chinese overseas studies. In 2007, Professor Wang donated an addi-tional 3,000 books to the Centre. Other scholars and organisations were inspired by Professor Wang to contribute towards building a resource on

---

[46]Welcome Speech by Dr Su Guaning, President of NTU, at the International Society for the Study of Chinese Overseas (ISSCO) VII International Conference, NTU News Hub, 7 May 2010.

Chinese overseas at CHC. The Lin Wo Ling collection, the Cheah Heng Sin Collection, the Yeap Chong Leng Collection and a collection from the Ministry of Education of the People's Republic of China were among some of the valuable donations received by the CHC.[47]

The Way Forward

On 1 November 2013, the second anniversary of CHC's move to NTU as an autonomous institute, Professor Zhou Min, the Tan Lark Sye Chair Professor of Sociology and Head of the Sociology Division at the NTU's School of Humanities and Social Sciences was appointed Director of the CHC by NTU President Professor Bertil Andersson.

Professor Zhou is an internationally known scholar in the social science fields of international migration, Asian America, and the Chinese Diaspora. Prior to taking up the tenured professorship at NTU in July 2013, she was Professor of Sociology & Asian American Studies and the Walter and Shirley Wang Endowed Chair in US-China Relations and Communications at the University of California, Los Angeles, USA. She joined NTU because of her passion for research on the Chinese diaspora.

"I came to Singapore with an eye on the CHC as a platform, from which to launch impactful projects," she told the *CHC Bulletin*. Professor Zhou sees Singapore as the centre of the Chinese diaspora as it is at the nexus of the East and West, and there is strong interest and support from the government and local communities for Chinese heritage preservation and the development of the study of Chinese overseas as an academic field. She hopes to leverage on the strategic location of Singapore at a major research university and at the centre of the Chinese diaspora and on her own position as NTU's tenured chair professor to fulfil CHC's mission in creating, advancing, and curating the global body of knowledge concerning the Chinese overseas.[48]

Brimming with ideas, Professor Zhou shared her five-year strategic plan with this writer in an exhaustive interview in December 2014. In her

---

[47] *CHC Bulletin*, Issue 3, (June 2004), p. 49.

[48] "New head for NTU Chinese Heritage Centre", *The Straits Times*, 16 October 2013; "周敏想让华裔馆 '站在巨人肩膀上'" (Zhou Min wants CHC to 'stand on the shoulders of giants", 《联合早报》, 15 October 2013; "Interview with Professor Zhou Min, the new Director of the Chinese Heritage Centre", *CHC Bulletin*, Issue 20, (July 2014), pp. 1–4.

view, two urgent issues require attention. One is the insufficient public acknowledgement of the tremendous contributions that people of Chinese descent have made to societies and economies around the world historically and in contemporary times. Ample work has been done to document the sufferings, oppressions, struggles, and losses of the Chinese overseas, but not enough to acknowledge their triumphs, dignities, achievements, and impactful contributions to humankind. The other urgent issue is the risk of the generation lost — the gradual detachment of younger generations from their Chinese roots, not only in mother tongues but also in cultural tradition and heritage.

The CHC is in an ideal position to address these urgent issues through rigorous research. It can draw on the institutional strengths of NTU and tremendous manpower from NTU's faculty and students to promote CHC's active research agenda, which should focus on not just the past but the present as well, assembling all the pieces of information on Chinese that have dispersed in all directions into one integrated whole. With a strong foothold in Southeast Asia, the CHC should go beyond the region, setting its sights on the world.

Professor Zhou's faculty position at NTU would also enable her to strengthen the ties between CHC and the university and to build a platform that is beneficial to both. With the assistance of the faculty at NTU, the CHC can stimulate students' interest in research and involve them in the Centre's projects. The students can help to inject an incredible amount of energy into CHC while the Centre can help them rediscover their roots and make their learning experience at NTU richer and more meaningful. Professor Zhou elaborated,

> Young people have many ingenious ideas and their way of seeing the world may be different from ours. Their originality, creativity and unique perspectives can contribute to new understanding and stimulate new research. I would like to showcase some of their work at the CHC.

Another important thrust in the strategic plan is to reach out to local communities and help connect Singaporeans to their Chinese heritage and to the nation's multicultural identity. In addition to a rigorous research agenda, the CHC will also focus on public education and community service, acting as a bridge between the university and local communities, especially the local Chinese community.

The CHC plans to build a "Youth Engagement & Community Service" programme. This programme aims to stimulate and inspire young people, NTU undergraduates in particular, to serve the local community in preserving Chinese cultural heritage and appreciating multiculturalism among the younger generation. Such an experience will enrich learning while nurturing a strong civic sense in young people. The CHC will also seek greater partnerships with Chinese clan associations and other cultural organisations to promote intercultural exchange and cultural events.

Much has been accomplished in less than a year. In January 2014, Huang Yao Foundation supported the Centre's new translation programme for the study of the Chinese overseas which aims to introduce English readers to research works on the Chinese diaspora translated from Chinese. A team of NTU students led by Professor Zhou is working on the first project under the programme — the translation into English of *The History of the Chinese in Malaysia and Singapore,* written in Chinese by popular cartoonist, painter and scholar Huang Yao and first published in 1967.[49]

In March 2014, the Wang Gungwu Library launched the Early Textbook Digital Project. Nanyang Spectrum — the NTU's student-run TV station reported that the introduction of QR-coded rare textbooks at the Wang Gungwu Library's Special Collection of early Chinese textbooks was well-received by the technology-savvy NTU students who use their smartphones to save the information for research projects.[50] In November 2014, the CHC received a Heritage Participation Grant from the National Heritage Board to digitise the contents of the Early Textbook Collection, making it available online and readily accessible to researchers and interested individuals in Singapore and worldwide.[51]

Responding to demand from local communities and overseas visitors, the CHC has launched a package tour programme. This programme is designed to enhance the overall educational experience of overseas visitors during their visit in Singapore and to foster ties between the CHC and

[49] "华裔馆获四万余元捐赠翻译黄尧《马星华人志》(CHC obtains $40,000 donation for translation of Huang Yao's *History of the Chinese in Malaysia and Singapore*)", 《联合早报 (*Lianhe Zaobao*)》, 25 January 2014.

[50] "Wang Gungwu Library introduces QR-coded textbooks", *Nanyang Spectrum*, 26 March 2014.

[51] *CHC Bulletin*, Issue 21, (December 2014), p. 26.

overseas counterparts. This inaugural programme includes both a standard package (including CHC museum visit and a bus tour on the NTU campus), serving local schools and communities in Singapore and the region, and a tailored package (including CHC museum visit, a bus campus tour, and thematic workshops/lectures), meeting the special needs of various tourist groups from China and elsewhere. While this programme aims to introduce Singapore's diverse cultures, local fares, and places of interest, it also encourages self-discovery through active learning, helping participants build character and self-confidence and nurture their leadership skills and team work spirit.[52]

On 1 June 2014, the CHC Faculty Advisory Committee was established. Comprising 25 NTU faculty members from multidisciplinary fields whose areas of research and teaching are related to the study of Chinese overseas, the Committee functions as a think tank and its main role is to provide insight and advice to the CHC director on matters relevant to research, teaching, community outreach, and the development of CHC. With greater integration into NTU, the CHC strives to promote the development of the study of Chinese overseas as an academic field via research, teaching, and public education.[53]

The story has come full circle. Six decades ago, Nanyang University offered the first courses on overseas Chinese to university students; today, the CHC, recognised and well-established as an authority in the study of Chinese overseas, is an integral part of NTU and aspires to embody the Nanyang spirit just as Nantah once did.

---

[52] *CHC Bulletin*, Issue 21, (December 2014), p. 4.
[53] "Establishment of the CHC Faculty Advisory Committee", *CHC Bulletin*, Issue 20, (July 2014), p. 31.

CHAPTER 5

Chinese Philanthropy
Past and Present

CHEW Kheng Chuan

When We were a Community, a Colony, but not yet a Country

For any Chinese in Singapore, in China, and perhaps the world over, who was born before the last 50 years, Tan Kah Kee (陈嘉庚) (1874–1961) was a revered first name in Chinese philanthropy. He is famously associated with the founding of the Chinese High School (华侨中学) in Singapore (now Hwa Chong Institution) (新加坡华侨中学) in 1919 and Xiamen (Amoy) University (厦门大学) in China in 1921. As a community leader he was a founding member of the Singapore Chinese Chamber of Commerce & Industry (新加坡中华总商会) in 1906, led the Singapore Hokkien Huay Kuan (新加坡福建会馆) and chaired the Ee Hoe Hean Club (怡和轩). Many schools in Singapore (and in China) were founded by him — Tao Nan (道南), Ai Tong (爱同), Nan Chiau (南侨), Chong Fu (崇福) and Nanyang Girls' High School (南洋女中). He was also a key benefactor of the Anglo-Chinese School (ACS) (英华学校) and Raffles College.

His business empire was at its height in the 1920s but was felled by the Great Depression of 1929 and his company was wound up in 1934. Regardless, he continued supporting the schools he had started. Tan was also a social activist who was involved in humanitarian relief during catastrophic flooding in Fujian and Guangdong in the early 1900s. Between 1937 and 1941, he led the China Relief Fund in Southeast Asia for war victims in the Sino-Japanese War. In 1939 he mobilised overseas Chinese volunteers to transport military supplies to China via an overland route through Burma. When Tan Kah Kee died in his hometown of Jimei in Fujian province in China in 1961, the government of China honoured him with a state funeral, and its legendary premier Zhou Enlai (周恩来) was one of his pallbearers.

This essay is primarily about the last 50 years (1965–2015) of philanthropy in Singapore, and its practice in the Chinese community here, to coincide with our first 50 years as a nation. But we were a city before we were a country. And we are a majority community in this country that has a history that stretched 150 years before our beginnings as a nation.

Earlier in our history, even before Tan Kah Kee, there was Tan Tock Seng (陈笃生) (1798–1850) who founded the hospital in 1844 that today bears his name. There was his son Tan Kim Cheng (陈金钟) (1829–1892) who was responsible for rebuilding and funding the hospital (and who was Singapore's plenipotentiary to the Thai Kingdom and famously introduced Anna to the King of Siam). Tan Chay Yan (陈齐贤) (1871–1916), Tan Tock Seng's grandson and Kim Cheng's nephew, made a significant contribution in 1905 to found the Straits Settlement and Federated Malay States Government (SSFMSG) Medical School, the precursor of the King Edward VII Medical College. Tan Kim Cheng's grandson Tan Boon Liat (陈武烈) (1875–1934), was one of the founders of Tao Nan School in 1906. This line of philanthropy continues today from Boon Liat's son-in-law Seow Poh Leng (萧保龄) (1883–1942) to his great-grandson Richard Seow Yung Liang (b.1962), Chairman of the Board of Governors of ACS.

There was also Tan Kim Seng (陈金声) (1805–1864), and his grandson Tan Jiak Kim (陈若锦) (1859–1917), who was the prime mover of a donation drive in 1905 that raised $87,000 (of which he contributed $12,000) to establish the SSFMSG Medical School, as aforementioned, the precursor of the King Edward VII Medical College and the first incarnation of the National University of Singapore. Kim Seng Road and its offshoot Jiak Kim Street today bear their names. Tan Kim Seng contributed $13,000 in 1857 for the construction of the first reservoir and waterworks in Singapore. To commemorate Kim Seng's public works philanthropy the Municipal Commissioners erected a fountain and named it the Tan Kim Seng Fountain in 1882. This fountain at Fullerton Square was moved to the Esplanade Park in 1925 and gazetted as a National Monument in 2010.

They were all notable philanthropists, not only in the spheres of education and civic and social welfare, but also socially and politically, with some supporting revolutionary movements in the "Motherland", and against wars of foreign aggression.

In more contemporary times, and carrying the philanthropic traditions to greater heights, Lee Kong Chian (李光前) and his Lee Foundation (李氏基金), have succeeded Tan Kah Kee (his father-in-law) as the present "first name in philanthropy" in Singapore.

Private philanthropy in Singapore's history has been notably expressed in the service of medical care and medical education. From the founding of the Chinese Paupers' Hospital which later became and stands today as Tan Tock Seng Hospital (陈笃生医院) (no longer a private hospital but part of the government-run and funded national healthcare system), to the founding of the National University of Singapore (first as the King Edward VII College of Medicine as mentioned) and to the latest naming of the third medical school in Singapore in 2011, the Lee Kong Chian School of Medicine at Nanyang Technological University (南洋理工大学李光前医学院). Not forgetting the landmark founding of Nanyang University itself in 1955 by the leadership of Tan Lark Sye (陈六使), philanthropy has been an abiding virtue of the Chinese community in Singapore.

Now with Nationhood

The practice of philanthropy in the Chinese community in Singapore in its 50 years of nationhood has also been active, significant, and substantial. More research is needed to confirm my personal observation but it would seem there has been substantially more private philanthropy in the last 15 years compared with the first 35 years of our nationhood.

From the turn of this new millennium 2000–2015, there has been a significant growth in the philanthropic landscape in Singapore. What is the level and scope of philanthropy today, in terms of how much is collected in donations from all private sources (individuals, foundations and charitable organisations, the public at large) to all charities and beneficiaries in a year?

The National Volunteerism and Philanthropy Centre (NVPC) (全国志愿服务于慈善中心) first started a bi-annual survey of giving in 2004. In that year, the total amount of giving in Singapore was recorded at $438 million. Two years later the quantum dipped to $341 million, possibly a response to a controversy that befell a particular charity (the National Kidney Foundation) in 2005. But in the next survey two years later in 2008, there was a three-fold increase to $958 million. Since then the annual quantum of private philanthropy in Singapore has crossed the billion-dollar mark. In the latest 2014 survey it stood at $1.25 billion. Although these are national surveys of all communities in Singapore it can safely be taken that the Chinese community accounted for the majority of such giving and likely more than the 76% share of the figures, reflecting more than its composition in the total population.

Here is an interesting contextual aside in comparative global rankings. Singapore's population today is 5.4 million. The United States' population is 64 times of Singapore's, at 320 million. Singapore (GDP US$364 billion) is recently the wealthiest GDP per capita country in the world (US$55,000 per person compared to the USA's US$53,000 per person), whereas the US is the wealthiest country in the world (GDP US$16 trillion). Singaporeans give S$1.2 billion annually. Americans give 456 times as much — US$400 billion annually, on an absolute basis. On a per capita basis, Americans give eight times more than Singaporeans annually, S$1,713 per person compared with S$226 per person.

However, in comparing philanthropy it seems to me that absolute numbers are more meaningful than the per capita numbers, because giving is observed to be "lumpy" and not evenly spread out. That is to say, even as the absolute number of donors in a community grows, a small number of donors give a disproportionately larger share of the total amount of donations.

As my experience has been that of a fundraiser for tertiary institutions, this chapter of philanthropy in the Chinese community will focus on the field of higher education. While education is perhaps the key beneficiary of philanthropy in Singapore, philanthropic individuals, foundations and charitable organisations do of course support many other areas and causes. They contribute importantly to social welfare and the needy, medical research and treatment, humanitarian disaster relief, ethnic self-help groups and Chinese clans, religion, causes in the arts and cultural development, and international outreach.

The Chinese community has always looked to education as a means to uplift their lives in terms of increasing social mobility between generations. Investment in higher education by way of giving generously to its cause has therefore not been a difficult sell.

In 1991 the Universities Endowment Fund (UEF) (大学捐赠基金) was set up by the government to tap private philanthropy for the National University of Singapore (NUS) (新加坡国立大学) and Nanyang Technological University (NTU) (南洋理工大学). Its target was to raise $250 million[1] in 10 years. It was a very unfamiliar idea, since for the prior four decades, the responsibility for funding higher education had rested squarely on the government's shoulders.

In the first three decades of nationhood, very large donations were not easy to come by. Notably, the Shaw Foundation made a gift of $5 million and the Kuok Foundation did likewise to NUS. Two buildings were named after these foundations for their substantial gifting.

One of the early major gifts of $3.68 million to the UEF was a bequest of the late Chairman of the Ban Hin Leong Group Mr Lim Seng Tjoe (林生珠) (1906–1993). He had served on the boards of the Chinese High School, Nanyang Girls High School and Chung Cheng High School. He was also the President of the Sian Chay Medical Institution, a charitable TCM (traditional Chinese medicine) clinic serving the community. In recognition of his gift, NUS' largest lecture theatre LT27 at the Faculty of Science was named the Lim Seng Tjoe Lecture Theatre in 1995.

The estate of Lee Wee Nam (李伟南) (1881–1964) made a gift of $10 million to NTU in 2001 and its main library was named the Lee Wee Nam Library in his honour. Lee Wee Nam's family owned the Four Seas Communications Bank (四海通银行) (later bought over by the Overseas Chinese Banking Corporation OCBC 华侨银行) and he served as President and Vice-President of Ngee Ann Kongsi (义安公司) between 1920 and 1964.

---

[1] The UEF's purpose was to establish an endowment of $1 billion shared equally between the two universities. The Government however felt that this sum was too huge to be met by private philanthropy alone. Therefore it decided to furnish half that amount, $500 million, as a seed fund, and then challenge the universities to raise half of the remaining $500 million, to which it would offer a one-for-one matching grant. Thus the universities had to raise $250 million and $750 million would be provided by government.

During the Sino-Japanese War he chaired the Teochew section of the China Relief Fund and for such involvement he was jailed and tortured by the Japanese Occupation army in Singapore. His nephew Lee Hiok Kwee (李毓奎) (1930–1992) made a gift of $17 million to NUS in his will which was executed in 2002 and a building of the NUS Faculty of Science was named the Lee Wee Kheng (李伟卿) building to honour his father, and a Life Sciences Laboratory in the building named after Lee Hiok Kwee the filial son.

Gifts in the philanthropic landscape began to take off after 2000. First there was the breath-taking $60 million gift which the Lee Foundation (李氏基金) made in 2002 to the National Library (国家图书馆). Fifty years earlier in 1953, its gift of $375,000 had founded the National Library, on the condition that it was to be a free public library. (In current dollars, it would be equivalent to $70 million today.)

In the last 15 years, a new trend has emerged. In the first year (2003) that NUS established its dedicated fundraising office (Development Office, using the American term) it met with unexpected success. It had hoped to raise $10 million in its first two years of operation. But in that first year it raised $111 million. Since that time, it has continued to raise between $100–150 million annually. With a generous government matching policy, its endowment coffers have grown to a very respectable $3.68 billion (as stated in its 2014 annual report), far exceeding the original $500 million target of the UEF.

Whereas in the first 35 years of nationhood, private philanthropy did not express itself with such large gifts, once NUS began to tap the generosity of the donor community, the trickle became a flood. Soon, major gifts at the level of $1 million were no longer newsworthy but achievable. Indeed, in the NUS experience, principal gifts (so-called for gifts above $1 million) came to be received in a steady stream.

In 2003, the Yong Loo Lin Trust[2] (杨潞龄医学院信托) made what felt like an unheard-of gift of $25 million to NUS to found the Yong Siew Toh Conservatory of Music (杨秀桃音乐学院). This was followed in 2005 by another spectacular gift of $100 million to the NUS medical faculty, which was subsequently named the Yong Loo Lin School of

---

[2]Strictly speaking, the Yong Loo Lin Trust is a Chinese Malaysian Trust, though it is domiciled and administered in Singapore.

Medicine (杨潞龄医学院) to honour its donor. In 2008 the Yong Loo Lin Trust made an additional gift of $25 million to the Yong Siew Toh Conservatory's endowment. All these gifts were matched dollar for dollar by the government, allowing the NUS endowment to grow by $300 million from this single donor alone.

The Lee Foundation has also given generously to NUS, as it does to many other causes and organisations. It made a $30 million gift in 2005 for the endowment of bursaries, scholarships and professorships. To recognise its gift, one wing of the University Hall at NUS, the seat of administration, was called the Lee Kong Chian Wing. Earlier in 2004, it had made a $50 million gift to the Singapore Management University (SMU) (新加坡管理大学), and in recognition of this gift SMU named its key faculty the Lee Kong Chian School of Business (李光前商学院). In 2009 the Lee Foundation made a $25 million gift to NUS to help establish the Lee Kong Chian Museum of Natural History (李光前自然历史博物馆), a successor to the Raffles Museum of Biodiversity at NUS which had been a museum mostly in name with no exhibition space, holding the collection of the former museum, with its famous skeleton of a whale.

The Lee Foundation was established in 1952 by Lee Kong Chian (1893–1967), not very long after his business fortunes recovered from the ravages of the Japanese War, helped by the booming price of rubber fuelled by the Korean War. It was said to have been established with an endowment of $3.5 million. When Lee died in 1967, half of his estate went to the Lee Foundation, to allow it to continue its good work, in the hands of his sons Lee Seng Gee (李成义), Lee Seng Tee (李成智), and Lee Seng Wee (李成伟).

The Lee Foundation gives not just to the cause of education, its beneficiaries are widely distributed in the areas of social welfare, addressing the needs of the destitute, the building of arts and cultural institutions, and medical education, research, treatment and healthcare. But it was in education that it gave substantially in absolute amounts, beginning in 1929, 24 years before the establishment of the foundation itself, to the Singapore Chinese Girls' School (新加坡华人女中).

In 1957 the foundation donated $1 million towards the new Nanyang University (Nantah) (南洋大学), fulfilling a pledge. In 1962 it donated $1 million to the Faculty of Medicine at the University of Singapore (later

NUS). In 1965 it donated $1 million to help set up the Institute of Medical Specialties at the Singapore General Hospital. It has also been a key benefactor of Chinese High School (华侨中学), Singapore Chinese Girls' School, St Theresa's Convent, Kuo Chuan Girls' School (国专女校) (named after Lee's father), Anglo-Chinese School (英华学校), Kong Hwa School (光华学校) (originally named for Lee Kong Chian with his gift of $300,000 in 1953, but renamed on his insistence) and Nan Chiau High School (南侨中学). While its record of major gift amounts are listed here, the Lee Foundation's philanthropic practice is to spread its largesse to a very wide range of causes. In one year it may disburse up to 2,000 grants, large and small, from four- to eight-figure amounts. More recently in 2011, it made philanthropic history in Singapore with the largest single gift of $150 million to NTU and the Lee Kong Chian School of Medicine (李光前医学院) was named in honour of its founder. Established as one of the most respected and best-endowed foundations in Singapore, the Lee Foundation is estimated to have donated over a billion dollars (in current dollars) since its founding.

The Shaw Foundation (邵氏基金), set up in 1957 by brothers Runme Shaw (邵仁枚) and Run Run Shaw (邵逸夫), has as its asset base the ownership of Shaw House and Centre (邵氏大厦) at the junction of Scotts Road and Orchard Road. Its current chairman is Shaw Vee Meng (邵维铭), the late Run Run Shaw's son. The Shaw Foundation supports the National Kidney Foundation (新加坡全国肾脏基金会), the Community Chest (共益金), the NUS Endowment (国立大学捐赠基金), and also in the field of the arts, the Singapore Repertory Theatre (新加坡专业剧场), and the Substation (艺术之家). Since 1948 they have made a tradition of giving gift parcels of food staples and an "ang-pow" to approximately 10,000 elderly folks in Singapore, Kuala Lumpur, Malacca, Ipoh and Penang. The "ang-pow" amount has been adjusted with inflation, from $2 in 1960, to $50 in 1985, to $100 from 2005. The foundation reports that since 1999, its annual budget for grant making has increased to almost $18 million and in its history, it has given away approximately $200 million.

There is a larger Shaw Foundation in Hong Kong, established in 1973 by Sir Run Run Shaw, supporting charitable causes mostly in Hong Kong and China but also in Britain and the US. It reports that since its inception it has made gifts of more than US$390 million. The Shaw Foundation made a gift of $10 million to NUS in 2005 to support the building of the Shaw Foundation Alumni House (邵氏基金校友会大厦) on campus.

The Lien Foundation (连氏基金)was founded by Dr George Lien Ying Chow (连瀛洲) (1907–2004) in 1980. Its present Chairman is his grandson Laurence Lien (连宗诚), and its Governor Emeritus is Dr Lien's wife of 40 years, Margaret Lien (连陈文贤). Philanthropically and in his civic service, Lien Ying Chow was associated with the founding of Nanyang University in 1955 (now NTU) and of Ngee Ann College (now Ngee Ann Polytechnic) (义安理工学院). He was the first Chairman of the National University of Singapore (NUS) Council from 1980 to 1992 and then its Pro-Chancellor thereafter. He had also served as Singapore's High Commissioner to Malaysia in 1966. But Lien Ying Chow was foremost the founder of the Overseas Union Bank (OUB) (华联银行), one of the Big Four Banks in Singapore until it was acquired in 2001 by Wee Cho Yaw's UOB (United Overseas Bank) (大华银行). In 2008 NTU renamed a road within its 200-hectare campus Lien Ying Chow Drive, in honour of the $27 million that the Lien Foundation had given to the university in earlier gifts.

In 2013 Margaret Lien made a gift of $12 million to NTU, engendering government matching that established a $30 million endowment which named the Margaret Lien Centre for Professional Success. Currently the Lien Foundation's key areas of focus are early childhood education, eldercare and environmental sustainability in water and sanitation.

NTU's predecessor institution is Nanyang University (Nantah). Nantah's founding in 1955 was nothing short of heroic, an outpouring of community pride and determination, and an expression of the community's most profound regard for education. Many prominent community leaders of the day supported and played key and critical roles, but Tan Lark Sye (陈六使) (1897–1972) has been called its founder. Tan came from Tong An county in Fujian province in China in 1914 when he was 17 years old. He worked for Tan Kah Kee and later established his own rubber-exporting firm, Aik Hoe & Co (益和树胶有限公司), when he was 28 years old. His business grew successfully and he became the President of the Singapore Hokkien Huay Kuan in 1949 and the Singapore Chinese Chamber of Commerce & Industry in 1950. He was a prime advocate for the setting up of a Chinese-language university to meet the aspirations for tertiary education of all students graduating from Chinese secondary schools throughout Nanyang

(Southeast Asia) but with no university to go to outside of China. (Many regional governments restricted travel to China in the early years of the People's Republic of China.)

The establishment of Nantah galvanised the entire Chinese community. With the community leaders as its champions, donors from all walks of life — from tycoons to taxi drivers to "taxi-dancers", from shopkeepers to students — responded to the call to give to this university of their future. The Hokkien Huay Kuan led by Tan donated 523 acres of its real estate for the university to be built. Tan Lark Sye himself announced an almost unimaginable $5 million leadership gift to Nantah. This writer conservatively estimates that the gift would be equivalent to $500 million today. Honouring his pledge in 1953 to match 10% of the total amount raised for Nantah, Lee Kong Chian's Lee Foundation contributed $1 million ($100 million in current dollars) in 1957.

Khoo Teck Puat (邱德拔) (1917–2004) was a banker and hotelier who began his career at age 17 with the OCBC Bank in 1933. He founded Malayan Banking Berhad in Malaysia (now Maybank) (马来亚银行有限公司) in 1960 but was ousted as its chief executive by the Malaysian government in 1967, though he remained a shareholder until 1976. He then went to Brunei and founded the National Bank of Brunei (NBB) (文莱国家银行) in 1965 but his ownership of NBB also came to grief in 1986. In the meantime he had acquired the Goodwood Park Hotel (良木园酒店) and other hotel properties in Singapore in 1968, and became the largest shareholder (13.51%) of Standard Chartered Bank (渣打银行) in Britain in 1986. When he died in 2004 in Singapore, he was listed as the wealthiest Singaporean by Forbes ranking.

In 1981 Khoo set up the Khoo Foundation (邱氏基金) with a $20 million endowment, supporting a range of charitable causes. But it was after his death that very substantial gifts were made by his estate, totalling $345 million. Duke-NUS Graduate School of Medicine received $80 million in 2007 and a new hospital in Yishun which opened in 2010 was named Khoo Teck Puat Hospital (邱德拔医院) with a gift of $125 million. His family also made the single largest gift of US$21 million received by Beijing University in China in 2006 for the construction of a gymnasium to be used in the 2008 Olympics held in Beijing.

Ng Teng Fong (1928–2010) (黄廷芳) built his fortunes in property development in Singapore and Hong Kong to become one of the wealthiest tycoons in Singapore at the time of his death. His company in Singapore, Far East Organisation (远东机构), is headed by his son Philip Ng (黄志达) while his eldest son Robert Ng (黄志祥) heads his SinoLand Group in Hong Kong (香港信和集团). The family of the late property tycoon has not formally set up a foundation in Singapore. Their philanthropic practices are predicated on their deeply held Christian beliefs.

In 2011 his family made a $125 million gift to Jurong General Hospital (裕廊综合医院) and it was renamed Ng Teng Fong General Hospital (黄廷芳综合医院). In 2013 the Ng family made a $10 million gift to the NUS Institute of Real Estate Studies to establish the Ng Teng Fong Professorship in Real Estate. In 2014, $52 million was given to Tan Tock Seng Hospital to establish the Ng Teng Fong Healthcare Innovation Programme.

Chinese Indonesian businessman Mochtar Riady (李文正), founder of the Lippo Group (力宝集团) made a gift of $21 million to NUS Business School (新加坡国立大学商学院) in 2007 and $5 million to SMU in 2011. In 2014, his son Stephen Riady (李棕), Singaporean by citizenship and chairman of property and hotel developer Overseas Union Enterprise Limited (OUE) (华联企业有限公司) made a gift of $30 million to NUS.

Goh Cheng Liang (吴钦亮), founder of the Nippon Paint Southeast Asia Group (立时集团) and ranked Singapore's wealthiest man by Bloomberg in 2015 with a net worth of $11.2 billion, established his Goh Foundation (吴氏基金) in 1994, giving especially to medical research and healthcare. In 2009 he made a gift of $12 million to NUS and the Viva Foundation for Children with Cancer. His substantial contributions have been made to the National Cancer Centre Singapore, with gifts totalling $63 million, the latest and largest being $50 million made in 2014.

Unusual amongst major philanthropists because he is not a businessman, retired professor of Statistics and author Dr Saw Swee Hock (苏瑞福), made a gift of $30 million in 2011 to his alma mater, crowning earlier giving to NUS of about $4 million. NUS named the Saw Swee Hock School of Public Health (苏瑞福公共卫生学院) in his honour.

Toh Kian Chiu (卓键水) (1927–2000) made his fortune in the construction industry and his Swee Constructions Pte Ltd (水建筑私人有限公司) was one of Singapore's earliest road builders. His earlier gifts to NUS provided scholarships for medical studies, but in 2013 the Toh Kian Chiu Foundation (卓键水基金) made a $20 million gift to the Lee Kong Chian Medical School at NTU.

The selective listing of philanthropists and foundations of the Chinese community above in the last 50 years is far from comprehensive, and no doubt suffers from many egregious omissions. I had wanted to give a picture, however incomplete, of "heroes of philanthropy" (borrowing the term from *ForbesAsia*) of the Chinese community in Singapore today and in its history. There is an academic paper written by Associate Professor Albert Chu-Ying Teo of NUS and his students called *Grant Making Entities in Singapore* first published in 2011. It lists 118 grant-making entities and is a creditable attempt to map the philanthropic landscape. However its survey is far from complete in its details. Clearly more research and writing on this subject need to be done.

The Chinese Development Assistance Council (CDAC)

The Chinese Development Assistance Council (CDAC) (华社自助理事会) was formed in 1992. It was an initiative of the Goh Chok Tong (吴作栋) Government, but it was founded as a partnership between the government and the two significant representative bodies of the Chinese community — the Singapore Chinese Chamber of Commerce & Industry (SCCCI) (新加坡中华总商会) and the Singapore Federation of Chinese Clan Associations (SFCCA) (新加坡宗乡会馆联合总会). The purpose of the CDAC is to address the educational standards and income needs of the bottom 20% of the community.

It was also founded on the notion that traditionally, people turned to their ethnic group to seek welfare assistance. The term "self-help" was a significant principle, and the "self" referred to was the ethnic community that one was a part of. On the other hand, after a quarter century of nationhood, Singaporeans were also very self-conscious of themselves as a multiracial society, and so there was an initial reservation from some quarters, whether such a concept was a historically retrogressive approach.

But the CDAC had been preceded by the formation of Yayasan Mendaki in 1982 and the Singapore Indian Development Association (SINDA) in 1991, both of which were defined by their ethnic-based identity. The absence of a Chinese self-help organisation might be misinterpreted as a discriminatory omission. Thus the SCCCI and SFCCA were roped in to establish the CDAC.

It was calculated that for the CDAC to fulfil its mission of uplifting the bottom 20% of its community base, it would require at the time of its formation, some $5 million per annum in operational expenditure, and perhaps an endowment of $50 million for its longer term needs. The government agreed to match the fund up to $10 million. Wee Cho Yaw (黄祖耀), in his capacity of the President of the SFCCA (a post he held from its founding in 1985 to 2010) was elected the Chairman of the Board of Trustees of the CDAC. The Chairman of the Board of Directors of the CDAC was a senior government minister, the first one being then Home Affairs Minister Wong Kan Seng (黄根成). The Patron was the Prime Minister.

The inaugural fundraising in 1992 collected $5.5 million. A second round of fundraising in 2014 raised an additional $17.8 million. The device to fund its operational budget however came from an "check-off" scheme whereby $0.50 (for monthly salary not exceeding $2,000) and $1 (for monthly salary of $2,000 and above) were collected from the monthly contribution of every employee unless one "opted out" and did not want to allow this automatic contribution. These monthly contribution rates were increased for the first time since the CDAC's founding, from $0.50 to $1 in the past to from $0.50 to $3 per month since January 2015 depending on one's salary. For the Eurasian Association it was increased from $2–$10 to now $2–$20, and for SINDA it was increased from $1–$7 to now $1–$30. Presently some $12 million is collected annually by CDAC from CPF members' contribution and the reserves of CDAC is reported to be $55 million.

The CDAC conducts tuition and enrichment classes for students and sponsors skills training for lower-skilled workers. It also provides programmes and assistance schemes for families and senior citizens. Approximately 50,000 students, workers and families from low-income households benefit every year from these CDAC's programmes and assistance schemes.

Incentives for Philanthropy

From the 1990s, the government has stepped into the landscape of philanthropy in very significant ways that have paradoxically both enhanced and overshadowed it. In 1991 the government began to provide matching grants for donations raised for the Universities Endowment Fund. Initially such matching benefitted only the universities. But in celebration of 50 years of nationhood, and having created great national wealth, the government very generously extended its matching grants to "institutions of public character" (IPCs) beyond the universities. Donations to arts and heritage organisations were also given dollar-for-dollar matching with the establishment of the $250 million Cultural Matching Fund (文化捐献配对基金) in 2014. Voluntary Welfare Organisations (VWOs) (志愿性福利机构) have their own $250 million Care and Share matching grants, and that has now been extended for another year to 2016 with a provision of another $250 million.

Even before this gratifying act of matching was extended to charities and non-profit organisations (NPOs) in the arts, heritage, culture and social welfare spheres, donors to IPCs have for more than a decade enjoyed substantial tax benefits. Every dollar given to a charitable cause (that had IPC status) enjoyed a 250% tax deduction from the donor's taxable income. For the SG50 window, this tax benefit given to donations to IPCs was increased to 300% deduction of taxable income. Looking at the fine print reveals further advantages: such tax benefits could actually be carried over for a period of five years, a fact not generally well-known.

Undoubtedly, this enlightened and highly generous tax incentive given by the government, and their act of matching of donations to, first the universities, and now extended for a qualified period to most IPCs, have served to greatly encourage the practice of philanthropy in Singapore.

Conclusion: The Evolving Philanthropic Landscape in Singapore

As one surveys the philanthropic landscape in Singapore over the last 50 years and extends the view past that time to its beginnings, a few observations arise that call for further consideration.

Philanthropy by individuals, foundations, or charitable organisations is seldom sufficient for the establishment and the sustainable operation and development of institutions or organisations serving the public good. Philanthropic support may significantly augment the budgets of these organisations but they rarely provide enough for their necessary ongoing sustenance.

There are exceptions that prove the rule. In the last 50 years the NKF (National Kidney Foundation founded in 1969 by Professor Khoo Oon Teik 邱恩德) and the KDF (Kidney Dialysis Foundation founded in 1996 by Dr Gordon Wu 胡应湘) come to mind. At the height of its fundraising success before it was felled by the 2005 "NKF Saga", NKF fundraising peaked at more than $70 million a year from public donations — that is, private philanthropy. This was for a single cause: to make kidney dialysis affordable for its base of about 2,000 needy patients, and it was such donations that enabled it to build reserves of $262 million.

Venerable institutions which are still largely independently funded and sustained by private philanthropy which have their founding in the past would include the Singapore Thong Chai Medical Institution (新加坡同济 医院) (founded in 1867) and Kwong Wai Shui Hospital (广惠肇留医院) (founded in 1910), though even with these institutions the government of the day had provided them with the gift of the real estate of their locations.

Other than a few notable exceptions, philanthropy and philanthropists do not seem to have founded institutions, Non Profit Organisations (NPOs), or charitable social service organisations (excluding the clan associations) that have not needed at some point to secure state funding for their sustenance.

Tan Tock Seng (陈笃生) had set up the Chinese Paupers' Hospital in 1844, but it took much further funding from other philanthropic sources, and growing aid from the government to get the hospital up and running. By 1961 Tan Tock Seng Hospital had become wholly run and funded by the government. Tan Lark Sye and the Chinese community had founded Nantah in 1955 with massive private funding, but by 1980 Nanyang University was merged with the University of Singapore to form the National University of Singapore, and the burden of funding was taken over by the state.

The Singapore Hokkien Huay Kuan set up its first school in 1849 and today six schools are affiliated with it. Similarly Ngee Ann Kongsi founded Ngee Ann Polytechnic (in 1963), as well as the secondary and primary schools that carry the Ngee Ann name. But with the advent of nationhood, the funding of these schools has gradually been taken over by the Ministry of Education and is no longer the sole burden of their founders.

More recently founded charity healthcare institution Ren Ci Hospital (仁慈医院) (1994), while actively raising funds, looks nonetheless mostly to government subvention for its $30 million annual expenditure (FY 2013).

The raising of approximately $80 million each year[3] from private philanthropy that is given to the Community Chest (part of the National Council of Social Services funded by the Ministry for Family and Social Development and the Totalisator Board) is used to give financial support to some 84 charities or VWOs operating over 200 programmes addressing children with special needs, youth at risk, people with disabilities, the elderly, and families in need.

In its history, philanthropy in Singapore by leading members of the Chinese community was munificent, ambitious, and borne of an abiding sense of altruism and civic duty. Ironically perhaps, with nationhood and an economically thrifty yet highly successful government growing ever more dominant, with its foundational socialist agenda to address the pressing needs for housing, education, and medical care, the state seemed to have stepped largely into the breach to tackle the most urgent and desperate social needs of its citizens, displacing in its wake, the urgency of private philanthropy.

The clans and the merchant class in the chambers of commerce carried on their good work in civic philanthropy, but with a certain measure of quietism, it would seem, in the ever-growing vigor of the state. In the 1960s, 1970s, and 1980s, public housing cleared the slums and squatters, public education propelled the people, and the provision of improving medical services grew apace. Did such energies displace the growth of the civic role of philanthropists in the community?

Then beginning in the 1990s, with the call by government to give to higher education, private philanthropy was re-ignited. However, the warm new light of philanthropy these last 15 years, have not been evenly cast on the social landscape.

Many areas of social welfare and civil society, with enormous needs but not yet able to compellingly communicate their visions and missions, have not yet found the key or keys to unlock the latent generosity and capacity of a new generation of donors and philanthropists.

---

[3] Figures obtained from the FY2013 report of the Community Chest of Singapore.

With the greatly increased wealth of these present times, there is substantial philanthropic capacity in our society. But its expression has been uneven. Million dollar gifts to the universities are routine. But arts, cultural and civil society causes are still underfunded.

Present day philanthropists in our community might take a leaf from their forebears, in believing more boldly in their abilities to create a future, and more ambitiously to be able to sustain a social cause close to their hearts.

They might look beyond a self-limiting sense of the mere augmentative possibility of their contributions. Their philanthropic acts, in concert with like-minded fellows, encouraged and incentivised by a wealthy government wanting to unleash new resources to co-create new civic institutions for the future, can achieve much. They can achieve with their own philanthropic acts, large and small, more than the dreams of their fathers.

Chapter 6

Chinese Social Clubs*

AU Yue Pak

Networking to establish the right *guanxi* (relationships) is a feature of Chinese business communities. The Singapore Chinese community is no exception to this. There is a host of social organisations catering to the interests of the different segments of the community. In this essay we examine the histories and activities of some of the more prominent private Chinese clubs in Singapore in the past 50 years.

There are many different types of Chinese associations and clubs. Besides clan associations, industrial and commercial organisations, cultural groups and sports associations, there are clubs formed for recreational purposes among the wealthy. As the following pages will show, these private Chinese clubs not only organised social and recreational activities, they also contributed immensely to the nation in terms of welfare, education and culture. Some of the clubs still play an important role in Singapore today.

The better known ones are: Ee Hoe Hean Club (怡和轩俱乐部), Chui Huay Lim Club (醉花林俱乐部), Tanjong Rhu Club (丹戎禺俱乐部), Singapore Chinese Weekly Entertainment Club (维基利俱乐部), Goh Loo Club (吾庐俱乐部) and Hoi Thin Amateur Dramatic Association (海天游艺会). A non-registered organisation, "Lau Pa Sat *Kopi Yew* (老巴刹咖啡友)" is also widely known in the Chinese community.

---

*This chapter was originally written in Chinese.

Ee Hoe Hean Club

Founded in 1895, Ee Hoe Hean is one of the most active millionaires' clubs when it comes to participating in national movements and social events. Its first chairman was Mr Lim Chwee Chian (林推迁). The Club was originally located at 28 Duxton Hill. It moved to 38 Club Street in 1911, before moving again to its present location at Bukit Pasoh Road in 1925.

When Ee Hoe Hean was first started, the majority of its members were from the Hokkien community. However, when Tan Kah Kee (陈嘉庚) took over as chairman in 1923, he expanded its activities and invited talents from all other dialect groups to hold important positions in the Club. Hence, Lim Nee Soon (林义顺), a Teochew, was elected the Club Chairman in 1931.

Since its establishment, Ee Hoe Hean Club has always taken an active interest in national affairs and social work. Not long after its founding, Ee Hoe Hean supported Sun Yat Sen's (孙中山) efforts to overthrow the Manchurian government. Club members such as Lim Nee Soon, Teo Eng Hock (张永福) and Tan Chor Nam (陈楚楠) were leading figures in the Chinese United League (同盟会 *Tongmenghui*). Ee Hoe Hean often hosted Sun Yat Sen when he visited Singapore.

In 1928, after a public outrage over a massacre of Chinese civilians by Japanese troops in Jinan, Shandong (known as the *Jinan Incident*), Tan Kah Kee led Singapore's Chinese organisations and schools in setting up the Shandong Relief Fund (山东惨祸筹赈会), to raise money for the victims. The Chinese community was urged to boycott Japanese goods and services.

In 1937, after the Lugou Bridge (also known as Marco Polo Bridge) Incident in the suburb of Beijing which marked the beginning of the Second Sino-Japanese War, the Singapore Chinese Relief Fund Committee (星华筹赈会) was set up under Tan Kah Kee's leadership. On 10 October 1938, Chinese representatives from other Southeast Asian countries gathered in Singapore and established the Nanyang Hua Chiau (overseas Chinese) China Relief Fund Union (南洋华侨筹赈祖国难民总会) to support the fight against the Japanese, with Ee Hoe Hean as the headquarters.

Ee Hoe Hean in the New Republic

After Singapore gained independence as a new republic in 1965, Ee Hoe Hean continued its passion for caring for the less privileged in society. It participated actively in philanthropic causes and contributed to public welfare and education.

In 1974 the Club initiated a $10,000 scholarship fund. In 1977, it donated $10,000 to the Tanjong Pagar Community Centre scholarship fund (丹戎巴葛联络所奖学金). In that same year, the Club donated $10,000 to the Singapore Chung Hwa Medical Institution's (中华医院) building fund. A year later, Ee Hoe Hean donated to the Nanyang Academy of Fine Arts (南洋艺术学院) as well as the Spyros disaster relief fund. In celebration of the Club's 100th anniversary in 1995, Ee Hoe Hean donated $100,000 to the Chinese Development Assistance Council (CDAC) (华社自助理事会), Kwong Wai Shiu Hospital (广惠肇留医院), Chung Hwa Medical Institution, and Tong Chai Medical Institution (同济医院).

Reconstruction of Ee Hoe Hean Building

In recognition of its past contributions, the National Heritage Board of Singapore (新加坡国家文物局) installed a plaque at Ee Hoe Hean to acknowledge and praise its efforts in the anti-Japanese and China Salvation Movement, as well as its continual involvement in community service and philanthropic activities after the war. The plaque was unveiled by then President Ong Teng Cheong (王鼎昌) in 1995.

In 1997 Ee Hoe Hean's building was affected by the construction of the MRT (Mass Rapid Transport) North-East line. After several years of inspection and evaluation, the Club decided to demolish and rebuild the old building while retaining its original facade. During the reconstruction the Club operated from the Singapore Sak Kho Club (新加坡适可俱乐部) and later from the Singapore Chinese Weekly Entertainment Club. The Tan Kah Kee Foundation contributed $1 million for the reconstruction work, while members of Ee Hoe Hean donated over $1.3 million.

The reconstructed Ee Hoe Hean building was re-opened on 8 December 2007. The ground floor of the building has been dedicated as The Pioneers' Memorial Hall. Photos, historical documents and information on Tan Kah Kee, Lim Chwee Chian, Lim Nee Soon, Lee Kong Chian (李光前), Tan Lark Sye (陈六使), Lee Choon Seng (李俊承), Ko Teck Kin (高德根), Soon Peng Yam (孙炳炎) are permanently displayed. Since its opening, the Memorial Hall has attracted numerous local and overseas visitors, as well as Singapore students.

The second and third floors of the Club are used for recreational, academic and social activities. Since the re-opening of the building, the Club has organised talks on different topics such as current affairs, economics, culture, history, medicine and health which have been well received by the public.

Since the reconstruction of its premises, Ee Hoe Hean has also made efforts to revitalise the Club by increasing membership and expanding activities. Under the chairmanship of Lim Cheng Joo (林清如), a lawyer, the Club has attracted more members from the professional and academic sectors of the community. However, it continues to restrict members to males and retains its tradition of holding "Hokkien porridge" lunches daily for members and their friends. As of February 2015, it has 355 members.

To encourage greater interest in the Chinese language among the young, the Club set up the "Ee Hoe Hean Chinese Book Prize" with $100,000 in 2008. The money is used to award students from 10 Special Assistance Plan (SAP) schools with outstanding performance in Chinese in their school examinations.

At the same time, to liven up the local cultural scene, Ee Hoe Hean launched a Chinese publication, *Yihe Shiji* (怡和世纪), which covers a wide spectrum of social and cultural topics. With a print run of 5,000 copies, the magazine is distributed free to members and friends of the Club. At the close of 2014, 24 issues had been produced. In recent years, *Yihe Shiji* began publishing essays submitted in English alongside their Chinese translations.

In April 2015 the Club celebrated its 120th anniversary with a public talk and a gala dinner. Reaffirming its support for cultural efforts by the Chinese community, Ee Hoe Hean donated $100,000 towards the Singapore Chinese Cultural Centre, currently under construction.

Chui Huay Lim Club

Founded in 1845, the Chui Huay Lim is one of the oldest Chinese clubs in Singapore. Its principal founder was Tan Cheng Bao (陈成宝), a leading member of the Teochew community. The club was a meeting place for rich and powerful Teochew businessmen.

Tan Cheng Bao used an *attap* house owned by his family at 190 Keng Lee Road as Chui Huay Lim's clubhouse. Upon the death of Tan in 1879,

10 members donated $400 each to make a total of $4,000 to purchase the land from the Tan family, and they turned it into permanent premises for the Club.

The founders hired first-class chefs to serve authentic Teochew cuisine to their members, attracting many Teochew businessmen to bring their guests to Chui Huay Lim for meals. Politicians and royal families from around the globe visited the Club, and many left beautiful calligraphy extolling the good food at the premises.

Board directors and members of Chui Huay Lim generously supported welfare and educational projects in China. After the Jinan incident in 1928, Chui Huay Lim held a charity *Han* opera performance with the Er Woo Amateur Musical and Dramatic Association (余娱儒乐社) at *Heng Wai Sun* opera house (庆维新剧院) to raise funds for the Chinese victims. Fundraising efforts were also organised to support China's war against the Japanese following the Lugou Bridge incident in 1937.

After Singapore became an independent republic in 1965, Chui Huay Lim maintained its traditional role. It is not only a meeting place for Teochew businessmen; its members also actively support philanthropic causes in the nation. When the Club celebrated its 150th anniversary in 1995, its members donated $100,000 to the National Kidney Foundation (NKF) (全国肾脏基金会), Singapore Tong Chai Medical Institution, Kwong Wai Shiu Hospital, Singapore Chung Hwa Medical Institution and Ren Ci Hospital (仁慈医院).

Rebuilding the Chui Huay Lim Club

In 1995, the Board of Directors proposed to reconstruct and develop the clubhouse and its 10,000 square metre land. After years of planning and discussions, the plan was finally submitted and approved by the Urban Redevelopment Authority (URA) in 2006. Under the plan, the land was divided into two parts. One half was used to rebuild Chui Huay Lim while the other half was "leased" to a contractor for construction of a residential condominium, with a lease period of 99 years. Profit from the lease was used to cover the construction cost of the new clubhouse.

In December 2011, the new Chui Huay Lim building was completed and re-opened in conjunction with the Club's 166th anniversary celebration.

The new building has a land area of 4,700 square metres. The main door has a traditional Chinese arch, but the whole building has adopted a modern style. The ground floor houses a Teochew restaurant and cafe, while the second floor contains a multi-purpose ballroom, suitable for banquets, conferences, talks and exhibitions. The third floor is used by the Club as its office, with meeting rooms and a library. The fourth floor has other facilities, such as a gymnasium and dance room. The roof top has a swimming pool and children's playground.

During its anniversary gala dinner, the Club donated $100,000 to the Special Education School set up by the Asian Women's Welfare Association (AWWA) (亚洲妇女福利协会特别学校), Lighthouse School (励航学校), Singapore Cheshire Home Residential Care (新加坡济世之家长久寄宿服务), Bright Hill Evergreen Home (光明山修身院) and Hospice Care Association (慈怀协会家庭护理中心). Each organisation received $20,000.

Various conferences, talks and exhibitions have been held at the new Chui Huay Lim building since its completion. Among them were the "Dr Wu Lien Teh (伍连德) International Conference cum Exhibition" held on 8 April 2014 and an art exhibition featuring the works of Teochew artists as well as private artworks of Teochew collectors which was jointly organised with the Teochew Poit Ip Huay Kuan (潮州八邑会馆) in conjunction with the Teochew Festival 2014. The two exhibitions received tremendous positive response from the public.

Today, Chui Huay Lim is not only a place for members to relax and exercise, it is also a meeting place of diverse cultures as usage of the club premises is not restricted to members.

Hoi Thin You Yi Hui (Amateur Dramatic Association)

Hoi Thin Amateur Dramatic Association (海天游艺会) started out as a recreational club for the Cantonese in Singapore. It was only after its relocation to Lim Teck Kim Road that the Club started accepting non-Cantonese as members.

Founded in 1918 by famous Cantonese figures such as Wong Ah Fook (黄亚福), Yow Ngan Pan (邱雁宾), Ng Seng Pang (吴胜鹏), Lu Mun Sek (卢文锡) and Fong Chong Cheng (方涌清), the organisation was originally known as *Qi Ying Shan She* (耆英善社). It was first located at Pagoda Street.

Hoi Thin was the first organisation to stage plays in Singapore. It put up stage shows to raise funds for flood victims in China, victims of the 1928 Jinan massacre, as well as for local charities.

Focussing on cultural performances in the Cantonese dialect, the association chose Hoi Thin as its name because the two words in Cantonese mean the ocean and the sky respectively. The founders hoped that their association would expand like a fish crossing oceans and thrive like a bird soaring into the sky.

In the Cantonese dialect, cultural performances are called *You Yi Hui* (游艺会). Since Hoi Thin was active in promoting cultural activities and raising funds through performances, its name was changed to *Hoi Thin You Yi Hui* (海天游艺会).

In 1937, after the Lugou Bridge incident, Mr Tan Kah Kee formed the Chinese Relief Fund Committee and supported China in fighting the war. Hoi Thin became the office of the Cantonese division of the Committee.

After the war ended in 1945, the Club purchased a building in Neil Road as a clubhouse but it had to relocate later, due to urban redevelopment of the area. In the 1960s, the club bought 2 Lim Teck Kim Road as its clubhouse.

In 1978, Hoi Tin celebrated its 60th anniversary by organising a charity performance of a famous Cantonese opera to raise funds for the expansion of the Tanjong Pagar Community Centre. The show raised nearly $250,000.

In recent years, the older generation of Cantonese opera enthusiasts has either passed away or retired, so public performances of Cantonese opera have ceased. Currently, Hoi Thin is mainly a place for members to gather and relax. The clubhouse is equipped with a karaoke system for its 76 members and their families to socialise and interact with one another.

Singapore Chinese Weekly Entertainment Club

The Singapore Chinese Weekly Entertainment Club was founded in 1889. Its founders were Peranakans and Singapore-born businessmen like Lee Choon Guan (李浚源) and Tan Chow Kim (陈秋金). It was the only club for the locally born entrepreneurs. Its clubhouse was a huge and luxurious bungalow in the heart of Chinatown. More importantly, the Club's management and members were all fluent in English and were, therefore, highly regarded by the British officials. Gradually, the Club accepted rich Chinese businessmen who were not born locally. One such member, Aw Boon Haw (胡文虎) who founded the world famous Tiger Balm, became its president.

When the colonial era ended, the social status of the local born English-educated businessmen dropped a few notches. Over time, Singapore Chinese Weekly Entertainment Club accepted more members with different backgrounds. Mandarin and Chinese dialects became more widely used among members and it gradually transformed into another millionaires' club of the Chinese community. It has a membership of about 200 currently.

The Club places much of its emphasis on member gatherings and leisure activities. Besides organising recreational events such as *mahjong* tournaments, it has also generously supported fundraising efforts in the Chinese community.

Goh Loo Club

Goh Loo Club (吾庐俱乐部) is located on Club Street, just beside the Chinese Weekly Entertainment Club. It was founded in 1905 by Soon Shi Teng (孙士鼎), Tan Tok Lian (陈卓然) and other Hokkien businessmen. It was named as "Gu Ji Le" (古寄乐) initially, but this was subsequently changed to Goh Loo Club in 1908. In the Hokkien dialect the name means "I love my home".

The Club has been largely inactive in recent years but it played an important role in the history of Singapore. On 27 February 1942 after the fall of Singapore, Japanese soldiers rounded up about a dozen prominent Chinese leaders who had not managed to escape and gathered them at the Goh Loo clubhouse. Among them were Tan Ean Kiam (陈延谦) (Goh Loo President at that time), Lim Boon Keng (林文庆), Lee Wee Nam (李伟南), Yeo Chan Boon (杨缵文), Wong Siew Qiu (黄兆珪), Tan Yeok Seong (陈育崧), Runme Shaw (邵仁枚) and Run Run Shaw (邵逸夫).

Lieutenant colonel Oishi (大石中佐) of the Japanese military forces threatened and forced these Chinese leaders to set up a Chinese Society (华侨协会), to extort $50 million from the Chinese in Singapore and Malaysia. Lim Boon Keng was compelled to assume the post of President and Tan Yeok Seong was appointed the Secretary.

Lau Pa Sat Kopi Yew

Besides registered groups with regular meeting places in the Chinese community, there are also non-registered groups, which have regular coffee meetings, lunch gatherings or golf games to keep in touch. The Lau Pa Sat *Kopi Yew* (coffee friends in the Hokkien dialect) is unique among the Chinese social clubs in many ways. It does not have a constitution or membership list; it has no election of office bearers but it has an undisputed "Chief" for the last 56 years, and it continues to meet every Sunday morning.

According to the Chief of the "Coffee Friends", Lok Chwee Hin (骆水兴) (96 years old in 2015), most of the original "friends" were running various businesses in the Telok Ayer area and they started to have coffee together to share and exchange market information every morning from around 1959. Lok Chwee Hin is a self-made man who left his impoverished village in Hui Ann, Fujian at 18 to join his father who had arrived in Singapore earlier. In 1945 he had saved enough to start his own company Tong Hin Pte Ltd.

These Coffee Friends are no average Joes. Besides ship chandler business tycoon Lok Chwee Hin, they include Kemenyan giant Kwa Chin Gar (柯千衙) (86 years old), grain and sugar king Tan Soon Guan (陈顺原) (93 years old), pepper king Chua Wee Keng (蔡伟卿) (90 years old), granite king Seah Ann Tong (谢安桐) (80 years old) and chemical industry leader Chang Wen Yuen (张文元) (82 years old).

As explained by Lok Chwee Hin, he started the informal gathering by handing over $1,000 to a proprietor of the coffee stall at Lau Pa Sat. The amount of coffee and *kaya* toast consumed daily would be deducted by the stallholder. Whenever the money ran low, Lok would top it up with another $1,000. Little did he dream that the daily gatherings would continue for nearly six decades.

Lok Chwee Hin mused that since the morning coffee "club" started, the first Lau Pa Sat stall it patronised had gone through several operators, but the payment system continued until the venue was later changed. He could not say (and neither was he interested in toting up) the total amount of coffee that had been served in the past decades.

The older *kopi yew* recall that at its peak in the 1970s and 1980s, there were 60–70 "Coffee Friends" every morning. However, as the Central

Business District (CBD) was re-organised, many of the old enterprises gradually moved out of the area. Over the years, some of the old friends retired, some became less mobile, and others died. The number of people who gathered for the morning coffee slowly decreased over time.

Eventually, the daily gathering was reduced to every Sunday and public holiday, from 9 to 11 a.m., after which some in the group would go to the Chinese Weekly Entertainment Club to rest, before going for lunch at some nearby restaurants. The Coffee Friends would take turns to host lunch.

In recent years, Lau Pa Sat underwent major renovation work, so the coffee gatherings were moved to the hall on the second floor of Weekly Entertainment Club. An elevator was specially installed by the Club, for the convenience of the elderly Coffee Friends. After coffee, they would order food from Maxwell Hawker Centre or adjourn to a restaurant for lunch.

At a recent visit to the Sunday morning coffee session at the Weekly Entertainment Club, this writer counted about two dozen attendees, half of whom were either wives, children or maids of the original *kopi yew*. The discussion of current affairs and mutual friends was lively and loud, and coffee was served by the staff of the Club.

"Coffee Friends of Lau Pa Sat" did not register as an organisation but this did not stop its members from contributing to social causes in the country. Whenever fundraising efforts were brought to their attention, the group would either contribute individually or under the name of the "Coffee Friends of Lau Pa Sat".

Many of the members hold leadership positions in the clan associations, schools or grassroots organisations. For example, Lok Chwee Hin, Kwa Chin Gar and Chang Wen Yuen have been board members of Nanyang Junior College (南洋初级学院), Chung Cheng High School (Main) (中正中学总校) and Chung Cheng High School (Yishun) (中正中学义顺分校), and have made generous donations to these educational institutions.

Lok Chwee Hin has seen Lau Par Sat Kopi Yew grow and decline over Singapore's first 50 years; he has no illusion that this unusual social club would still be meeting over coffee when Singapore celebrates its 100th anniversary.

Tanjong Rhu Club

In the 1950s and 1960s, the Tanjong Rhu Club located along the east coast of Singapore was a favourite haunt of Hokkien businessmen. But the bungalow which housed the Club was demolished in 1991 as part of the redevelopment of Tanjong Rhu and this historical organisation has been de-registered.

Among the older generations of Chinese businessmen, journalists and Nanyang University (Nantah) alumni, many remember Tanjong Rhu Club as Tan Lark Sye's headquarters for his social movement efforts, in the same way Tan Kah Kee had used Ee Hoe Hean Club as the centre for the South Seas China Relief Fund Union (南侨筹赈总会) before the Second World War.

Tanjong Rhu Club was formerly known as *Ting Chao Bie Shu* (听潮别墅) (literally, "Listening to the Tides Villa") or Waterside Villa. Before the Second World War broke out in 1942, Pang Cheng Yean (冯清缘), a leading Hokkien in the pawnbroking business, would often invite his friends and associates to his home by the sea. Over time, the number of people increased and the gathering place became known as the Waterside Villa.

It was a huge two-storeyed bungalow, with eight rooms on the second floor, and three halls on the ground floor. In 1947, Tan Lark Sye and several other prominent Hokkien businessmen decided to adopt it as the premises for the newly registered Tanjong Rhu Club. It was also where Tan Lark Sye and other members planned the founding of Nanyang University.

From 1953 when Tan Lark Sye first mooted the idea of a Chinese university, various fundraising activities for the setting up of Nantah were planned at the Tanjong Rhu Club. All groups and organisations which were interested in Nantah would go to Tanjong Rhu to meet Tan Lark Sye. At that time, Tanjong Rhu Club was tantamount to Nanyang University's office. Hiring of administrative and teaching staff, design of campus buildings and other issues were all discussed and settled at the Club.

At the end of 1949, Tan Kah Kee stepped down as Chairman of the Singapore Hokkien Huay Kuan (新加坡福建会馆), a major clan association in the country, and he was succeeded by Tan Lark Sye. From then on and until he stepped down as Chairman in 1972, all development plans of the Huay Kuan and the five schools it was running were also discussed at Tanjong Rhu Club.

After Tan Lark Sye's death in 1972, Tan Kong Piat (陈光别) assumed the post of President of Tanjong Rhu Club, with Lim Kok Gin (林国仁) as the Secretary and Koh Tin Kok (许镇国) as the Treasurer. At that time, Tanjong Rhu Club had over 200 members, but membership dwindled over the years. In the 1980s, the land lease of the clubhouse expired and the land was returned to the government. The Club continued to rent the building from the government.

By 1991, membership was reduced to 20. The members decided to return the Tanjong Rhu bungalow to the government, together with the registration license of the club.

Section 2
Community Issues

CHAPTER 7

The Evolution of the Chinese Language

LEONG Weng Kam

Introduction

Early Chinese immigrants in Singapore before Sir Stamford Raffles' arrival in 1819 were dialect speakers who came mainly from China's southern provinces. Historical records show that many among Admiral Zheng He's fleet in his seven historical voyages across the Western ocean more than 600 years ago were experienced craftsmen and seamen from Fujian province. Many of them remained in Malacca in the Malaya peninsula, as well as Java and Palembang in Indonesia, with some spilling over to Singapore after the expedition.

The majority of those who moved to Singapore many years later were from similar backgrounds. Most were poor and not educated. They included merchants and craftsmen from Fujian province who came in search of business and job opportunities. By the mid-1800s, some 30 years after Raffles' arrival, they had already formed more than half of the local population, helped by the large numbers who arrived following China's defeat by the British in the Opium Wars of the 1840s.

A census in 1860 showed there were 50,043 Chinese, forming 61% of the local population comprising also of Malays, Indians and Europeans. About a century later, their number shot up to over a million, forming over 75% of the local population by the 1950s.

Besides Fujian, they had also come from the other southern provinces, such as Guangdong and Guangxi, and Hainan Island as well. The Chinese dialects they had brought with them — from the initial Hokkien, Teochew and Cantonese — had increased to more than 12 by then to include Hakka or Khek, Henghua and even Shanghainese, spoken by the mostly skilful furniture makers and artists from Shanghai.

Even British and American missionaries who came to preach the gospel to the local Chinese population from the early 19th century spoke fluent Hokkien and Teochew in their attempts to win souls.

Mandarin was far from being the *lingua franca* of the Chinese in those early years. It was the spoken language of only the few better educated immigrants who were members of the intelligentsia. They included educationists and writers who moved to the British colony to work as home tutors and journalists for Chinese-language publications started by the community.

The dominance of the Chinese dialects in the community continued after the People's Action Party, came into power in 1959, and began to make radical changes to the Singapore education system and its language policies. It launched the Speak Mandarin Campaign in 1979 to encourage Chinese Singaporeans to replace dialects with Mandarin. The campaign, still on after more than 35 years now, has had a great impact on the languages used by the Chinese in Singapore ever since.

A Chinese Community Divided

From the very beginning, the Chinese population was not a united one. It was divided into disparate groups distinguished not only by the dialects they spoke, but also by the locations where they congregated, worked and lived.

For example, the Hokkiens from Fujian province were largely concentrated in the Telok Ayer area which was near to the sea port where their vessels arrived with spices and other goods they traded in then. The Teochews, the second largest group from Guangdong province, made Hong Kong Street and the present Clarke Quay area their base where they conducted their businesses. The Cantonese, the third largest group, also from Guangdong province, occupied the Kreta Ayer area near the present Chinatown, where they lived and worked, set up shops and restaurants. The Hainanese from Hainan island, known for their chicken rice till today, among other trades, set down roots in the North Bridge Road area.

Such divisions led to the creation of *bang* (邦) or dialect-based groupings in which the Hokkiens were the most dominant because of their larger numbers, followed by the Teochews and the Cantonese. This demographic composition is still the same today, more than 150 years later.

A census in 1990 showed the Hokkiens forming 42% of the Chinese population with 886,741 people, followed by the Teochews' 22%, with 461,303 people. The Cantonese population was third with 15%, comprising 319,322 people. The Hakkas and Hainanese were next, forming about 7% of the community each with 153,942 and 146,629 people respectively.

The top three Chinese dialects, led by Hokkien, were spoken by the majority of the Chinese population though there were those who spoke only English either because they went to English medium schools or were Peranakans or Babas, local or Straits-born Chinese whose forefathers married indigenous Malay women. They ended up speaking a mixture of Malay and English and some Hokkien, if at all.

Until the early 1970s, the Chinese dialects remained the common means of communication among Chinese Singaporeans at home, the marketplace, shops and offices, clan associations and even in army camps. Hokkien, the dominant dialect, was also the language of the business leaders simply because most of them were from the dialect group. It was in fact the *lingua franca* of the Chinese Chamber of Commerce — now known as the Singapore Chinese Chamber of Commerce & Industry (新加坡中华总商会) — set up by mainly Hokkien and Teochew business leaders in 1906.

Early Chinese Clan Associations and Schools

The early Chinese immigrants set up clan associations soon after they arrived in Singapore, mainly as self-help groups to look after their own clansmen. They were largely based on the Chinese dialect they spoke, though some were also formed from the common surnames they shared, or the provinces, counties, cities or even the villages where they came from in China.

The first clan association, Cho Kah Koon or *Cao Jia Guan* (曹家馆), was set up by a Cantonese who came from Taishan county in Guangdong province in 1819, the same year Sir Stamford Raffles founded Singapore. The man who founded the clan, Cao Ah Zhi (曹亚志), had worked for Raffles in Malaya as an informant and he in fact landed in Singapore as part of an advance party months before the British founder did.

For his good work, he was given land for a shophouse in Lavender Street to set up the first clan association, initially to provide help for his clansmen from Taishan. The clan and its premises remained till 1974 when the government acquired it for road expansion despite repeated appeals by the clan's leaders to preserve it.

Following Cho Kah Koon, clan associations both big and small and from the different dialect groups were formed one after another in rapid succession especially towards the late 19th century and early 20th century.

At its peak in the early 20th century, there were at least 500 clan associations on the island. Most became centres of activities for clan members and their families to meet, celebrate festivals and most important of all, worship their ancestors together at least once a year.

Members spoke mainly in the Chinese dialects, depending on the groups they belonged to. The management and annual general meetings of the clan associations were conducted in dialects.

Today, about 300 still exist, with the leading ones like Singapore Hokkien Huay Kuan (新加坡福建会馆), established in 1840 and Teochew Poit Ip Huay Kuan (潮州八邑会馆), which came much later in 1929, doing well with their memberships in the thousands and assets running into millions of dollars.

Back in the early days, not too long after Raffles came, clan associations and the wealthy, who though often illiterate themselves, began to think of providing education for the young after the basic needs of their clansmen, such as food and shelter, were met.

They started a form of home school or *shishu* (私塾). In 1829 there were at least three, two in Pekin Street and one in Kampong Glam. One to two dozen boys would gather in a residence or shophouse in such private schools to be taught by a tutor engaged either by a philanthropist or a clan association.

The Cantonese were believed to be the first to set up such *shishu*, followed soon after by the other dialect groups. By the mid-19th century, there were so many of them that one account stated there was at least one *shishu* on every street in Chinatown alone.

The students were taught basic Chinese classics such as *San Zi Jing* (三字经 Trimetrical Classic), *Bai Jia Xing* (百家姓 Century of Surnames) and *Qian Zi Wen* (千字文 Millenary Classic for Beginners). Later on, they would learn the *Xiao Jing* (孝经 Canon of Filial Piety), *Si Shu* (四书 Four Books of Teachings by Confucius) and *Meng Zi* (孟子 Book of Mencius).

Though the classic texts they studied were in written Chinese script, most tutors taught and read them in the Chinese dialects at the old-style schools during lessons in those days.

Chong Wen Ge (崇文阁), founded in 1849 by Tan Kim Seng (陈金声), a wealthy philanthropist, was among the better known *shishu* and developed to become the first school in Singapore supported by community and business leaders.

It was not until the early 20th century that these *shishu* began to expand and modernise, in response to events in China such as the May Fourth Movement, a cultural and political campaign started in 1919 by Chinese intellectuals who wanted to modernise society and learn from the West. The medium of instruction was switched from dialects to Mandarin and the curriculum of ancient classic texts was expanded to include modern Chinese works.

Such modern schools began to spring up all over town, supported by the different dialect groups. Yeung Ching School (养正学校), for example, was founded by the Cantonese in Park Road in 1905, moving to Club Street later in 1918. It was followed by the Hokkiens and the Teochews who set up Tao Nan School (道南学校) on Armenian Street and Tuan Mong School (端蒙学校) on Tank Road respectively a year later.

More wealthy business and community leaders such as Tan Kah Kee (陈嘉庚) came forward to support Chinese education and by the early 1910s, a few girls-only schools were established as well. They included Chung Hwa and Nan Hua Girls in 1911 and Nanyang Girls' School (南洋女子中学校) in 1917.

Tan Kah Kee founded Chinese High School, now a part of Hwa Chong Institution (华侨中学) in Bukit Timah, in 1919. It became a premier Chinese middle school in South east Asia even as early as the mid-20th century. Chung Cheng High School (中正中学), the other well-known Chinese middle school remembered for student activism in the 1950s and early 1960s, was founded later in 1939.

Except for the few top schools, such as Chinese High, Nanyang Girls and Chung Cheng High, Chinese dialects were commonly used among teachers and students in many of the early Chinese-language schools, especially those founded by the Chinese clan associations.

Chinese-Language Publications and Newspapers

Chinese-language publications including newspapers have a long history in Singapore. Among the first to circulate on the island was the *Chinese Monthly Magazine* (察世俗每月统纪传) to promote Christianity, produced and printed in Malacca in 1815. It was, interestingly, edited by an English missionary, William Milne, who was assisted by two Chinese xylographers from China. It lasted for nearly 10 years and was distributed in Singapore as well as the other Malayan states.

The first Chinese newspaper published in Singapore was the *Eastern Western Monthly Magazine* (东西洋考每月统记传), also edited by an Englishman, Charles Gutzlaff. It was originally published in Guangzhou, China, in 1833. Its editorial office moved to Singapore four years later in 1837. Besides promoting Christianity, the 12-page monthly also carried political, science and business news as well as commentaries. It ceased publication a year after the move to Singapore.

Singapore's first Chinese daily, *Lat Pau* (叻报) was launched in 1881 by See Ewe Lay (薛有礼). He was locally born and English-educated, and was working as a dealer at the Hong Kong and Shanghai Bank. Immigrants from Xiamen in Fujian province, his grandfather and father were both prominent figures in the Chinese community in early 19th century Singapore.

See Ewe Lay started the newspaper because he saw the Europeans publishing their own newspapers such as the English-language daily, *The Straits Times*, in 1845. He wanted to have one in Chinese as well to enrich the Chinese community and promote Chinese cultural activities. The paper, ideologically, was conservative, and even Confucianist, judging from its editorial and articles, written mainly by journalists and writers recruited from China. It ceased publication in 1932 due to the Great Depression of the 1930s.

At the turn of the century when the Qing Dynasty in China was on the decline, several Chinese newspapers were set up in Singapore either by revolutionaries and their overseas supporters or royalists to the Qing government wanting to quash any uprising against the Manchu emperor.

Among the firsts was *Thoe Lam Jit Poh* (图南日报) started in 1904 by Tan Chor Nam (陈楚楠), one of Dr Sun Yat Sen's (孙中山) ardent supporters in Singapore. But the newspaper lasted for only a year, due to lack of funds.

Another newspaper, *Zong Hui Ri Bao* (总汇日报) appeared the following year in 1905, financed by Tan Chor Nam and his like-minded friends, including Teo Eng Hock (张永福). But the newspaper was taken over by the Qing's royalists only after a year and changed its name to *Zong Hui Xin Bao* (总汇新报).

Other early Chinese newspapers published in Singapore to promote the Chinese revolution then included the *Chong Shing Yit Pao* (中新日报) in 1907, *Sin Chew Morning Post* (星洲晨报) in 1908 and the *Nan Ch'iao Daily* (南侨日报) in 1910. Many of these papers did not last long, because of the heavy financial costs needed to sustain them.

A serious and major Chinese daily to appear following the demise of the smaller papers was the *Nanyang Siang Pau* (南洋商报), started by business and Chinese community leader Tan Kah Kee in 1923. It was followed six years later by the publication of another major Chinese daily, *Sin Chew Jit Poh* (星洲日报), started by the Tiger Balm king Aw Boon Haw (胡文虎).

In 1960, another Chinese newspaper, *Min Pao* (民报), was established by Lai Kok Wah (黎国华). It lasted 24 years and ceased publication in 1984. In 1961, local businessman Leung Yun Chee (梁润之), founder of the Axe brand medical oil, started *Shin Sheng Yit Pao* (新生日报), but it closed in 1966.

After its closure, Mr Leung teamed up with Hong Kong novelist Louis Cha (查良镛), well-known for his martial arts books to start *Shin Min Daily News* (新明日报), an evening newspaper in 1967.

In 1983, after a major restructuring exercise of newspapers in Singapore, *Nanyang Siang Pau* and *Sin Chew Jit Poh* merged to become *Lianhe Zaobao* (联合早报). The same year, the newspaper group published another evening daily, *Lianhe Wanbao* (联合晚报).

Today, all the three Chinese newsapapers — *Lianhe Zaobao, Lianhe Wanbao* and *Shin Min Daily News* — enjoying a combined circulation of more than 350,000 copies daily, belong to Singapore Press Holdings, a media conglomerate which also publishes *The Straits Times, Business Times, The New Paper, Berita Harian* and *Tamil Murasu*, in addition to weeklies for school children both in Chinese and English.

Rise of the Chinese Language and Birth of Nanyang University

A strong Chinese newspaper industry, especially after the end of World War II, also saw a rapid rise of Chinese-language schools during the period. There were nearly 350 Chinese primary and secondary schools in Singapore by 1950, all privately run, by community leaders or clan associations. Together, they had a total enrolment of almost 70,000 students, accounting for almost 58% of the total school-going population then. Chinese-language schools were certainly at their peak, with enrolment much higher than the 34% of students (about 40,000) in the English-language stream.

Though the Chinese dialects were still widely spoken by the Chinese community at large, standards in some of the better Chinese schools, such as Chinese High and Chung Cheng High, were high as they recruited some very good teachers from China, including artists trained by the top art schools.

The Singapore schools also attracted a large number of students from the neighbouring countries who wanted to have a good Chinese secondary school education. Well-known leftist student activist turned workers' union leader, the late Lim Chin Siong (林清祥) from Johor was among those who came to study at Chinese High in the early 1950s. He led Chinese middle school students to protest against the colonial government's education policy before going into politics.

The 1950s was also a time of political upheavals and turmoil. Anti-colonial sentiments were strong among workers and Chinese middle school students.

The People's Action Party, led by Lee Kuan Yew (李光耀), a young, English-educated lawyer then, was formed in 1954. It had the support of left-wing trade unionists and politicians like Lim Chin Siong and the largely dialect-speaking Chinese population.

Hokkien was the most popular language spoken at political rallies during elections then, followed by Mandarin. PAP leaders like Lim Chin Siong and Ong Eng Guan (王永元) spoke fluent Hokkien and could sway the crowds with their eloquence. Lee Kuan Yew soon realised that he had to master the Hokkien dialect to win elections. He started learning Mandarin in earnest in his early 30s, engaging tutors and making speeches in the language. Later, he had to pick up Hokkien as well after he realised that the dialect was even more effective in reaching out to the masses.

After leading the PAP to win the 1959 general election to form the government, Lee continued to make speeches in Hokkien until 1979 when he launched the Speak Mandarian campaign. Learning Mandarin became his life-long passion. Through weekly lessons he learned to speak the language well with the help of tutors for the next 50 years. He was still at it before his last hospitalisation and death in March 2015, aged 91.

In 1949, the Chinese Communist Party claimed victory in the civil war against the Nationalist Kuomintang and proclaimed the founding of the People's Republic of China. Thereafter the doors to tertiary education at Chinese universities in the mainland were shut to Chinese middle school graduates in Singapore because the British colonial government imposed restrictions on travel to and from the communist nation. Those who left for China were not allowed to return.

The Chinese middle school graduates could not go to the University of Malaya in Singapore because its classes were all conducted in English.

Moreover, the travel restrictions imposed by the British also meant the source of teachers needed for the hundreds of Chinese-language schools in Singapore was effectively cut.

That prompted the Chinese communities in Singapore and Malaya to suggest that they should set up a Chinese university of their own in Singapore as early as 1950.

Rubber magnate Tan Lark Sye (陈六使), President of the Singapore Hokkien Huay Kuan which represents Chinese from the southern Fujian province in China, was the leading proponent. He was supported by Lee Kong Chian (李光前) and Ng Aik Huan (黄奕欢), both also wealthy businessmen and leaders from the same Hokkien clan association.

Together, they formally proposed the plans for the university at a joint meeting of the association's executive and supervisory committees in January 1953. The idea received overwhelming support from both the Chinese communities here and across the Causeway.

Leading by example, Tan Lark Sye, pledged $5 million (a hefty sum in the 1950s) himself and a 500-acre piece of land from the Hokkien clan association in Jurong for the university. His initiatives were followed immediately by enthusiastic support from all sectors of the Chinese communities in both Singapore and Malaya, from wealthy merchants to the working class, all contributing to the cause.

They included Singapore's 1,577 trishaw riders contributing a day's earnings in April 1954. Until today, this donation drive of the trishaw riders is used by many writers and commentators to illustrate the widespread support given to the Chinese university.

Despite initial objections from the British colonial government and many difficulties along the way, the first batch of 330 students started their courses at the newly opened university on 15 March 1956, which made history for being the first Chinese-language tertiary institution outside of Greater China at the time.

Its official launch two years later on 30 March 1958 was a day of great celebration as it marked a peak in Chinese language education in Singapore. Nanyang University was a source of pride for the Chinese community here and even in neighbouring countries.

Nobody then expected the university to last only 25 years when it had to merge with the then University of Singapore to become the National University of Singapore in 1980. The events which unfolded following the university's formation may give some clues.

New PAP Government and Language Policy Changes

The 1956 All-Party Report on Chinese Education which was initiated by the colonial government to solve problems faced by Chinese-language schools ended up laying the foundation for Singapore's bilingual education policy later rolled out by the PAP Government.

Though its recommendations were not formally implemented because of the uncertain political situations in the late 1950s, it was a roadmap of sorts for the PAP, which took over the government after the 1959 general election, having won 43 of the 51 seats in the Legislative Assembly.

One important recommendation the Report made was the need for a second language in Singapore schools. This was compulsory in both primary and secondary schools after Singapore's independence in 1965.

When PAP took over the government in 1959, it inherited an education system which was in favour of the English-language schools, as the other vernacular schools, including Chinese-language schools, had been left very much on their own by the British. Its first priority was to make the education system more equitable.

At the time 51% of the 330,000 students in primary and secondary schools were in English-language schools, 43.5% in Chinese, 5% in Malay and 0.5% in Tamil.

One of the first things the new PAP government did was to raise literacy levels by increasing the number of schools in all language streams. Between

1959 and 1965, a total of 72 new schools were built, increasing total enrolments in both primary and secondary schools to 473,000 during the period.

Next was the attempt to unify the different language streams by streamlining the school curricula and textbooks so that all taught a common set of national values. In the process of "Malayanisation", textbooks for all language streams were then written with a Malayan perspective so that students would orientate towards Singapore, not England, China, Indonesia or India.

A new Singapore Examination Board was also set up which gradually unified the examinations of all the language stream schools. By November 1960, the Primary School Leaving Examination (PSLE) for schools of all the four language streams was introduced.

Then came the proposal to change the Chinese middle schools' 3–3 system — three years of secondary school followed by another three years of pre-university — to the 4–2 system of the English secondary schools — four years of secondary school and two years of pre-university. There was initial resistance to the change by the Chinese middle school students who even staged a boycott of examinations, but in the end the change was effected in the early 1960s.

After Singapore's independence in 1965, it became compulsory for all schools to teach a second language to all students irrespective of the language stream they came from. Those from the English stream were required to take English and a second language which could be Chinese, Malay, Tamil or a choice of other Indian languages. Those from the vernacular language stream would have to take English as a second language.

All the changes resulted in tighter control of the Chinese medium schools, as most began receiving funding from the Ministry of Education.

In his 2012 book, *My Lifelong Challenge — Singapore's Bilingual Journey*, Singapore's founding Prime Minister Lee Kuan Yew revealed that he also tried to neutralise strong opposition to the changes from some of the schools by setting up another teachers' union and parents' associations to counter the leftist Singapore Chinese Teachers' Union (新加坡华文教师总会) then.

Student protesters to the changes were expelled and school principals and teachers found sympathetic to the leftists were either transferred or demoted.

In the book, the late Mr Lee said it took quite some years before the Education Ministry could assert full authority over these former private Chinese medium schools; many chose to close in defiance.

By 1971, Secondary Four students from all the four language streams were able to sit for a common GCE "O" Level examination.

There was also a re-organisation of the schools, particularly the Chinese medium ones. The smaller ones with dwindling enrolment were told to merge with one another or with a bigger school.

Integrated schools were introduced in the 1960s in which teachers and students from two or more different language streams were brought together to break down racial barriers and promote universal education. In the morning the classrooms could be used by those from the Chinese stream and in the afternoon students from the English, Malay or Tamil stream would take over. But they would come together during school assemblies or recess time, physical education classes or extra-curricular activities. The first such integrated school, Bukit Panjang Government School (武吉班让政府学校), was started in 1960. More followed it till the late 1970s.

The integrated schools, many located in public housing estates inadvertently caused many of the small Chinese medium schools in the villages and rural areas to close because of falling enrolment. The students found it more convenient to attend the integrated schools because of their proximity to their homes.

As a consequence of all the changes and the emphasis on the importance of English as the common language to unite all the different races, as well as having higher economic value, enrolment in Chinese schools began to slide rapidly from the early 1960s. By 1983, enrolment in Chinese primary schools had dwindled to only 2%.

SAP Schools and National Stream Schools

The threat of Chinese schools going extinct was so real that by 1978, the Singapore government introduced the Special Assistance Plan (SAP) schools, to groom at least a number of ethnic Chinese students among their cohorts who would be effectively bilingual in English and Chinese and able to practise and appreciate traditional Chinese values.

The schools selected for the exercise were all previously well-known Chinese schools with a rich history and good track records, particularly with regard to their students' academic performance.

Students in these schools were allowed to take both English and Chinese at first language levels. To qualify for admission, students had to have high PSLE scores especially in the English and Chinese languages.

Nine schools were selected to be the first SAP schools in 1979. They were: Chinese High School, Nanyang Girls' High School, Dunman High School (德明政府中学), River Valley High School (立化中学), Chung Cheng High School (Main), St Nicholas Girls' School (圣尼各拉女校), Catholic High School (公教中学), Anglican High School (圣公会中学) and Maris Stella High School (海星中学). Two more schools, Nan Hua High School (南华中学)and Nan Chiau High School (南侨中学) joined the list in 2000 and 2012 respectively making a total of 11.

Subsequently, 15 primary SAP schools were identified. They included secondary SAP schools with primary schools, such as Catholic High, Maris Stella and St Nicholas Girls. The others included Nanyang Primary (南洋), Ai Tong (爱同), Maha Bodi (菩提) and Pei Hwa Presbyterian (培华长老会).

Like the SAP schools at the secondary level, English and Chinese were taught at first language levels to their students.

After nearly 40 years, SAP schools are a success, judging from their popularity and the number of schools wishing to be elevated to be SAP schools.

Today, several of these SAP schools are among the top secondary schools in Singapore, comparable in academic results with premier schools such as Raffles Institution, Anglo Chinese School and Raffles Girls' School.

Another change which had great impact on Chinese stream students was the introduction of the National Stream, albeit progressively from the early 1980s, which made English the language of instruction in all schools by 1987.

All students from then on studied English as the first language and their mother tongue languages — Chinese, Malay or Tamil — as a second language, with the exception of those in SAP schools.

Though the change was supposed to be gradual, it still took many students, especially those in Chinese stream schools, by surprise.

Almost overnight students in Chinese stream schools found their textbooks changed from Chinese to English, and Chinese teachers struggled to teach science subjects in English while still referring to their old Chinese textbooks.

It was a painful transition and many, unable to cope due to inadequate ability in the English language, had to drop out of school or found themselves unable to further their studies at the tertiary level during the 1980s.

The thinking behind this change was that since English is a common language for use across all races and it could help connect Singapore to the world, it had to be made the main language of instruction in schools, apart from the mother tongue languages.

After nearly 30 years, National Stream is no longer an issue, but many Chinese community leaders worry about falling Chinese standards and waning interest in the use of Mandarin among students.

The Speak Mandarin Campaign

Believe it or not, the 1979 campaign to encourage Chinese Singaporeans to stop using dialects and speak Mandarin instead had something to do with a report on Singapore's education system presented by then Deputy Prime Minister Goh Keng Swee (吴庆瑞) just a year before.

In his report, Dr Goh pointed out that the proliferation of Chinese dialects spoken by the Chinese population had actually hindered students' learning of English and Chinese in school.

Then Prime Minister Lee Kuan Yew realised that Chinese Singaporeans had to make a choice between Mandarin and the dialects if they wanted to reduce the burden of their children who were already learning two languages, Mandarin and English, in school.

The Speak Mandarin Campaign was launched in September 1979. At its launch, Mr Lee asked Chinese Singaporeans whether they wanted English–Mandarin, or English–dialect for their children as most of them were already sending their children to English stream schools then.

Mr Lee was a fierce advocate of Mandarin who saw no value in the Chinese dialects. He believed that Mandarin is a far more superior spoken language than Hokkien or any other Chinese dialect.

Hokkien or any of the other Chinese dialects is not congruent with the Chinese written script. Only Mandarin is. So if we were to learn a spoken Chinese language, he argued, it should be Mandarin which has the same written script taught and understood by the more than 1.3 billion people in China and Chinese in the other parts of the world. With Mandarin, Chinese Singaporeans would be able to communicate across different dialect groups and interactions within the Chinese community would become much easier.

If Hokkien prevailed and became the *lingua franca* among the Chinese here, he feared the standard of written Chinese would go down.

The reasons for dropping the use of dialects for Mandarin were convincing but unsurprisingly there was opposition to the campaign in the early years. Many argued that Chinese dialects should be preserved, and that they in fact also helped in the learning of Mandarin.

In the early years of the campaign, promoters of Mandarin were so aggressive that dialect programmes were all banned from radio and television and even in the cinema. Old clansmen at the Chinese clan associations began to speak in Mandarin too, as did grandfathers and grandmothers when speaking to their grandchildren.

After nearly 40 years of the campaign, the aim to get Chinese Singaporeans to stop speaking dialect has been achieved. It has changed the language speaking habit of Chinese Singaporeans, from the dialects to Mandarin indeed.

But the worry now is that the young are not speaking enough Mandarin and communicating mainly in English instead.

That is perhaps why the campaign is still very much alive, at least to remind the young of the importance of Mandarin.

Chinese Language Teaching Reviewed

The Chinese language, its falling standards, how it is being taught in schools and whether it is spoken widely among the young are talking points in the Chinese community and will probably continue to be in the years ahead.

These issues have prompted the government to constantly review how Chinese is being taught in the schools over the years.

There have been at least three major reviews, the first in 1992, led by the late former Deputy Prime Minister Ong Teng Cheong (王鼎昌) who later became Singapore's first elected President, the second in 1997 by then Deputy Prime Minister Lee Hsien Loong (李显龙) and the third in 2004 by former Director-General of Education Wee Heng Tin (黄庆新).

The Ong Teng Cheong Review was released after the 1991 general election when the ruling PAP lost four Parliamentary seats and suffered a drop in popular votes. At the party's review of the election results, one reason cited was that Chinese educated voters were so unhappy with the government's language policies which lowered both the standard and status of Chinese that they had voted in protest for the opposition.

Among the review committee's recommendations were to change the name CL2 to Chinese language and CL1 to Higher Chinese to correct the previous wrong impression that Chinese is not an important subject in school.

It also called for a revision of the teaching materials such as textbooks to be more up-to-date in an effort to improve learning and the appreciation of Chinese culture and values.

Hanyu pinyin or romanised Chinese, it suggested, should be taught as early as in Primary One and the use of dictionaries for essay writing examinations should be allowed for primary school pupils.

Other recommendations included increasing the weightage given to reading and listening comprehension in examinations, encouraging more students with flair for the language to study Chinese and Chinese literature at the higher level in their GCE "O" level examinations.

The key recommendation of the Lee Hsien Loong's 2004 review was the introduction of an alternative Chinese Language B syllabus at the upper secondary school and junior college levels. The syllabus offered simpler texts and a smaller vocabulary to learn and was meant for students still weak in Chinese after secondary two. They needed only to pass Chinese at this lower level to qualify for admission to junior college or university later.

Other recommendations included revising Chinese textbooks to the pre-1991 standards and encouraging more students to take up Higher Chinese from as early as Primary Four.

The most important recommendation from the Wee Heng Tin's review report was the suggestion of a modular approach to Chinese language teaching in schools. It has a core curriculum for all students but those found to have little contact with Chinese at Primary One could do bridging modules first before joining the core module later. Reinforcement modules would be introduced in Primary Three for students who need better support in order to cope. Those with strong interest in Chinese and the ability to do so are offered enrichment modules from Primary One to Primary Six for them to achieve a higher level of competency in the language.

Most of the recommendations were accepted and implemented.

Conclusion

In this short review of the usage of the Chinese language by the Chinese community in Singapore, I have tried to show that it has been radically transformed over the last 200 years or so. From being spoken in dialect forms by the early Chinese immigrants, most of them illiterate, it is now mainly spoken in Mandarin by the majority of Chinese Singaporeans, some studying the language at a high level in schools and even universities.

Singapore's Chinese newspapers and publications have also had a long history. Singapore Chinese literature is still growing, albeit amidst a much smaller group of writers and enthusiasts. Television programmes in Mandarin, both news and entertainment ones, are widely watched by Chinese Singaporeans, their viewership surpassing even English-language programmes. Mandarin remains the most popular spoken language among Chinese Singaporeans.

The evolution of the Chinese language in Singapore may be traced to government language policies which resulted in a National Stream school system where English is the main language of instruction in all schools and tertiary institutions.

With 75% of Singapore's population being ethnic Chinese, the rise or decline of the Chinese language, whether spoken or written, has and will always be a sensitive topic for discussion. More reviews on how Chinese should be taught and studied in school are to be expected in the future as Chinese Singaporeans are still passionate about the language.

As the Founding Prime Minister Lee Kuan Yew had pointed out in his book, *My Lifelong Challenge — Singapore's Bilingual Journey*, Singapore's language policy must never stop changing in order to keep up with the times and development around the world. In his own words:

> The bottom line is that our education system must evolve and adjust as the situation changes. No policy is cast in stone. If the Chinese language grows in economic value and parents and students want to learn more Chinese, our system must accommodate them. The choice, however, must be exercised by parents and students, and not by the government.

CHAPTER 8

New Immigrants from China
*Boosting Bilateral Relations**

ZHOU Zhaocheng

Right from the start, the Chinese population in Singapore has comprised people of different origins and backgrounds. Shortly after Sir Stamford Raffles founded Singapore in 1819, many Chinese from the Malay Peninsula and Indonesia moved to the island. From the mid-19th century, Chinese immigrants from the southern coastal provinces of Fujian and Guangdong constituted a significant part of Singapore's population. From the early 20th century till 1970, the proportion of the Chinese population in Singapore remained largely unchanged, but there was a major change in its composition. There was a sharp decline in the number of non-local-born Chinese within the community. The figure dropped from 76.4% in 1921 to 64.2% in 1931, to 42.3% in 1947, to 32% in 1957, and then went further down to 23.4% in 1970.[1] The change in these data can be attributed to Singapore's morphological evolution from a colony to an independent state, as well as the changing emigration trends of mainland China.

After the 1980s, the number of Chinese migrating to Southeast Asia, Europe, the United States and other places grew steadily. As the number of emigrants increased, the official Chinese agencies dealing with overseas Chinese affairs began referring to them as *xin yi min* (新移民 new migrants) instead of *huaqiao* or *huaqiao huaren* (华侨/华侨华人 overseas Chinese). The new term *xin yi min* was first coined by the government departments of China to refer to Chinese citizens who emigrated overseas after the

---

* This chapter was originally written in Chinese.
[1] Saw Swee Hock, *The Population of Singapore*. (Singapore: ISEAS, 1999), p. 33.

economic reforms and "opening up" of China. However, the term has not replaced "overseas Chinese". Rather, it appears to refer to a sub-group within the larger community of overseas Chinese.[2] The number of Chinese immigrants to Singapore has fluctuated at various periods, reflecting the socio-political changes in the region as well as Singapore's relationship with China.

Singapore and China established diplomatic relations in 1990. As bilateral political and economic exchanges increased, and with the lavish praise Deng Xiaoping accorded Singapore during his southern tour in 1992 as well as the construction of the Suzhou Industrial Park in 1994, Singapore's reputation in China rose considerably. It became one of the main destinations for Chinese emigrants. Moreover, with China's booming economy and growing regional influence, Singapore rediscovered and vigorously promoted the economic value of the Chinese language. As Singapore and China developed new opportunities for cooperation in areas such as economics, transport, culture, education and language, the emergence of "new immigrants" among Singaporean Chinese became increasingly noticeable.

In the 1980s there was a surge of Hong Kong emigrants to Singapore, as China and Britain began talks on the 1997 return of Hong Kong. Another factor was the 4 June 1989 student demonstration in Beijing. The Hong Kong immigrants formed their own social groupings and they became part of the "new immigrants" in Singapore.

In Singapore, scholars define "new immigrants" as migrants from mainland China who have become Singapore citizens or permanent residents after the 1990s. However, in the common usage of the term among the community at large, xin yi min generally include Chinese from mainland China who are working or studying in Singapore and have yet to receive permanent residency.

As Singapore's immigration policy focuses strongly on attracting foreign talent, most new immigrants are admitted through employment, further studies recruitment and scholarships. They are highly educated and transnational, unlike past immigrants to Singapore. Therefore, some scholars have proposed the concept of transnational Chinese as

[2] Wang Gungwu "New Chinese immigrants: How and why are they new?" in Liu Hong and Huang Jianli, eds., *The Greater Vision and Direction in the Research on Overseas Chinese.* (U.S.: Global Publishing Company, 2002) p. 326.

the immigrant groups who in the process of moving overseas, maintain multiple relations connecting their (or their parents') birthplace with the country they reside in. Their social circle traverses geographical, cultural and political boundaries. Being transnational migrants, they speak two or more languages; have immediate family members, social networks and careers in two or more countries; and maintaining frequent cross-border exchanges becomes an important means of livelihood for them.[3]

Today, the new Chinese immigrants in Singapore clearly possess this multinational characteristic. Due to the globalisation of science and technology, electronics, biology, pharmacology and other research skills, career choices have also become more globalised. Singapore's immigration policy was also developed in response to such globalisation trends, thus a major characteristic of new immigrants is that they possess portable, transnational skills. Local criticism that some of these new immigrants regard Singapore as a springboard to Europe, America and other countries is, in fact, an affirmation of their transnational capabilities.

Singapore's meritocratic policy creates a favourable environment for new immigrants who are prepared to work hard to achieve social status. At the same time, it enables new immigrants to integrate into the local culture and society.

New Immigrants and Singapore Society

There are no exact figures, but based on daily interactions and personal experience, it is not difficult to come to the conclusion that there is a considerable number of immigrants from China in Singapore.

One can determine this largely due to the differences between Singapore Chinese and Chinese from China. It is generally easy to distinguish between a new immigrant from China and a Singapore-born Chinese. These differences include accent, clothing and style of dressing, as well as behaviour. Such judgmental first impressions are often not far from the truth. However, a deeper understanding of the paradigms, logic and behavioural styles, as well as other subtle influences affecting the *xin yi min* can only be achieved

---

[3] Liu Hong, *The Evolution of the Post-war Singapore Chinese Society: Emotions of the Natives, Regional Networks, Global Vision*. (Xiamen: Xiamen University Press, 2004), p. 215.

if the two groups reach out and interact, relate and become more exposed to each other over time.

The differences between the two groups raise two issues. Firstly, although Singaporean Chinese and the new immigrants from China speak the same language and are of the same race, the former are traditionally from the southern Fujian and Guangdong provinces whereas many of the latter group come from northeast China and Inner Mongolia. This makes it easy and also natural for the two groups to begin distinguishing themselves and establishing distinct identities. As a consequence, the Chinese community becomes divided into "us" and "them". How each person responds to and faces such differences directly affects how these two groups of people view and relate with each other. It is reinforced when negative social practices or behaviour of individuals are generalised as applying to the whole group.

The new immigrants in Singapore can generally be classified into the following categories — those who have become Singapore citizens, those who have received permanent residency, those who have specialised skills and possess the Employment Pass, students in a wide range of educational institutions, those who were brought into Singapore as labourers and possess the Work Permit, those who hold long-term Social Visit Passes due to marriage or are accompanying their children studying in Singapore, and those here for the short term (including street prostitutes etc.). The first four groups are able to reside in Singapore in the long term. Those who hold the Employment Pass or study here are also able to gain permanent residency more easily. From the legal viewpoint, new immigrants refer to those who have obtained permanent residency or citizenship. The last three groups belong to the other end of the spectrum and tend to interact with the lower rungs of Singapore society. Misunderstandings and strife are more prone to arise from these groups.

The problem is that most Singaporeans do not see the differentiations among the new immigrants. The tendency is to regard all seven groups of Chinese immigrants as a single one. The upper-middle class *xin yi min* are extremely sensitive to being tarred with the same brush. This unhappiness over being lumped with the other social groups is seldom expressed openly but it rankles the better educated and better qualified new immigrants.

Because of limited human resources, the Singapore government is compelled to rely on foreign labour. This foreign labour comprises specialists and professionals, as well as labourers who generally belong to the lower rungs of the social ladder and are not highly skilled. They include a large number of construction workers, maids and service workers holding work permits. In the context of a low population replacement rate, the foreign talent policy is often intertwined with debates on boosting population growth.

With an increase in the number of Chinese labourers being employed in coffee shops, food courts and factories, complaints have arisen from some low-income citizens, i.e. that the new immigrants who are willing to accept lower wages and longer work hours have stolen their jobs. Such sentiments gradually evolve into resentment against Chinese migrants.

Immigration has always been a political issue. The increase of Chinese immigrants has even been interpreted as a deliberate move by the PAP government to dilute opposition strength and reduce the voice of English-educated Singaporeans who often criticise the government and are dissatisfied with the ruling party. It is argued that by increasing the intake of new immigrants, the PAP can bolster their electoral chances because the Chinese from China are more "obedient" and have lived under political control for a long time.

Being a cosmopolitan nation, the people of Singapore interact with a great number of foreigners in their daily life. Whether they like it or not, Singaporeans have to deal with the impact and conflicts, as well as integration and assimilation of immigrants. Paradoxically, Singaporean Chinese often accord a higher degree of tolerance for cultural differences with other races than towards Chinese immigrants who speak the same language and belong to the same race. One reason could be the deliberate distance Singapore set between itself and communist China during its early founding years, in terms of ideology and contact between the citizens of the two countries. Other contributory factors are the superiority complex some Singaporean Chinese have subconsciously built up, the disdain that those strong in the English language have towards the Chinese-speaking world, China's later development, regional differences of the new immigrants, as well as some of the poor habits that Chinese people have, amongst others.

At the same time, many Chinese immigrants have little knowledge of Singapore's history and its cultural and social background. Despite speaking the same language and being of the same race, there is a great, covert disparity between the Singapore born and new immigrant Chinese. In particular, the Chinese-speaking and English-speaking communities hold very different perceptions and feelings towards Chinese and the Chinese culture. English-speaking Chinese generally have less contact with and understanding of the Chinese immigrants than the Chinese-speaking community.

Within their respective social circles, both Singapore-born Chinese and new immigrants from China often voice their grievances and difficulties with sarcasm and disdain for the other group. They seek solace and comfort for their "collective suffering". However, they may also be subtly and unconsciously reinforcing their existing negative impressions. These are the undercurrents flowing in the two communities. For example, "study mamas" (mothers who accompany their children studying in Singapore) often face direct rejection when looking for a place to rent due to their negative social image. Some Singaporeans even refuse to rent to any Chinese from China. This elevates the undercurrents into direct discrimination and conflicts between the two groups. The outstanding performances of students from China also generate complaints from local students and parents who fear they might be deprived of opportunities amidst such intense competition.

Clearly, making judgemental conclusions of a whole community without detailed consideration, or deliberate ignorance of the different layers of mentalities and opinions due to differing social experiences, educational background and income levels is unfair. Yet such thinking has become so common many fail to recognise it in themselves.

From a historical perspective, the growth and decline of Chinese immigrants to Singapore reflect the socio-political events at various periods and also mirror the evolution of Singapore's relations with China.

Today, the higher educational level of China's emigrants is very different from what it was in the past. Professionals and students account for a large proportion of the overseas Chinese population. Many are rich and affluent. In recent years, as China's economic growth began to be a stimulus for Southeast Asia's, a "Chinese fever" has risen, leading Singapore to actively promote the economic role of the Chinese language. Singapore and

China thus have new collaborative opportunities in several areas such as economics, transport, culture, education and language, amongst others.

As a consequence, immigrants from China have become increasingly self-confident and secure in their perceptions, even to the extent of becoming complacent at times. Many no longer look up to Singapore or consider themselves as recipients. Instead they see themselves as contributors who have helped meet Singapore's needs.

Singapore's emphasis on the teaching of the Chinese language and the importance it attaches to the rise of China enhances the confidence of Chinese immigrants. Their knowledge of Chinese not only creates a special niche for them, it affords them a sense of superiority in fields where the Chinese language is used. The greater emphasis given to the Chinese language has given immigrants from China relatively more opportunities for survival as well as room for expression. Providing Chinese tuition is one of the easiest means for Chinese immigrants to make a living in Singapore. In other fields where the Chinese language is applied, they naturally develop a sense of superiority and tend to criticise Singaporeans for their low mastery of the Chinese language.

Due to the interdependent relationship between the Chinese community and Chinese language media, Singapore is the only independent country outside of China (including Hong Kong, Macao and Taiwan) where Chinese language media is a part of the mainstream. For Chinese immigrants, they have a convenient platform for expression, participation in public and social events, and publication of their views on local society and lifestyle, and a channel to provide the perspective of new immigrants and gain the attention of the main society. This may lead to resonance or rebuttals from native Singaporeans. Once certain commentators are labelled "Chinese" or "Singaporean", the disparity will be widened as each seeks to establish their self-identity.

However, in Singapore's political and social environment, the term "new immigrants" only denotes the background of a large group of people. The group is not a fully formed community with vested interests. It will not likely become a specific group lobbying for rights or political status. The paradox is that in comparison with other foreigners, this does not give impetus for the integration of Chinese immigrants into the Singapore society. With the ease of Internet communication and convenience of travel, the costs of connecting with their birthplace are greatly reduced for migrants. Concurrently, networking opportunities and capacities are greatly enhanced. As such, their birthplace and place of residence can be easily bridged, whether temporally or spatially. While this has facilitated their continued attention on China's development and current affairs, it also presents a new challenge in their assimilation efforts.

"Three New's" and "Two Differences" among New Immigrants from China[4]

It is often said that China's new migrants have "three new's" (三新) and "two differences" (两异.) The "three new's" are a new era, new immigration patterns and education level, as well as new places of origin. The two differences are a greater space for public opinion and the government's better understanding of new immigrants. Compared with new Chinese immigrants in other countries, those in Singapore exhibit the "three new's" but have greater development opportunities in the "two differences".

The "three new's" of Singapore's *xin yi min* reflect their cosmopolitan nature as compared to those who arrived in the 19th and early 20th centuries. The first "new" is a new era. Singapore's "new immigrants" migrated after China's economic reforms. The second "new" refers to the fact that most of the new immigrants have higher levels of education and migrate by studying overseas or are skilled professionals employed to work overseas. The third "new" refers to the change in the geographical origin of the immigrants. In earlier days, immigrants mainly came from the Fujian or Guangdong provinces while the new immigrants come from a wider array of places.

The rapid growth of new Chinese immigrants in Singapore has had significant impact on the local Chinese community. At the same time, technological advancements have enabled new interactive relationships between country of residence and country of origin. All these have impacted local society and culture.

---

[4] Translated from the original Chinese idiom 三 心 两 意 which means "undecided or unfocussed". By replacing two words with the same sound, but different meaning, the title of this section becomes 三 新 两 异.

One of the "two differences" between new Chinese immigrants in Singapore and those in other countries is the relatively larger room for expression here. Singapore uses Mandarin as part of its mainstream media. It is therefore more convenient for new immigrants to participate in discussions of social and public events. The influence of Singapore's *Lianhe Zaobao* and other Chinese media in mainland China has also expanded the scope of expression for new immigrants.

To help new immigrants integrate smoothly into society, the Singapore government's REACH (Reaching Everyone for Active Citizenry @ Home) group, clan associations and other organisations often run dialogue sessions with senior government officials or politicians. It is not difficult for the voice of the new immigrants to be heard.

The second of the "two differences" refers to the bigger contributions that new Chinese immigrants in Singapore make due to the close and unique bilateral political and trade relations between Singapore and China. Today, new immigrants work in a myriad of economic fields, including finance, trade, education, culture, arts, construction, manufacturing, and media, among others; some have achieved great success in Singapore. As economic and trade relations between Singapore and China prosper, new immigrants can play the useful role of middlemen. Their achievements, in turn, further strengthen bilateral business relations.

The new immigrants in Singapore have set up associations for their members to interact, provide mutual help, socialise and gather in an organised manner. At the same time, they have maximised business opportunities and trade cooperation by pooling their background knowledge, resources, professional skills and networks. The greatest push for the formation of these associations is to promote social networking and business collaboration. This is very different from the clan associations set up in the past, whose main role was social assistance.

The "two differences" are special characteristics of new Chinese immigrants in Singapore. These characteristics affect the relationship and interaction between new immigrants and Singapore society, as well as the civil and social relationships between the two countries in a special way. The rapid growth of new Chinese immigrants has already created new ways and perspectives on identification, as well as new interactive relations between country of residence and country of birth. Many of these changes are the result of the transformations in the organisational methods and patterns of activity of the new immigrant associations.

The Social Role of New Immigrant Associations

One of the reasons that Singapore is able to attract a large number of new immigrants is the appeal of its successful development. Other factors are its Chinese majority, the nation's prosperity, security and stability. These are the historical and cultural pull factors for overseas Chinese immigrants. Another factor is Singapore's open policy towards foreigners. Singapore's immigration policy takes into consideration factors such as economic growth, social circumstances and population growth. Under this policy, immigrants accepted into Singapore tend to be highly skilled in technology, scientific research and other high value-adding areas. They are familiar with the operations of a modern economy and are capable of leveraging upon Singapore's multinational environment to realise their personal career goals in step with the Republic's development.

The new immigrant associations help the *xin yi min* to expand their social and economic networks and participate in commercial and trading activities. Singapore's position as a regional centre and its frequent exchanges with the various parts of China also provide business opportunities for the new groups. At the same time, their familiarity with China and latest economic developments facilitates the linking up of Singapore's and China's resources. Singapore's founding Prime Minister Mr. Lee Kuan Yew said in October 2001,

> In order to better understand Chinese people, I decided to recruit intelligent Chinese from China to work and study in Singapore so they can understand Singaporeans and become part of Singapore. When Singaporeans invest in China and there are Chinese who reside in Singapore among the company's team, they can help us understand the situation in China. It will then be easier to see results from the Singaporean company's investment.[5]

---

[5]Lee Kuan Yew speaking at the Q&A session during the "Ministerial Forum" held at the National University of Singapore, *Lianhe Zaobao*, 16 October 2001.

Besides being engaged in the fields of science and technology, trading, services and other economic sectors, the new immigrants are also active in the cultural and educational sectors. They also contribute towards the knowledge economy as part of the research teams in the higher institutes of learning. In the social sphere, new immigrants actively participate in the programmes of the local Chinese community and even help shape the cultural scene by setting up their own associations. These new organisations not only add diversity to the local Chinese dialect groups, they have also made the use of the Chinese language more widespread.

Whether the associations are formed by new immigrants who have become Singapore citizens or permanent residents or by Chinese who do not have such residence status, they all have to face the issue of cultural integration. They have to deal with the twin challenge of accepting, and being accepted, by Singaporeans. The Singapore government is concerned about how new immigrants are integrating into society. The new immigrant associations can and need to be platforms that help promote the social integration of *xin yi min* into Singapore.

At the first anniversary celebration dinner of the Hua Yuan General Association (华源会) in May 2002, then Deputy Prime Minister of Singapore, Lee Hsien Loong noted that new immigrants

> need to integrate into our society and become part of our nation's family. Organisations such as Hua Yuan General Association of New Immigrants from China need to ensure that their members do not rest on their laurels and become a closed group, slowing down integration into our society.[6]

The new immigrant associations and traditional clan associations have established mutually beneficial relationships. On one hand, the older clan associations assist the new immigrants with integration into Singapore; on the other hand, new immigrant organisations use their members' knowledge and connections to promote exchanges between Singapore and China.

---

[6]Speech by then Deputy Prime Minister Lee Hsien Loong, *Lianhe Zaobao*, 12 th May 2002.

Some of the older clan associations in Singapore such as Singapore Chin Kang Huay Kuan (新加坡晋江会馆) and Sam Kiang Huay Kwan (三江会馆) are actively recruiting new immigrants to join them as members or directors. The leaders and members of many clan associations have business dealings with China and the new immigrant members can help them understand the culture and thinking of the Chinese people as well as aid local companies in doing business with the Chinese.

Organisational Characteristics of New Immigrant Associations

A comparison of the older clan associations and new immigrant organisations shows that they have distinctly different characteristics.

(1) Traditionally clan associations are organised based on locality or kinship ties. For example, the Singapore Hokkien Huay Kuan (福建会馆) and Kwangtung Hui Kuan (广东会馆) were set up according to the birthplace and dialect origin of the immigrants; the Singapore Lee Clan General Association (李氏总会) and Federation of Chen Clan Association (陈氏总会) were established based on surnames and kinship ties.

   The new immigrant associations, however, are only based on locality (provincial/dialect groups) because of the limited number of immigrants sharing the same surnames, and the debilitated kinship-based clan culture in mainland China. Examples of such clan associations are Tianjin Association (天津会), Shanxi Association (山西会), Shandong Association (齐鲁会), Shaanxi Association (陕西同乡会), Guizhou Association (贵州同乡会).

(2) While partly based on locality, some new immigrant groups have stepped beyond their geographical boundaries. Tian Fu Association (天府会), established in February 2000, was originally set up for new immigrants from Sichuan, but there are now no restrictions in the geographical origin of its members. Hua Yuan General Association, established in May 2001, accepts all new Chinese immigrants as members regardless of their provincial and dialect backgrounds. These associations promote interaction among new immigrants from different provinces by

organising various activities. They also act as networking bridges between China and Singapore businessmen.

(3) University alumni associations are another platform for the new immigrants. There are many graduates of Chinese universities in Singapore and thus there is a member base for the setting up of Chinese universities' alumni associations in the country. Currently, there are already more than 20 universities that have set up alumni associations, including the renowned Peking University (北京大学), Tsinghua University (清华大学), the South China University of Technology (华南理工大学), Shanghai Jiao Tong University (上海交通大学) and other science and engineering universities.

(4) As Singapore and China's trade relations become increasingly closer, new immigrant associations are playing an intermediary role, thus contributing towards bilateral business cooperation.

Some new immigrants with business backgrounds have established locality-based trade associations. For example, the Zhejiang(s) Entrepreneurs Association (新加坡浙商协会) and Jinshang Business Club (Singapore) (新加坡晋商商会) were established for commercial purposes.

A Brief Introduction to Some of the New Immigrant Associations

Listed below are some of the better known *xin yi min* organisations.

The Kowloon Club (九龙会)

The Kowloon Club was set up on 6 April 1990 with the purpose of giving members a platform for providing mutual assistance, social interactions and opportunities for getting to know local Singaporeans. Its members comprise Hong Kong immigrants and Hongkongers working in Singapore. There are more than 4,700 families among its members. In addition to providing guidance and assistance to new immigrants, the Kowloon Club has also begun giving back to society and participating in charitable and community activities including the Singapore Chingay parade, Golden Jubilee National

Day Preview, Istana Presidential Palace Open House Charity Sales, Sentosa Mid-Autumn Festival Charity Fundraiser, as well as visits to Malay Muslim Children's Homes.

Tian Fu Association (Singapore) (天府会)

The Tian Fu Association (Singapore) formerly known as "Tian Fu Clan Association" was one of the first new immigrants' associations set up after diplomatic relations were established with China. Approved by the Singapore Registry of Societies on 3 February 2000, the Association now has about 2,300 members. Originally, members of the Tian Fu Association were mainly immigrants from Sichuan. Later, the Association expanded its membership criteria. There are now new immigrants from Beijing, Shanghai, Tianjin, Xi'an, Zhejiang, as well as the north-east regions. The Association provides a platform and place for networking and social interaction. Most of the members are professionals and highly-educated; 99% of members have university degrees and more than 30% have done further studies in Singapore. There are more than 600 families in the Tian Fu Association and almost 70% of them have become Singapore citizens.

Every year, more than 400 people attend its annual general meeting, forums and Mid-Autumn Festival celebration. The Association also maintains close ties with more than 10 old and new immigrant associations such as the Singapore Chinese Chamber of Commerce & Industry, Singapore Federation of Chinese Clan Associations, Teochew Poit Ip Huay Kuan, Sam Kiang Huay Kwan and Singapore Amoy Association. It also participates in large-scale activities organised by other organisations.

Tian Fu Association has also donated to charities and worthy causes in Singapore and China. These include donations to the Chinese regions hit by earthquakes ($240,000) and the Islamic Religious Council of Singapore (MUIS) in 2009 ($10,000). They also donated funds for the construction of a primary school after the Sichuan earthquake (RMB1.2 million).

In 2010, Tian Fu Association also donated $60,000 for the 25th anniversary of the Singapore Federation of Chinese Clan Associations. The Association also awards scholarships and bursaries to children of members as well as other new immigrants. To date, 128 students have benefitted from these awards.

Hua Yuan Association (华源会)

The Hua Yuan Association was officially registered on 4 January 2001. Members are not limited to any particular province or dialect group. Any new immigrant from China can join as a member. Hua Yuan Association's objective is

> to help members better integrate into Singapore's multiracial society, facilitate communication and information exchange among members; promote the spirit of mutual help and camaraderie; enhance friendship and exchanges between members and other associations; enrich the lives of members and their families with a variety of leisure activities; and promote cultural and trade relations between Singapore and China.

Hua Yuan Association has set up eight sub-groups — volunteers, education, arts, sports, business, publicity, science and technology and academic exchange, and public relations and activities.

Tianjin Association (天津会)

The Tianjin Association was registered on 11 September 2007. It collaborates closely with the other new immigrant organisations in social activities such as the Mid-Autumn festival.

Shanxi Association (Singapore) (新加坡山西同乡会)

The Shanxi Association was incorporated on 30 April 2010. Its members consist of Shanxi people from all walks of life. Shanxi Association has organised various events, such as an East Coast 10 km Walk, Thousand People Spring Roll event and annual Chinese New Year Members' dinners.

Shaanxi Association (Singapore) (新加坡陕西同乡会)

The Shaanxi Association was established on 20 August 2011. Its main objectives are to help Shaanxi immigrants integrate into Singapore's multiracial society, organise and participate in social welfare activities, and promote business, cultural and technological exchanges between Singapore and Shaanxi.

Shandong Association (Singapore) (齐鲁会)

The Shandong Association (Singapore) was an initiative launched by new immigrants from the Shandong province and was officially established on 1 November 2012. It aims to enhance relationships between Shandong immigrants and Singaporeans, aid in the integration of new Shandong immigrants into Singapore society, and promote cultural, educational, science and business exchanges and collaborations between Singapore and Shandong.

Zhe Jiang(s) Entrepreneurs Association (新加坡浙商协会)

The Zhe Jiang(s) Entrepreneurs Association was registered on 1 February 2013 and inaugurated on 1 May. Set up by businessmen from Zhejiang, the Association focuses on promoting economic ties between the province and Singapore.

Jinshang Business Club (Singapore) (新加坡晋商商会)

The Jinshang Business Club (Singapore) was inaugurated on 8 November 2013. The club aims to promote Jin (Shanxi) culture and business activities and cultural exchanges between Singapore and Shanxi.

He Fei Association (合肥会)

The He Fei Association was formally established on 30 June 2013. According to its website, the association serves as a platform to promote commercial, technological, cultural and educational exchanges between Singapore and the city of Hefei in Anhui province of China. Its objective is to help the immigrants from Hefei to integrate fully into Singapore.

Guizhou Association (贵州同乡会)

Officially registered on 29 July 2013, the Association comprises Chinese nationals from Guizhou. It aims to be the platform for social gatherings and information exchange among Guizhou people, provide mutual support and facilitate integration of members into Singapore's multiracial society. The Association actively promotes cultural exchanges between Singapore and Guizhou.

Chinese Universities' Alumni Associations in Singapore

The earliest Chinese university alumni association set up in Singapore can be traced back to 1947 when the Xiamen University Alumni Association was registered. Others were founded more than 10 years ago, such as the Shanghai Jiao Tong University Alumni Association established in 1999. The Peking University and Tsinghua University Alumni Associations of Singapore have also been around for several years. In recent years, Sun Yat-Sen University, Fudan University, South China University of Technology, and Harbin Institute of Technology have successively set up alumni associations here as well.

In the past, the Chinese university alumni associations in Singapore generally organised gatherings for meals and recreational activities. As most alumni members were concentrated in the National University of Singapore and the Nanyang Technological University of Singapore, many Chinese university alumni activities were initiated by the alumni of these two universities. As technological entrepreneurship and trade investments increased, the Chinese universities' alumni associations also began organising activities in these areas. More details on the various university alumni associations are as follows:

— Tsinghua Alumni Association (Singapore) (清华大学校友会) was offi-
  cially registered on 26 April 2007.
— Xiamen (Amoy) University Alumni Association (Singapore) (厦门大
  学校友会) was formally established on 16 October 1947. However, as
  Singapore students no longer went to study in Xiamen University after
  the 1950s, most of the members of the Alumni Association today are
  Chinese alumni who migrated to Singapore after the 1990s.
— Fudan University Alumni Association (Singapore) (复旦大学校友会)
  was officially set up on 11 August 2012.
— Harbin Institute of Technology Alumni Association (哈尔滨工业大学校
  友会) was formally incorporated in February 2014 and held its inaugural

dinner on 31 August. The Association has managed to obtain information of nearly 400 alumni working, studying and residing in Singapore, among whom a considerable number are alumni who have come to Singapore for further studies through the Singapore-China educational exchange programmes.

— Peking University Alumni Association (Singapore) (北京大学校友会) was officially registered on 28 July 2008.

— Shanghai University Alumni Association (Singapore) (上海大学校友会) was registered on 26 April 2012.

— Shanghai Maritime University Alumni Club (Singapore) (上海海事大学校友会俱乐部) was officially incorporated on 29 November 2011.

— Shanghai Jiao Tong University Alumni Association (Singapore) (上海交通大学校友会) was registered on 18 March 1999.

— Zhejiang University Alumni Association (Singapore) (浙江大学校友会) was approved and set up on 2 June 2000.

— Tongji University Alumni (Singapore) (同济大学校友会) was registered on 24 August 2007.

— Tianjin University Alumni Association (Singapore) (天津大学校友会) was incorporated on 25 November 2009.

— Dalian Maritime University Alumni Association (Singapore) (大连海事大学校友会) was formally established on 1 November 2012.

— Sun Yat-Sen University Alumni Association (Singapore) (中山大学校友会) was officially set up on 2 June 2014.

Conclusion

As new immigrants live in the Internet era where transport and communications have achieved tremendous advancements, the costs of maintaining contact with their place of birth have been considerably lessened while the speed of communication has increased. This facilitates new immigrant associations in helping members strengthen relationships, organise activities, as well as interact with the outside world and home country. New immigrant associations are playing a bigger role and gaining greater status in Singapore society due to a number of factors.

The first factor is the importance that the Singapore government places on the integration of immigrants into society. The new immigrant associations are viewed as important channels and intermediaries for the resolution of conflicts during the integration process.

Secondly, as more new immigrants achieve personal success, and as more of them begin playing leading roles in the community, their influence also increases. This, in turn, has a positive impact on the associations they represent.

The third factor is the importance of improving bilateral ties by the Chinese and Singapore governments. Because the new immigrants and their associations have long and special relationships with China's local authorities and businesses, they are able to play important roles in building bridges between China, their land of birth, and Singapore, their country of adoption.

CHAPTER 9

Chinese Religious Traditions in Singapore
Buddhism, Taoism and Christianity

HUE Guan Thye and Kenneth DEAN

Introduction

Singapore is a multi-ethnic, multi-religious society, which has enjoyed a long period of religious harmony. Because of its immigrant history, Singapore is home to the world's major religions — Buddhism, Taoism, Christianity, Islam and Hinduism. The believers of these faiths have co-existed harmoniously throughout the five decades of the Republic.

This success is in part due to government regulations and policy. Ambassador at Large Tommy Koh has published an overview of government policies on religion over 50 years.[1] Prime Minister Lee Hsien Loong (李显龙) referred to the long history of harmonious co-existence between religious and ethnic groups as one of the greatest accomplishments of the Singapore state and society at the 25th anniversary banquet of the Taoist Federation on 19 April 2015. A month later he reiterated the importance of government regulation of harmony among religions for Singaporean society.[2]

While policy is certainly important, another vital aspect of the story is the response of Singaporeans to these policies, as well as their interactions in everyday life. From this perspective, the successful harmony between religious

---

[1] Tommy Koh, "Miracle on Waterloo Street", *The Straits Times,* 21 February 2015.
[2] Lim Yan Liang, "'Unrealisitic' to say religion is no longer sensitive issue: PM says", *The Straits Times,* 13 May 2015.

and ethnic communities is partly the legacy of the long history of globalisation, stretching back hundreds of years before the founding of Singapore. In the port cities where migrant groups and religious communities from India, China and the Middle East lived side by side with one another and with native communities of Southeast Asia for centuries, the communities tended more often to practise mutual inclusiveness than resort to exclusiveness and strife. Indeed, many scholars have pointed out that religious and ethnic intolerance and conflict in South and Southeast Asia was a by-product of the rise of post-colonial nation-states, many of which insisted on imposing hard boundaries between ethnic and religious communities.

In today's multiracial and multi-religious Singapore, it is common to see temples, churches and mosques in close proximity to one another. Sometimes, multiple temples join up to form a "united temple". Buddhist and Taoist temples can be found on different floors of the same building. Even more exceptional are hybrid temples such as Luoyang Dabogong (洛阳大伯公宫), at Loyang Way where a Chinese temple stands next to a Hindu shrine, with an Islamic keramat in between, all in the same temple complex.

In the secular state of Singapore, religious freedom is enshrined in the constitution. Article 15 of the Republic's Constitution guarantees all citizens the right to practise, and to propagate their religions. Religious harmony is enforced by the provision in the Penal Code that makes it an offence to deliberately use words to offend people of another religion. In 1990 inter-religious respect and tolerance was further codified with the enactment of the Maintenance of Religious Harmony Act. The Act provided for the establishment of a Presidential Council for Religious Harmony, comprising religious and lay leaders to advise the President on issues affecting religions. Shortly after the September 11 terrorist attacks in the US, the Singapore government set up Inter-Racial and Religious Confidence Circles (IRCC) in all constituencies. The IRCCs organise a wide range of activities at the grass-roots level to encourage greater interactions among the different ethnic groups and religions. At the apex is a National Steering Committee chaired by a minister and comprising leaders from the different faiths and major civic organisations. Some scholars have commented that this is a form of pre-emptive harmonisation.[3] The government has been even-handed in its

---

[3] Lai Ah Eng, *Religious Diversity in Singapore*. (Singapore: ISEAS, 2012.)

respect for the major religious traditions, four of which have been allotted one public holiday each annually: Christmas, Vesak, Hari Raya Puasa and Deepavali are days of rest for all Singaporeans.

Since the establishment of the Republic of Singapore, the government has closely regulated but nonetheless allowed the construction of hundreds of temples, mosques and churches, while balancing the limited land resources of Singapore for a host of other needs. Although the government has remained strictly secular and has pursued modernisation with manifest results, it has allowed space for the religions to flourish. Most religious sites are however only issued a 30-year lease. Thus many religious communities continuously work to raise funds to extend their leases, or to pay for a move to a new location. Such policies inevitably generate some tension within the religious communities.

As our contribution to the deeper study of the diversity of religious expression in the Chinese community of Singapore, over the past five years, we have conducted a survey of 800 Chinese temples and Buddhist monasteries of Singapore's Chinese community. We present some of the results of our survey in this chapter. We also look at the findings of the 2010 census to explore the impact of education, gender, income and housing on religious adherence among Singaporeans of Chinese heritage.

The 2010 census found that Chinese Singaporeans made up 73%, or 2.4 million, out of the total of 3.2 million citizens (a figure which does not include over 1.5 million permanent residents and work permit holders). Of these 2.4 million, 1.8 million or three quarters (75.8%) claim a religious affiliation. Just over a million identified themselves as Buddhists (43%), while 340,000 listed themselves as Taoists (14.4%). Another 472,636 (20.2%) identified themselves as Christians [155,515 Catholics (6.6%) and 317,121 Protestants (13.5%)]. Some half a million (24.2%) claimed to be free-thinkers. Probably as a result of inter-faith marriages, there were 8,332 Chinese Muslims, 312 Chinese Hindus, 56 Chinese Sikhs, and 7,888 Chinese members of "other religions". From these figures, we can see that religious affiliation in the Chinese community of Singapore is still strong, with three in four professing a religion. The combined numbers of Buddhists and Taoists (57.4%) remain higher than the figures for Chinese Christians (20.2%) or the free-thinkers (24.2%).

These numbers reflect a dramatic shift over the past 50 years. In the early years of the Republic the vast majority of Chinese identified themselves as Buddhist or Taoist. Self-identifying Buddhists rose from 34.3% in 1980 to 53.6% in 2000, but dropped to 43% in 2010. Percentages for Taoists showed the opposite movement, from 38.2% in 1980 to 10.8% in 2000, but increased to 14.4% in 2010. Christianity among Chinese Singaporeans has slowly but steadily risen, from 10.9% in 1980 to 16.5% in 2000 to 20.1% in 2010. The absolute number of Chinese Christians has doubled in 30 years, increasing at a steady pace throughout this period. Partly in response to secularisation and modernisation, the number of free-thinkers also rose steadily, but slightly more slowly, from 16.4% in 1980 to 18.6% in 2000 to 21.8% in 2010. The number of Taoists dropped dramatically in the 1990s, only to gradually recover as the leaders of the religion developed new strategies to reach out to younger people and get more people to participate in their religious traditions.

One important aspect of the outreach efforts has been the role of religious groups in providing social services such as healthcare, scholarships, charity to the poor, burials and commemorative spaces for the dead, etc. In their own ways, the various religions and their believers have made significant contributions towards helping the less privileged in Singapore.

Singaporeans' religious affiliation is largely ethnically structured. For instance, in 2000, 99.6% of Singapore Malays were Muslim, 55.4% of Singapore Indians were Hindu, and 64.4% of Singapore Chinese practised Chinese religions (Buddhism and Taoism).[4] Another key variable is the correlation between religious affiliation and several socio-demographic factors, including ethnicity, gender, age, education and socio-economic status.[5]

The religious affiliations of adult Singapore residents remained relatively stable over the last three decades. However, the Chinese ethnic group experienced the most significant shifts in religious affiliations between 1990 and 2000. While both Buddhism and Taoism were traditional longstanding Chinese religions, Buddhism became more widespread over the past two decades and surpassed Taoism as the main religion of the Chinese. In 2000,

---

[4] *Census of Population 2000: Advance Data Release.* (Singapore: Singapore Department of Statistics, 2000), p. 36.

[5] For a detailed analysis that covers many of these issues for all different major religious communities of Singapore, see Tong Chee Kiong, *Rationalising Religion: Religious Conversion, Revivalism and Competition in Singapore Society.* (Leiden: Brill, 2007.)

54% of the Chinese population identified themselves as Buddhists, and this was a major increase from 34% in 1980 and 39% in 1990.

Figure 1 suggests that the growth in the Buddhist population from 1990 to 2000 came mainly at the expense of Taoism which experienced a decline in the number of followers. However, what also stands out is the more recent decline in the proportion of Singaporeans subscribing to Buddhism, from 42.5% in 2000 to 33.3% in 2010. This was the religion's first dip in 30 years. In contrast, the percentages in the other faiths either held steady or grew slightly over the last decade. *The Straits Times* reported that "The decline in Buddhism over the past decade may be traced to the rise of churches, more people wanting to choose their own faith or the lack of one, and greater clarity between Buddhism and Taoism."[6]

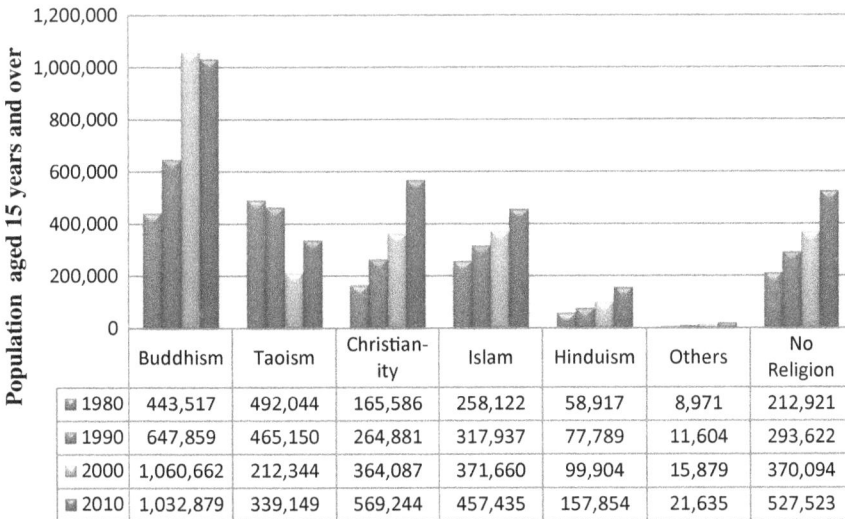

	Buddhism	Taoism	Christian-ity	Islam	Hinduism	Others	No Religion
1980	443,517	492,044	165,586	258,122	58,917	8,971	212,921
1990	647,859	465,150	264,881	317,937	77,789	11,604	293,622
2000	1,060,662	212,344	364,087	371,660	99,904	15,879	370,094
2010	1,032,879	339,149	569,244	457,435	157,854	21,635	527,523

Y-axis: Population aged 15 years and over

Figure 1. Religion and ethnicity from 1980 to 2010.
Source: Census of Population 2000: Advance Data Release No. 2 — Religion (Singapore: Singapore Department of Statistics, 2000), p. 1; *Census of Population 2010: Advance Census Release* (Singapore: Singapore Department of Statistics, 2010), pp. 13–15.[7]

As pointed out earlier, religion in Singapore is closely associated with ethnicity. The latest census in 2010 shows that 97.7% (1,009,158 Singapore residents) of the followers of Buddhism in Singapore are Chinese. Only

---

[6] Yue Feng, "Shedding light on decline in Buddhism", *The Straits Times*, 14 January 2011.
[7] The chart in this article was designed by the authors. For further readings, see Lai Ah Eng, ed., *Religious Diversity in Singapore*. (Singapore: ISEAS, 2008.)

2.3% of the Buddhists in Singapore are Indian or of other races. The 2010 census also indicates that there were more females (517,996) than males (491,163) who identified themselves as Buddhists. There are 26,833 more Chinese female Buddhists than Chinese males. In the Singaporean Chinese community, the level of religious affiliation is positively correlated with age: the higher the age, the higher the level of religious affiliation. Conversely, the younger the age, the higher the proportion reporting no religion. As for Buddhism, it is popular across all age groups but there are higher concentrations of Buddhists amongst the older adults aged 45 years and over.

Buddhism seems to have attracted a sizeable group of followers from all levels of education. The fastest growth was among those with below secondary qualifications. Over the decade, there was a sizeable increase in the proportion of Buddhists among high-school graduates. Their share in the high-school graduate population increased from 15% in 1990 to 24% in 2000. In absolute terms, the number of high-school Buddhists increased fourfold between 1990 and 2000, in contrast to a 1.7 times increase for the high-school Christians. Among those with post-secondary qualifications, the Buddhists have become the largest group with significant gains in the absolute and relative sizes of their population.

Cultural factors, as manifested through the language spoken at home, have a strong influence on the religious affiliation of the resident population. Singapore residents who have adopted English as their home language appear to have greater exposure to the influence of Christianity. Thus, in 2000, Christians formed the largest group among the English-speaking population. In contrast, Buddhism and Taoism, as traditional Chinese religions, are more popular among the Mandarin and dialect-speaking population.

Residents of private apartments and houses tended to have larger representations of Christians and free-thinkers than HDB flat dwellers. In comparison, the bulk of HDB dwellers are Buddhists or Taoists. The findings for self-identifying Buddhists hold for those who affiliate themselves with Taoist temples as well (Tong 1998). Tong points out that most of these structural elements are reversed when it comes to the rising Chinese Christian population.

Buddhism in Singapore

Buddhism in Singapore includes different canonical Buddhist traditions — Mahayana, Theravada and Vajrayana — co-existing and interacting with one another. Rather than fully reflecting the theology of their canonical traditions in the institutions and practice of Buddhism in Singapore, most of the Buddhist temples and organisations follow a pattern based upon the nationality or cultural background of the founding monk or laity. Hence, the diverse origins of Buddhism in Singapore can be traced to the following nations and cultural regions: China, Taiwan, Myanmar, Sri Lanka, Thailand, and Tibet. Within Singapore, we have surveyed 72 Buddhist temples and monasteries, as well as between 30 to 60 folk Buddhist temples.

Mahayana Buddhism in Singapore

Buddhism is currently a dominant religion in Singapore, with over 1 million adherents. There are 72 Buddhist monasteries and temples distributed across the country. Respected and accomplished Singapore born Buddhist monks like Kwang Phing (广品), Kwang Sheng (广声), Wai Yim (惟俨) and Fa Zhao (法照), provide strong leadership to the Buddhist Sangha. Vesak day (the 15th day of the 4th lunar month) was made a national holiday in 1955. To this day it is celebrated by hundreds of thousands of devotees who visit Buddhist monasteries and temples to personally "wash the Buddha" (浴佛) and pray for blessings. Since the establishment of the Buddhist College of Singapore in 2006, Buddhist monasteries can now train their own monks and nuns. This current success story depends on a 150-year history of the evolution of monastic institutions in Singapore. Let us have a quick look at this historical development.

The majority of early Chinese immigrants to Singapore came from southern and southeast China. They belonged to various different dialect groups including Hokkiens, Teochews, Cantonese, Hakkas, Hainanese, Hockchias, Foochows and Henghuas. Since the early 19th century, the various dialect groups have set up their own associations and temples along the Singapore River bank.

In general, the religion brought in by the Chinese immigrants was syncretic in nature — a mixture of Taoism, Confucianism and Buddhism. For instance, in the Hokkien temple Thian Hock Keng (天福宫) on Telok Ayer Street, the patron deity is the Goddess of the Sea (Mazu, 妈祖), but among the secondary gods in the temple are Avalokitesvara (Guanyin Pusa, 观世音菩萨) and Confucius (孔子). As for the Hakka temple Hock Teck See (望海大伯公庙) on Palmer Road, the main deity is the Great Uncle (Dabogong,

大伯公), while the secondary gods include the Most High Lord of the Dao (Taishang Laojun, 太上老君) and Avalokitesvara. In the Teochew temple Yue Hai Qing Miao (粤海清庙) on Phillip Street, the main deities are the God of the Dark Heavens (Xuantian Shangdi, 玄天上帝) and the Goddess of the Sea (Mazu), but the secondary god is Avalokitesvara.

Hence, although Buddhism is generally considered to be the major religion in Singapore, Vivienne Wee argues that "the word 'Buddhist' is actually used as a religious label by [a] variety of people in Singapore whose religious practices and beliefs do not necessarily correspond to those prescribed by the Buddhist Scriptures".[8] This is even more clearly the case with the 30 to 50 temples considered as "folk Buddhist". Some of these temples are dedicated to a combination of gods from the teachings of Buddhism, Taoism and Confucianism. Others combine worship of the Buddha or Guanyin with devotion to the Unborn Eternal Mother (Wusheng Laomu, Xiantian Dao 无生老母, 先天道).[9]

The earliest record of Buddhist monks in Singapore can be found on a wooden tablet in Hang Sun Teng (Pavilion of the Eternal Mountain, 恒山亭), the institution overseeing the Hokkien cemetery in early Singapore. Carved in 1836, this tablet sets out the temple regulations laid down by the management committee. It spells out that the resident monk of the temple should collect monthly donations from Chinese, Siamese and Annamese sailing ships to pay for the temple's incense and candle offerings. If any ship owner refused to contribute, any deceased sailor on his ship would be prohibited from burial in the temple's cemetery grounds.

By the early 20th century, there were more reports of Chinese monks visiting Singapore. Ven. Xian Hui (贤慧) and Ven. Xing Hui (性慧) were on transit while returning from their pilgrimage to Ceylon and India. Ven. Tai Xu (太虚) (1890–1947) came to Singapore as part of his lecture tour to Europe and Ceylon. Ven. Yuan Yin (圆瑛) (1878–1953) and Ven. Ci Hang (慈航) (1893–1954) were invited to deliver Dharma lectures to the general public in Singapore. Ven. Zhuan Dao (转道) (1872–1943) came to raise

---

[8] Vivienne Wee, "Buddhism in Singapore", in Ong Jin Hui, Tong Chee Kiong and Tan Ern Ser, eds., *Understanding Singapore Society*. (Singapore: Times Academic Press, 1997), p. 130.
[9] Marjorie Topley, "The Great Way of Former Heaven: A Group of Chinese Secret Religious Sects", *Bulletin of the School of Oriental and African Studies, University of London,* Vol. 26, No. 2 (1963), pp. 362–392.

funds for the construction of a Dharma college for the Sangha in China. The spread of canonical Buddhism was largely due to these Chinese monks.

Ven. Zhuan Dao played a significant role in the propagation of the Dharma in Singapore. Born in Nan'an, Fujian Province in China, he was ordained at the age of 20.[10] The monk first came to Singapore in 1912 to raise funds for the establishment of a college for Sangha training at Nanputuo Monastery in Xiamen (厦门南普陀寺闽南佛教僧伽院). While in Singapore, he built the Phor Toh See (普陀寺) at Yan Kit Road on land donated by a lay Buddhist. In 1921, he returned to Singapore to preach the Dharma. After receiving generous gifts of land and financial support from another lay Buddhist, he founded the Phor Kark See (菩觉寺) at Bright Hill Road in order to provide accommodation for visiting monks from China. Five years later, he assisted in the establishment of the Chinese Buddhist Association (中华佛教会), the first lay Chinese Buddhist organisation in Singapore. In 1934, Ven. Zhuan Dao helped to organise the Singapore Buddhist Lodge (新加坡佛教居士林) along with Mr Lee Choon Seng (李俊承) (1888–1966) and several other lay followers. By the time Ven. Zhuan Dao passed away in 1943 at the age of 72, he had laid a firm foundation for the development of Chinese Mahayana Buddhism in Singapore.

The earliest Chinese Buddhist monastery in Singapore was the Shuanglinsi (Double Grove Monastery, 双林寺) in Kim Keat Road. The construction of the monastery began in 1898 and was only completed a decade later in 1909 with the support of Mr Low Kim Pong (刘金榜 1837–1909). Mr Low was from Xiamen and he became rich and successful from dealing in traditional Chinese medicine and private banking.[11]

According to an entry in the gazette of the Xi Chan monastery (福州怡山西禅寺) in Fuzhou, both Mr Low and his son had an unusual dream. They dreamt of a golden man arriving from the west. In 1898 Ven. Xian Hui was passing through Singapore on his return trip to China after spending six years on a pilgrimage to Ceylon. Mr Low felt that the golden man in his dream must be Ven. Xian Hui and therefore requested him to stay in Singapore. Ven. Xian Hui accepted his invitation. Subsequently, Mr Low

---

[10] Guang Yi, "Zhuang Dao Lao Heshang Zhuan (The Biography of Master Zhuang Dao)", *Nanyang Fojiao* (Nanyang Buddhism), Vol. 4 (1969), p. 20.

[11] Song Ong Siang, ed., *One Hundred Years' History of the Chinese in Singapore.* (Singapore: University of Malaya Press, 1967), pp. 107–110.

donated 15 acres of land to build the Shuanglin Monastery. This monastery was modelled after the Xi Chan monastery in Fuzhou. All the building materials were imported from Fujian province. Ven. Xian Hui passed away two years later in 1901 and Mr Low died in 1909 before the monastery's opening ceremony.[12] This monastery remains an important centre for Buddhism in Singapore, and is now, after extensive renovations, one of the most beautiful and graceful Buddhist sites in the nation.

The largest Chinese Buddhist monastery in Singapore is the Kong Meng San Phor Kark See Monastery (光明山菩觉寺) founded by Ven. Zhuan Dao in 1921. It was built in the middle of a rubber plantation in Bright Hill Road. The subsequent abbots, including Ven. Hong Choon (宏船 1907–1990), Ven. Yan Pei (演培 1917–1996) and Ven. Kwang Sheng (广声), contributed to the expansion of the monastery and played a pro-active role in propagating the Dharma. It is currently one of the major Buddhist monastic centres in Southeast Asia.

In the attempt to make Singapore a model international Buddhist hub, the monastery founded the Buddhist College of Singapore (BCS) in 2005 and received its first cohort of students in August 2006. The first Buddhist training institution in Singapore, the founding purpose of the BCS is to contribute to the development of Chinese Buddhism and its spread in the English-speaking world. This is accomplished by nurturing its students to be effectively bilingual in English and Mandarin, grounding them in Buddhist doctrine and knowledge while instilling in them the ability to promulgate the faith and to engage in academic research.

After Singapore became independent in 1965, the Societies Act of 1966 required all Buddhist monasteries and temples in Singapore to be managed by their own registered Management Committees. The religious organisations were to run their premises and conduct their activities based on their constitutions. However, these temples continue to have strong links with and support from Buddhist organisation such as the Singapore Buddhist Federation (新加坡佛教总会), the Chinese Buddhist Association, the Buddhist Union (佛教会) and the Buddhist Free Clinic (新加坡佛教施诊所). The networks connecting the main Buddhist institutions of Singapore have now expanded across Southeast Asia and China.

---

[12] Lim How Seng *et al.*, eds., *Sile Guji* (*Singapore's Historical Relics*). (Singapore: Nanyang Xuehui, 1975), pp. 49–52.

The Singapore Chinese Buddhist Laity and Lay Buddhist Organisations

In the 1940s, a number of Chinese lay Buddhists such as Lee Choon Seng (李俊承 1888–1966), Zhuang Duming (庄笃明 1892–1947) and Khoo Seok Wan (邱菽园 1884–1941) played a pivotal role in promoting Mahayana Buddhism in Singapore. Among the Chinese laity, Mr Lee Choon Seng deserves special mention. Mr Lee Choon Seng was born in Yong Chun in Fujian and left China as a young man to join his father in Negri Sembilan, Malaya. Later, he came to Singapore to set up his own business. He became a key director of the Overseas Chinese Bank Corporation (OCBC) bank and was one of the leaders in the Chinese community of Singapore from 1930s to 1960s. Mr Lee was not only actively involved in the propagation of Buddhism, he also helped to set up the Singapore Buddhist Lodge and the Singapore Buddhist Federation.[13]

The Singapore Buddhist Lodge (SBL) was established in 1934 thanks to the collaborative efforts of Ven. Zhuan Dao, Ven. Swee Teng (瑞等), Mr Lee Choon Seng, Khoo Seok Wan, Zhuang Du Ming and others. Initially, the SBL was set up as a sutra publication and distribution centre to circulate Chinese Mahayana sutras in Singapore. This centre later founded the Lian Serh Sutra Chanting Society. Mr Lee Choon Seng donated a double-storey house located at 26 Blair Road to the Lodge for its activities. With generous financial support from Mr Lee, the SBL expanded very quickly and soon had a membership of over 100, with many of the members coming from the Chinese social elite.

Besides promoting Mahayana Buddhism, SBL also carried out welfare activities such as providing financial support to the poor and the elderly.[14] Today, SBL is located at Kim Yam Road and is among the largest lay Buddhist organisations in Singapore. It provides three free meals daily to several thousand people as well as rice and cooking oil to Yayasan Mendaki and the Singapore Indian Development Association (SINDA). For the past 10 years, it has invited representatives from other faiths to share the celebration of Buddhism's most important annual event, Vesak Day, in Little India.

---

[13] Li Jun Cheng, *Jueyuan Xuii (A Postscript to Complete Enlightenment)*. (Singapore: Nanyang Publication, 1956), p. 61.

[14] "Jue Yuan Li Jun Cheng Lao Ju Shi Shi Lue (A Brief History of the Old Lay Buddhist Li Jun Cheng)", *The Meeting Report of Singapore Buddhist Federation: 1st January to 31st December 1966* (Singapore: Singapore Buddhist Federation, 1967), p. 30.

Little India's Vesak day celebrations have become an excellent opportunity for people from different faiths to network and to share experiences and knowledge with one another.

The Singapore Buddhist Federation (SBF) is the umbrella Buddhist organisation of Buddhist temples and monasteries in Singapore. On 31 July 1949, Mr Lee Choon Seng took the initiative to invite representatives from all the mainstream Chinese Buddhist temples to the SBL to discuss the formation of a nation-wide Buddhist organisation. A preparatory committee was set up after all representatives showed their support. Subsequently, the SBF was officially registered on 30 October 1949. Mr Lee was elected as the Chairman.

The five guiding objectives of the SBF were to promote world peace, to promote the Dharma, to expand Buddhist education, to carry out welfare services (such as scholarships for students), and to raise the quality of Sangha members.

SBF took over the management of the Maha Bodhi Primary School (菩提学校) in 1950. MBS had been established two years earlier on 20 January 1948. In 1950, the school principal Ms Pitt Chin Hui (毕俊辉) and the management committee decided to place the school under SBF. In 1982 SBF set up Manjusri Secondary School (文殊中学). In 1952, SBF set up a Buddhist cemetery of 110 acres at Chua Chu Kang Road. In 1955, SBF and representatives from Theravada Buddhist organisations successfully petitioned the government to have Vesak Day gazetted as a public holiday in Singapore. After Mr Lee stepped down in 1964, Ven. Hong Choon (1907–1990), the abbot of Phor Kark See Monastery, succeeded him as Chairman. Ven. Hong Choon was succeeded by Ven. Kwang Sheng. The current Chairman of SBF is Ven. Kwang Phing. As of 2013, the SBF has 128 institutional members.

Singapore's third Buddhist school is Mee Toh Primary School (弥陀学校), built in 1954 largely through the efforts of Ven. Kong Hiap (广洽 1990–1994) the abbot of Leong San Si (龙山寺) in Race Course Road. The school has since been relocated to Punggol.

The Buddhist Free Clinic was established in 1969 by Ven. Hong Choon and Ven. Siong Khye (常凯). This clinic provides medical consultation and medication for a nominal fee. The Singapore Buddhist Free Clinic now has branches at Geylang West, Tanjong Pagar, Redhill, Delta, Ang Mo Kio,

Jurong East, and Sembawang to provide medical care and rehabilitative services.

Buddhist, Sectarian and Redemptive Religious Movements

The Kwan Im Thong (观音堂) in Waterloo Street traces its origins to the Teachings of Prior Heaven (Xiantianjiao), a redemptive society that worships the Buddha and the Unborn Mother (Wusheng Laomu), which spread across China and subsequently to Southeast Asia in the late Qing dynasty.[15] The main temple hall is dedicated to the worship of Guanyin. The temple has a constant stream of worshippers and its charitable foundation is one of the wealthiest charities in Singapore. In 1991 the "Kwan Im Thong Hood Cho Temple-NKF (National Kidney Foundation) Dialysis Centre" was set up in Simei. Since then the temple foundation has been contributing $1.5 million to it annually. The Kwan Im Thong has also supported education through endowing professorships at the National University of Singapore (NUS). It has engaged in many other forms of charity as well, making major contributions to society.

Other groups of Chinese temples are affiliated to the Teochew Shantang (潮州善堂) and the Dejiaohui (Association for the Teachings of Virtue, 德教会). The former has 12 temples in Singapore. These all worship the Song dynasty Buddhist monk Song Dafeng (宋大峰祖师), who is credited with founding the movement. Historical records suggest that the Shantang began to get involved in charitable works during the Ming dynasty. This temple network spread to Thailand, Malaysia and Singapore with the migration of Teochew merchants and labourers. The temples practise spirit writing (扶箕、鸾笔) to encourage morality and good works, and participants chant scriptures dedicated to Master Song Dafeng. The Shantang have organised many free traditional Chinese medical clinics around Singapore. They were also at the centre of the Blue Cross medical teams that cared for the sick and wounded Singaporeans during the Japanese Occupation. The Shantang have also donated substantial sums to the NKF.

Dejiao is a more recent religious movement that started before World War II in Chaozhou (Teochew) and spread to Southeast Asia in the 1950s and 1960s. Their temples are dedicated to the leaders of all the world's great

---

[15] Marjorie Topley, "The Great Way of Former Heaven: A Group of Chinese Secret Religious Sects", *Bulletin of the School of Oriental and African Studies, University of London*, Vol. 26, No. 2 (1963), pp. 362–392.

religions. Spirit writing enables these deities to communicate with their worshippers. Dejiao has 12 temples in Singapore. They are also actively involved in charitable works and support the provision of medical services, old age care, scholarships, and other worthy causes.

One of these temples established the Thye Hua Kwan Moral Society (THK, 太和观), a non-profit voluntary welfare organisation in 1978. This organisation provides community-based social, health, and educational services to all, regardless of race, language, and religion. Currently, the THK group of charities operates more than 50 centres and services which include the Ang Mo Kio-Thye Hua Kwan Hospital (AMK-THKH) and the Thye Hua Kwan Moral Charities (THKMC). They also run four welfare homes, five family service centres, 14 senior activity centres, and several centres for early intervention for infants with disabilities.

Theravadea Buddhism in Singapore

There are 19 Thai Buddhist temples and religious institutions with some 80 resident monks in Singapore. The oldest Thai temple in Singapore is the Wat Ananada Metyarma. It was completed in 1925 and is located at Jalan Bukit Merah. The current Chief Abbot, Ven. Chao Khun Phra Tepsiddhivides, is also one of the Buddhist leaders involved with the Inter-Religious Organisation (IRO), an organisation that promotes religious understanding and harmony in Singapore.

After a major renovation which took 11 years (1975–1986) to complete, Wat Ananda Metyarama was given the authority to ordain monks. The construction of a three-storey extension to house the library of Buddhist sutras, Dharma classrooms, and a meditation hall was completed in 1996. This temple was partially sponsored by the Thai Government, but all the other Thai temples in Singapore were either built by the monks or by lay followers, including many Chinese supporters.

Other significant Thai Buddhist monasteries in Singapore include the Sakyamuni Gaya Temple, with its 50-feet high standing Buddha and its reclining Buddha, built by Ven. Vuthissara in 1927. Ven. Vuthissara conducted rites of worship and explained Buddhist philosophy to interested visitors until his death at the age of 94.

Wat Palelai was founded in 1963 by Madam Mary Yap. The Branch Temple at Bedok Walk was completed in 1973. The purchase of land was funded by contributions from Thai, Malaysian, and Singaporean Buddhists. Sattha Puchaniyaram Buddhist Temple was first established at Holland Road in 1963. Ven. Phraku Saddhanukul, alias Foo Hong Kim, a Singaporean, received his ordination in Alor Star, Kedah, Malaysia. Soon after he returned to Singapore from his Buddhist studies in Penang and Bangkok, he rebuilt the Holland Road temple. In 1984, the temple relocated to its present site (Bukit Batok), due to a road widening project.

Wat Uttamayanmuni Thai Buddhist Temple is closely affiliated with the Kelantanese Thai monastic chapter in Malaysia. In 1962, Jao Khun Khron was invited to visit Singapore. Mr Tan Khe Wat, a Singaporean, offered 2.5 hectares of land to him to build a Thai temple in Singapore.

Singhalese and Burmese Sangha, Temples, and Organisations

There are presently two Sinhalese temples in Singapore, namely Sri Lankaramaya and Mangala Vihara. An earlier small Sinhalese temple was located at Outram Road. The first Sinhalese Buddhist organisation was the Singapore Buddhist Association (SBA), founded in 1923. The SBA was set up by the prominent Ceylonese monk — Ven. M.M. Mahaweera Maha Nayaka Thero (1913–2002). In 1939, he bought land in Outram Road and built a new temple on it. He also started a Sunday Dharma school and organised the Pali Section of the SBA.

Many English-educated Chinese, especially the Peranakans, were attracted to the Outram Road temple. Hence, bigger premises were urgently needed. Subsequently, Ven. Mahaweera collected donations to build the Sri Lankaramaya at St. Michael's Road in 1952. With a stupa, a Bodhi tree, Buddha images, and an Ordination Hall, the temple is considered a complete monastery under the Theravada tradition. Since its foundation, many Sri Lankan monks have come to Singapore to serve in the temple.

The Mangala Vihara in Eunos Road was established primarily to serve the Peranakan and English-educated Chinese Buddhist community. This temple was also founded by Ven. Mahaweera Maha Nayaka Thero and was built on land donated by Madam Chew Quee Neo. The monastery was competed in 1966.

The Burmese Buddhist Temple (BBT) is the only Burmese temple in Singapore. The present BBT was built in 1990 to replace the previous small BBT at 17 Kinta Road. From its humble beginnings, the BBT gradually expanded as a result of the untiring efforts of U Kyaw Gaung, also known as

Khoo Teogou, a Burmese practitioner of traditional medicine. Its magnificent marble Buddha image is the biggest outside Burma. Besides Dharma classes and religious festivals, Burmese traditional celebrations such as New Year (Thingyan) are regularly held in the temple.

Vajrayana Buddhism in Singapore

Vajrayana Buddhism, more commonly known as Tibetan Buddhism, is a comparatively recent entrant to Singapore. In fact, the first Tibetan Buddhist organisation was only established three decades ago. There are now 42 Tibetan Buddhist organisations in Singapore.

The Singapore Buddha Sasana Society, the first Tibetan Buddhist organisation in Singapore, was founded in the 1970s. When the society bought their first premises at 9 Topaz Road, Ven. Sakya Trizin sent Ponlop Lama Tashi Tenzin, one of the highest ranking monks in the order, to guide the members in their understanding of the Buddha's teachings. Ponlop Lama Tashi Tenzin was the Principal of the Tantric College of Sakya Monastery in Tibet and he became the society's first resident monk. The society had to move a second time (to Geylang) as a result of land acquisition for the expansion of the Pan Island Expressway. In 1990 the temple finally moved to its current new home, Sakya Tenphel Ling, which was constructed at 5 Pasir Ris Drive 4.[16]

The Karma Kagyud Buddhist Centre (KKBC) was founded in 1981. In 1979, Ven. Kunzig Shamar Rinpoche visited Singapore. With his encouragement and advice, a committee headed by Mr David Chee Kim Swee was formed in preparation for the founding of KKBC in Singapore. In 1981, the Registrar of Societies approved the registration of KKBC. In 1990, Rinpoche initiated the search for a new location to cater to the expansion of the centre's activities and in December 1991, KKBC relocated to its present location, in Geylang.

The Amitabha Buddhist Centre (ABC) was officially established in January 1989. It is affiliated to the Foundation for the Preservation of the Mahayana Tradition (FPMT), an international, non-profit organisation

---

[16] Singapore Buddha Sasana Society, accessed on 10 December 2010: http://www.sakyatenphelling.org.

founded by Lama Yeshe. The FPMT is devoted to the transmission of the Mahayana Buddhist tradition worldwide through teaching, meditation and community service. While he was on retreat in India, Rinpoche had a very strong instinct about having a Dharma centre in Singapore. The feeling became so overwhelming that by the end of his retreat, he was determined to go to Singapore and establish a Dharma centre, which he did in 1985. ABC today offers opportunities for the study and practice of Tibetan Buddhism through public talks, the publication of free Dharma books, Buddhist study courses, meditation classes, pujas, animal liberation rituals, community service, recreational activities, retreats, and pilgrimages.

If the Theravadin Buddhist monasteries appear to have appealed largely to Peranakan and English-educated Chinese, the same may not be the case for Tantric or Tibetan Buddhism in Singapore. As in many modern societies in the West, or in Taiwan, or even in contemporary China, many younger, highly educated Chinese Singaporeans are turning to Tibetan Buddhism in search of an alternative to overly commercialised culture.

Finally, there are several global Buddhist organisations or Buddhist sectarian groups active in Singapore, such as the Taiwanese Human Realm Buddhist organisation Ciji (Merciful Salvation), the Fagu (Dharma Drum), and Foguang (Buddha Radiance) temples. Redemptive religious movements like the Yiguandao have a presence in Singapore as well, with an estimated 80,000 followers and 1,000 household sacred spaces, as well as unofficial temples. Japanese Buddhist movements like Soko Gakai also have temples and activities in Singapore. Soko Gakai has participated in national events like the National Day parade.

Taoism in Singapore

Taoism in Singapore can be discussed narrowly in terms of the Taoist Ritual Masters, their liturgical troupes and rituals. Taoist ritual masters from each of the main dialect communities of Singapore are still active today, performing rituals in hundreds of temples dedicated to the local gods of the different regional pantheons. More broadly defined, Taoism includes temples dedicated to locally, regionally and nationally known gods. These temples maintain close ties with Taoist ritual specialists, and often host their own temple keepers and spirit mediums. The Taoist Federation of Singapore, founded 25 years ago, is an organisation that represents these temples and their communities of worshippers. These are the people who primarily identify themselves as Taoists in the Singapore Census, although it is important to recall that many Chinese Singaporeans see little distinction between worshipping Buddha and worshipping regional or local gods.

Taoist temples, many of them built in the early days of the British settlement of Singapore in 1819, can mostly be traced to the founding temples in Fujian and Guangdong. These temples were mainly dedicated to the deities worshipped by the different dialect groups that migrated to Singapore. Each dialect group has its own unique tradition of Taoist ritual. These ritual specialists were invited to consecrate new temples and to celebrate the birthdays of the gods. Many temples in Singapore also have spirit mediums of the resident deities and communicate with worshippers in the name of the gods.

Our survey located over 500 (Taoist) temples. Of these, over 350 are now housed in 68 united (or combined) temples. With the exception of a small number of temples on the register of historical monuments or with freehold land, these temples have had to relocate every 30 years to make way for urban redevelopment. The survival of these temples is a testimony to the vitality and power of the ritual traditions that underlie them, which create community even when their membership is scattered across Singapore. We also found a large number of spirit mediums operating within Housing & Development Board (HDB) flats. Some observers have estimated that there could be more than 1,000 of these. Some of these mediums raise enough funding over time to set up temples to their deities.

In very general terms, there were four phases in the development of Taoism in Singapore (1819–1911, 1911–1965, 1965–1985, 1985–2015). From 1819 to 1911 each of the Chinese dialect communities built several hundred temples dedicated to the gods of their home villages in Southeast and Southern China. Temples were also the gathering places and focal points of each dialect group. Many clan associations sprouted from temple grounds. Towards the end of this period, some Chinese leaders such as Cheang Hong Lim (章芳林) (1841–1893) tried to build temples that would encourage the different dialect communities to come together, such as Giok Hong Tian (Temple of the Jade Emperor, 玉皇殿). Another temple that appealed to common surname groups across dialect divides was the Po Chiak Keng Tan Si Chong Su (保赤宫陈氏宗祠) at Magazine Road.

The second period between 1911 and 1965 saw the rise of the Chinese Chamber of Commerce and the support of many Singapore Chinese elites for nationalism and even revolutionary socialism in China. During this period, Chinese elites, including early SCCC business leaders, English-educated Confucian scholars like Lim Boon Keng (林文庆 1869–1957), and reformist Buddhist leaders all tried to transform society in the name of progress by attacking Chinese folk religion. Nevertheless, local temples continued to flourish up to World War II. During the Japanese occupation, religious groups like the Teochew Shantang managed to continue to provide support to the community through the Blue Cross.

After the establishment of the Republic of Singapore, the Government introduced a Master Plan for Urban Development, created satellite towns and passed the Land Acquisition Act in 1966, giving it control of all land except freehold land. During this third phase of very rapid change (1965–1985), hundreds of Chinese temples were forced to move, sometimes multiple times, to make way for urban development projects. Most temples were granted only a 30-year lease and had to find ways to raise funds in anticipation of another move at the end of the lease period.

Many temples simply closed their doors. Others joined forces to survive. This was the period that saw the first of the "united temples" such as the Five-fold Combined Temple (伍合庙) in Tao Payoh, built in 1974. Later, united temples would have as many as 13 different temples merged under one roof, each setting up a shrine to its own deity, all placed in a row. This kind of arrangement has recently led to calls for the construction of a high-rise temple complex which could accommodate a temple on each floor. Whether or not this idea eventually materialises, it makes evident the space pressures under which the Chinese temples of Singapore operate.

Clearly the Government was deeply engaged during this period in building an economically successful new Singapore. Nevertheless, it provided some space for religious organisations in its planning and established auctions for the purchase of spaces set aside for religious uses in each of the

16 new satellite towns. But the long-term effect of these policies was to encourage many temples to move from town centres to industrial zones, or to relocate to freehold land in Geylang. The rapid industrialisation of Singapore, urban redevelopment and displacement of many villages and temples, and the emphasis on English language education for a globally engaged workforce all had a debilitating effect on the Chinese temples and associations, which went through a long period of decline during this phase. However, developments inside China, especially the Cultural Revolution, encouraged some temples to persevere, as they feared that their ancestral traditions might be lost in their home villages in China.

The fourth phase began in the mid-1980s and culminated with the establishment of the Singapore Taoist Federation (新加坡道教总会) in 1990. In response to the dramatic drop in numbers of Taoists, many Chinese temples decided to get together to propagate the Taoist faith. The founding Chairman of the Singapore Taoist Federation was Master Tan Kok Hian (陈国显). Since 2002, the Chairman has been Mr Tan Thiam Lye (陈添来).

During this period many temples and associations returned to China to rebuild their founding temples, ancestral halls and Buddhist monasteries. The Koo Chye Ba Sheng Hong Temple (韭菜芭城隍庙) helped rebuild the Anxi City God Temple (安溪城隍庙) in Anxi, Fujian, from which it had divided incense at its founding in 1918. With the subsequent rise of the Chinese economy, many of these networks became even more powerful. In November 2014, the Singapore Lam Ann Association (南安会馆) and the Hong San See Temple (凤山寺) purchased two seats on a jet to fly a statue of their patron deity, Guangze Zunwang (The Revered Lord of Broad Compassion, (广泽尊王) from Fujian to Singapore. The god was then paraded around all the branch temples in Singapore. This is just one example of the transformation of the Chinese Taoist temple system in Singapore in recent years.

A final example is the rising importance of the Nine Emperor God celebrations (九皇诞), which were attended last year (October 2014) by the Prime Minister and several other Ministers. These celebrations involve large processions (mostly on lorries) to the sea. Like all religious events, such public processions are strictly regulated. Nevertheless, the presence of government leaders at these events suggests the increasing importance attached to Taoism.

The Chinese temples in Singapore participate actively in charitable work, providing support for many local community as well as national initiatives. Some support hospitals and elderly care centres such as the Bo Tian Welfare Services Society. Some temples such as the Doutian gong and the Zhenren gong hold major events to raise funds for charity, as does the Sanhuang Wudi spirit medium altar.

Chinese Christians in Singapore

Over the past five decades, increasing numbers of Chinese Singaporeans have become members of different Protestant Christian and Catholic denominations. The Christian community has also made crucial contributions to the development of Singapore over the past 50 years, especially through church-supported educational institutions, hospitals, as well as other welfare organisations. Some students of global Christianity have pointed out that for many people in Asia, conversion to Christianity is regarded as a kind of conversion to modernity. Christianity is often seen as being compatible with science and progress. Christianity became the model for the reform of Buddhist organisations, and a partner with the secular state in the rejection of popular religion as superstition and an obstacle to progress.

The Christian movement in Singapore can be divided into three periods — the early period of the establishment of the Catholic dioceses and the various Protestant denominations (1819–1965), the rise of liberal social doctrines of the 1960s, and the rise of Pentacostal prosperity doctrines from the 1990s. From the point of view of the Singapore secular state, the swift increase in the numbers of Christians in Singapore could potentially lead to the disruption of religious harmony and multiculturalism due to proselytising. The Government imposed strict limits in 1987 on Catholic groups which had adopted third-world liberation theology critiques of the negative effects of global capitalism. Some church figures were subsequently arrested.

The later rapid rise of the Pentacostal Church movement relates to its ability to adapt to the view of the state when it comes to promoting progress, while also fitting in with the overall trends of global capitalism (i.e., interpreting prosperity as a sign of God's favour). However, the Pentacostal movement also has a strong emphasis on proselytising (through what they called the Global Spiritual Warfare), which is a source of concern to the Government.

Despite these issues, Christianity continues to flourish in contemporary Singapore, and the current discussions between Pentacostal and evangelical leaders of the church indicate that they are taking a serious look at the calling of the church to address social issues once again.[17]

Conclusion

In the 19th century, Singapore's Chinese community members were mostly firm believers in deities related to their home dialect regions. However, due to the efforts of many Buddhists monks and lay people during the 20th century, Mahayana, Theravada and Vajrayana schools of Buddhism were successfully transmitted to Singapore. Contemporary Singapore has seen over a hundred years of historical Buddhist influence that has greatly enriched the city's culture, literature and arts. Other religious traditions have also flourished, though there have been many struggles on a day-to-day basis for the survival of particular temples in the face of rapid urban development. The deeper question remains whether the state project of secularisation and modernisation can open up to a broader understanding of the variety of modes of human flourishing. For this to happen, Buddhist as well as Christian, Taoist, Islamic and Hindu religious leaders will have to lead the way by engaging in inter-faith dialogue as well as participating in conversations with secularists and government planners. Such dialogue must seek to reframe the question of Singapore's future evolution, by exploring the wealth of resources within its rich and diverse religious heritage.

---

[17] For further information, see Bobby E.K. Sng, *In His Good Time: The Story of the Church in Singapore 1819–2002* (3rd edn.). (Singapore: Bible Society of Singapore, 2003); Daniel Goh, "State and Social Christianity in Post-colonial Singapore", *SOJOURN: Journal of Social Issues in Southeast Asia*, Vol. 25, No. 1 (2010), pp. 54–89; Terrence Chong and Hui Yew Feng, *Different Under God: A Survey of Church-going Protestants in Singapore.* (Singapore: ISEAS, 2013.)

Section 3

Chinese Visual & Performing Arts

Chapter 10

Towards a Nanyang Culture

CHOO Thiam Siew

During the 1970s and early 1980s, when Singapore was pre-occupied with nation-building by concentrating on economic growth, the arts and culture were given less attention. S. Rajaratnam, one of the ministers in the first cabinet who rose to be Deputy Prime Minister even warned that Singaporeans only knew "the price of everything and the value of nothing". This was the stage when Singapore was often but erroneously described as a "cultural desert".

Today, financial assets continue to be a major measure of success, but past efforts (notably begun in the late 1990s) to make Singapore a vibrant Renaissance City are bearing fruit. With government prodding and support and a growing talent pool, the arts community is buzzing with new ideas and innovations. The iconic Esplanade by the Bay, the new National Art Gallery and the Singapore Chinese Cultural Centre currently under construction all attest to the national focus on turning Singapore into an arts and entertainment hub.

The palpable excitement among arts practitioners has also infected the Chinese-speaking community. The references to *xinyao* (新谣) and Nanyang culture by Prime Minister Lee Hsien Loong in his National Day rally speech in 2014 has stirred considerable interest and discussion in the Chinese arts community.

Xinyao, literally meaning "new song" or "Singapore song", generally refers to the movement spawned in the 1980s by young Singaporeans which created a new genre of songs that depicted their hopes and aspirations. Distinguished by their inclusion of local terms and places, these

Chinese songs gained a wide following in the 1990s and formed the spring-board of many Singapore songwriters. The songs penned by Liang Wern Fook (who was awarded a Cultural Medallion for his contributions to the music scene) and many others, continue to be popular today.

In the following four essays, we try to show the development of four major art streams in the Singapore Chinese community — painting, callig-raphy, music and dance.

Dr Bridget Tan's contribution on Chinese painting points out that the idea of a Nanyang style was mooted by our artists as far back as the 1940s. Wong Joon Tai, who began teaching calligraphy after he retired from gov-ernment service, is optimistic that this traditional Chinese art form will continue to thrive in modern Singapore.

Terence Ho's essay on the development of Chinese orchestral music highlights the efforts by the Singapore Chinese Orchestra to infuse elements from our multiracial environment as well as our regional neighbours into its compositions and performances. Edmond Wong, whose wife is Creative Director of the Dance Ensemble of Singapore, is passionate about the need to balance tradition with modernity in the local cultural scene.

The fact is that Singapore's Chinese art practitioners have long recog-nised that their cultural roots are tied to the region, geographically called Southeast Asia and historically better known as "*Nanyang*" (南洋). While China's art forms and practices had influenced the Singapore Chinese immi-grant community, and while they would continue to shape our future artistic developments, today's Singaporeans recognise that these influences have to be adapted to be in sync with our multiracial and multicultural nation.

Slowly but surely, the Singapore Chinese are evolving our own visual and performing arts. They would continue to be known as "Chinese" paint-ings, music or dance, but they would include components from our non-Chinese compatriots as well as our regional neighbours. In short, the Singapore Chinese cultural identity needs to be an amalgam of our Chinese traditions and our multiracial environment.

The Singapore Chinese Cultural Centre, scheduled for completion in late 2016, intends to play a catalytic role in this metamorphosis and be a centre of resources and activities to promote our local culture.

CHAPTER 11

The Transformation of Chinese Visual Arts in Nanyang*

Bridget Tracy TAN

The diversity of visual art reflects Singapore's plural communities in the last 100 years. In the field of Chinese painting what is not often acknowledged is how the national fervour nascent in the first republic of China in the early 20th century was catalytic in endeavours to create a new, indigenous art centred in this region popularly referred to as Nanyang.

Many of the Chinese artists who travelled to Southeast Asia returned to China after a while. But for those who stayed, their artistic journeys incorporated the modernisation and revolutionary mood so often acknowledged in Chinese art history. The immigrant artists also brought with them the many layers of Western ideas and methodology that had influenced Chinese art in past centuries.

The increase of Jesuit missionaries during the Kangxi reign (1661–1722) of the Qing dynasty brought with it Western art techniques, including drawing and perspective. Archival evidence demonstrates particularly the incorporation of Western perspective into Chinese painting, providing a new and stimulating form of realism in traditional Chinese art of the time.[1] Even before this, Western influences had found their way into Chinese painting as noted by the early Qing painter, Wu Li (吴历 1632–1718). Wu himself

---

* All paintings in this essay were obtained from the Collection of the Nanyang Academy of Fine Arts (NAFA) and reproduced with permission.
[1] John W O'Malley *et al.*, eds., *The Jesuits II: Cultures, Sciences, and the Arts, 1540–1773*. (Canada: University of Toronto Press Incorporated, 2006), pp. 263–264.

was a baptised Catholic missionary who had travelled to Europe before returning to the Yangtze Delta to paint.[2] It cannot be overstated that long before the establishment of the international settlement in Shanghai as one centre of modern art in China, Western ideas, technology and art had already infiltrated Chinese culture and the arts.

In 1935, the Singapore Society of Chinese Artists (新加坡中华美术研究会) began life as the Salon Art Society in Malaya, with a membership numbering less than 15 due to its restrictive membership eligibility. All members had to be graduates of the Shanghai School of Art and the Xinhua Art Academy, institutions that reached their peak within the international settlement in Shanghai during the first republic. With the name change and official registration in 1936, the Society drew a larger membership that absorbed the waves of migrants arriving into Malaya from the Chinese mainland, Taiwan and Hong Kong. The lineage of these artists can be clearly traced back to the May Fourth and corresponding New Culture Movement of the first republic. Modernism in art and painting was advocated to stimulate changes in society and culture. It was the catalyst to modernise Chinese communities within China as well as the ones formed by those who had left China and arrived in Malaya before World War II. The prevalent trends and philosophies hinged around democratic values, individualism, as well as reinterpretations of ancient teachings with notable influence on Chinese culture and identity, such as Confucianism, Buddhism and Taoism.

The first two decades of the new republic saw greater infusion of Western influence through Japan and France. Japanese artists were brought in to teach Western drawing techniques. Concurrently China sent artists to Japan for cultural immersions that included exposure to the modern art of Europe. The first 20 years of the new century spawned art schools and colleges across many Chinese provinces. Art academies such as the Xiamen Meishu Xuexiao (厦门美术学校) (f. 1923), China Academy of Art (中国美术学院) (f. 1928), Shanghai Meizhuan (上海美专) (registered 1915) and later Xinhua Yishu Zhuanke Xuexiao (新华艺术专科学校) (f. 1926) taught both Western and Chinese traditional art practices.[3] The artists we refer to

---

[2] Richard M Barnhart *et al.*, *Three Thousand Years of Chinese Painting*. (New Haven, London & Beijing: Yale University and Foreign Languages Press, 1997), p. 264.
[3] Michael Sullivan, *Art and Artists of Twentieth Century China*. (California: University of California Press, 1996), pp. 42–46.

as the pioneer generation of Singapore such as Chen Wen Hsi (陈文希), Chen Chong Swee (陈宗瑞), Lim Hak Tai (林学大), Liu Kang (刘抗) and Cheong Soo Pieng (钟泗宾), among others, were trained in these schools. Their journey to Singapore (or what was then Malaya) in the 1930s introduced their cross-cultural training to the Straits.

The teaching of art was commonplace in Chinese schools such as Hwa Chong Institute formerly Chinese High School (华侨中学) that was founded in 1919 by the philanthropist and businessman Tan Kah Kee (陈嘉庚) and Chung Cheng High School (中正中学), founded in 1939 by a Hakka descendant, Aw Boon Haw (胡文虎). The pioneer generation artists taught part-time at these schools, but also conducted private lessons in art. In 1938, they were co-opted as specialist teachers in the newly founded Nanyang Academy of Fine Arts (NAFA) (南洋艺术学院).

At NAFA, training for fine arts was divided into two main categories: the foundations of Western art such as painting and drawing, and the foundations of Chinese painting and calligraphy. Mediums such as charcoal, pen, ink, pastels, watercolour and oil were covered in Western art training. Chinese painting was taught largely through traditional genres of birds and flowers, landscapes and bamboo, all typical subjects one might encounter today (Figures 1 and 2).

While the Western elements can be traced to the Modern European influences that had proliferated in early 20th century China, the Chinese paradigms are slightly more layered. In general, Chinese painting in the Straits drew from the traditions of the Lingnan (嶺南畫派) and Shanghai (海上画派) "schools". These "schools" broadly encapsulated the changing strains of traditional Chinese painting between the Ming and Qing dynasties. Historians have traditionally referred to this process and practice as the modernisation and revolution of Chinese painting. The artists of these new styles such as Gao Jianfu (高劍父), Wu Changshuo (吴昌硕) and He Tianjian (贺天健) for instance, advocated a more casual air in execution (as opposed to the rigidity of ancient Chinese painting and its strict traditions) and the need to inject greater realism that reflected a true response to the local environment (as opposed to the academic rigours of old paradigms that focused on stock subject matter and techniques of representation).

In the Straits Settlements, the Chinese paintings of Chen Wen Hsi and Chen Chong Swee often manifested the Lingnan school concept, articulating

Figure 1. Chen Wen Hsi, Bamboo and Birds, c. 1980s, Chinese ink and colour on paper, 45 × 34.5 cm (by Courtesy of NAFA).

Figure 2. Che Cheng Lin (车澄霖), 1987 Bird on Rock, Chinese ink and colour on paper, 140 × 69 cm (by Courtesy of NAFA).

looser brushwork, daring expressionistic techniques and in some instances, local flora and fauna as well as local landscape profiles (trees, coastlines and rural pathways for example).

During the first half of the 20th century, the Straits welcomed many Chinese artists, such as Xu Beihong (徐悲鸿), Liu Haisu (刘海粟), Guan Shanyue (关山月), Pan Shou (潘受) and Wu Tsai Yen (吴在炎), some of whom stayed on and settled in Singapore. In those early decades, the Chinese artists also brought with them mastery of Western realism, Western techniques of mathematical perspective and subtlety in tonal values. Additionally, their foundation in Chinese mediums allowed for an expansion of the literati forms that included seal carving, calligraphy, poetry writing and ink painting. In some instances, particularly in the work of Chen Wen Hsi and Cheong Soo Pieng (Figure 3), ink painting even became infused with more abstract concepts found in Modern European art forms, such as cubism.

With the different influences established within Malaya, the artists felt poised to seek out a vernacular in visual art that would adequately reflect their new experiences within the region. This confidence to extend Chinese

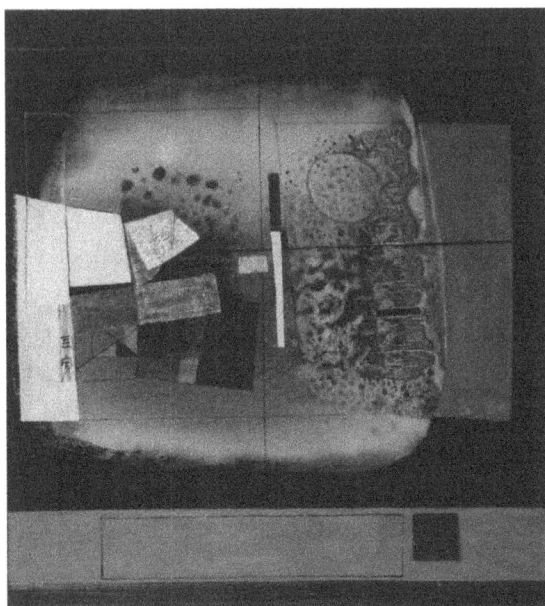

Figure 3. Cheong Soo Pieng, Composition 1, 1973, oil and mixed media on canvas, 100 × 92 cm (by Courtesy of NAFA).

art into the region was boosted by the newly established NAFA, led by its dynamic principal, Lim Hak Tai (林学大). As its name suggested, Nanyang would be the core of NAFA's artistic extension to the region.

As a start, Lim issued a manifesto of sort, outlining six principles that could shape the future of local visual arts in the region. Art had social and cultural as well as political premises. Art needed a role that would offer social bonds within the community and advance thought, learning and growth in a fledgling society like Malaya. These six principles were consolidated and fleshed out in 1955.

i. Fusion of cultures of the different race (融混各族文化风尚).
ii. Bridging of Eastern and Western art (沟通东西艺术).
iii. Diffusion of the scientific spirit and social thinking of the 20th century (发挥二十世纪科学精神, 社会思潮).
iv. Reflection of the needs of the peoples of the Federation of Malaya and Singapore (反映本邦人民大众需求).
v. Expression of local tropical flavour (表现当地热带情调).
vi. Fulfillment of educational and social needs (配合教育意义, 社会功能[4]).

Broadly speaking, Nanyang refers to Southeast Asia. Geopolitically, this incorporates the Indo-Chinese region of Vietnam, Thailand, Cambodia, the Malay Peninsula, Singapore and Indonesia. The NAFA artists sought to establish a "Nanyang" style, incorporating the local landscape, the indigenous people and their lifestyles, their dress, their habits and their daily lives. In 1952, the famous Bali expedition took place. Liu Kang, Chen Wen Hsi, Chen Chong Swee and Cheong Soo Pieng travelled as a quartet along the Malayan Peninsula, Borneo and the Indonesian islands. Bali is often highlighted because the island greatly inspired the artistic style they began to innovate as "Nanyang" in spirit and in visual consonance (Figure 4).

In Bali the four artists met and became acquainted with the Brussels born Adrien Le Mayeur, who had set up his art and final home in the island. The practice and work of Le Mayeur offered parallels to the Modern

---

[4] Low Sze Wee, "Lim Hak Tai — Art and Life", *Crossing Visions*. (Singapore: Nanyang Academy of Fine Arts, 2011), p. 37. For more on the history of Lim Hak Tai's experiences and compatriots as well as the genesis of NAFA with the assistance of Chinese businessmen and Chinese artists, Low's essay covers a good spectrum of this development.

Figure 4. Chen Chong Swee, 1952, Bali Landscape, watercolour on paper, 47 × 81 cm (by Courtesy of NAFA).

European masters the four were familiar with, such as Paul Gauguin, who had sought alternative experiences other than the current civilisation to fuel and create a new language in art.[5]

After their return, the four artists held an exhibition of their new works at the British Council. The show was a critical milestone in the development of the "Nanyang" style, a style that was reflective and took its inspiration from the region, but native to Singapore. It was not uncommon to find visual markers reminiscent of batik lines and colouring, or the rudimentary form and feel of wood carving as well as the more decorative elements of indigenous symbols, such as that from Sarawak and Sabah. Additionally, scenes of daily life, such as fishing along the coast; women in local dress in markets; houses with attap roofs, tall coconut trees and sandy rural areas became subjects of all mediums, whether Chinese ink, oil painting or pastels. Many of these works used Western perspective defining spatial compositions as

---

[5] Gauguin ventured into French Polynesia in the late 19th century, where he explored some of the islands and studied their communities. He developed a new vocabulary in his paintings, employing the simple and primitive quality of the local populace as well as their lifestyles to create an alternative modern painting set apart from that found in Europe.

well as tonal values to reflect colours in tropical light. But they also included deft qualities of brushwork and expressionistic variety found in Chinese painting of the literati. The new artworks moved toward a concrete realisation of the Singapore artists' search for a regional expression in their creations.

After World War II and in the 1950s and 1960s, the visual arts community expanded considerably. NAFA had reopened by 1946 in new premises to accommodate the larger number of students. The graduates of this generation benefitted from cultural forays into Europe and in some cases, America. In the late 1950s and early 1960s, graduates such as Wee Beng Chong (黄明宗), Tew Nai Tong (张耐冬) and Chia Yu Chian (谢玉谦), were able to travel to Paris where they studied at the Ecole Nationale des Beaux Arts de Paris. Other artists of this generation also went on to London to further their studies after obtaining their diplomas from NAFA. The exposure to the world art trends in cities such as London and Paris led to a significant Western slant in the iconography of Singapore art in the 1970s and early 1980s. Key artists of this period included NAFA graduates Anthony Poon (方谨顺), Ng Eng Teng (黄荣庭), Thomas Yeo (姚照宏) as well as artists who had travelled to America, such as Goh Beng Kwan (吴珉权). They returned with different strains of a new, worldly post-war art that included, but was not limited to abstraction (Figures 5 and 6).

By the 1980s, Singapore was defining its own cultural domain and artistic landscape. Commissions for sculptures and artworks in corporate and government buildings, as well as public spaces, initiated a platform for "Singaporean" art that reflected the multiracial and multicultural population. These second generation artists displayed both Western and Chinese art traditions. Artists such as Shi Xiang Tuo (施香沱), Fan Changqian (范昌乾), Huang Baofang (黄葆芳) (Figure 7), brought into their ink paintings characteristic local realism and local flavour through their subject matter as well as execution styles. They incorporated conventional ink painting techniques but adapted the principles of realism and naturalism to re-invigorate and distinguish their art. Conversely, artists such as Lim Yew Kuan (林友权), Thomas Yeo and Tay Chee Toh (郑志道) (Figure 8) to name but a few, created new iconographies in abstraction derived from Western principles or decorative elements from Southeast Asia that would classify their evolution as practicing artists in the new nation of Singapore. Still,

Figure 5. Tew Nai Tong, Nude 3, 2007, oil on canvas, 92 × 92 cm (by Courtesy of NAFA).

Figure 6. Thomas Yeo, The Dive, 1974, acrylic on canvas, 140 × 112 cm (by Courtesy of NAFA).

Figure 7. Huang Baofang, Niah Caves, Chinese ink and colour on paper c. 1968, 51 × 31cm (by Courtesy of NAFA).

Figure 8. Tay Chee Toh, 1972, Untitled, Batik painting, 90 × 117 cm (by Courtesy of NAFA).

their experiences and physical artworks do not definitively illustrate a concrete "Singapore" style, and rightly so. In the momentum of the 50 odd years since the end of World War II and self-government, as well as independence, the visual arts of Singapore has only just begun assimilating historical gravitas into a coherent concept that will guide our cultural satellites into the new century of national identity and independence.

In extrapolating those academic paradigms of Western and new Chinese painting (that is unrelated to Chinese pop art of the 1990s[6]), the artistic community and literati understood clearly that the physical journey into Nanyang could not be complete without its parallel journey in their own artistic practices.

In 1989, the report from the Advisory Council on Culture and the Arts recommended that a national arts council be created to steward funds and operational policies designed to "spearhead and coordinate cultural promotion".[7] In brief, the formation of the National Arts Council as well as the National Heritage Board in the 1990s provided a foundation on which culture would be nurtured and promoted. The visual arts were but one genre within the cultural domain. The mid-1990s and the early part of the new millennium saw the rapid emergence of museums, studios and platforms with which visual arts could be further nurtured and developed. Grants and subsidies were extended to practicing artists and arts groups to further their practice and contribute to society's cultural input and social bonding through both visual and performing arts.

During this time, visual arts began to transcend the conventions of traditional painting, drawing and sculpture, accommodating international influences. The climate of fracture and uncertainty following the Cold War (the 1950s and 1960s) that affected much of Southeast Asia artistically and culturally proliferated in the region, including Singapore. Over

---

[6]It can be largely presumed that following the end of the Cultural Revolution in China in 1976, Chinese art underwent a reformation and revival that blossomed in the mainland and the US as Chinese pop art of the mid-1980s and 1990s. This genre bore resemblances with German neo-Expressionism (many of the contemporary Chinese artists travelled to Germany for education and exchange from the late 1980s and 1990s) as well as American Pop art, both of which did have an impact on the Chinese artists of the pre- and post-Cultural revolution.

[7]Ong Teng Cheong et al., Report of the Advisory Council on Culture and the Arts, April 1989, Point 6.

206 I 50 Years of the Chinese Community in Singapore

the next few decades in the 1990s and early 2000s, new hybrid genres of multidisciplinary practice were not uncommon, mixing performance with visual arts expressions. New media also rose to the forefront, incorporating photography and moving visuals such as video and projections.

While in 1979, the Cultural Medallion had been instituted by the government as the highest national award for artists contributing to the nation, it was only in 1992 that the new National Arts Council instituted the Young Artist Award, a national level equivalent to the Cultural Medallion.[8] This new award focused on younger artists aged 35 and under, whose works were gearing up for energetic and forward-looking practices with a highly global face in interpreting the rich plurality of visual arts socially and ethnically.

Increasingly, such new vibrant practices have today grown to include film and hybrid installations of the sculptural, photographic and auditory (music and sound). The conventions of painting and sculpture as primarily established during the early years in Nanyang have evolved into a more mature level of established practices and consistent expression. Side by side with this, new media has extended the reach into the highly public domain, accessible by mass media and the internet around the world.

Although graphic and applied arts in the visual realm had been offered in 1974 in formal courses at the only arts school then in Singapore, the Nanyang Academy of Fine Arts, the late 1990s saw a transformation in its visual arts offerings. Visual communications including advertising and fine art photography as well as animation and video or screen media were introduced as part of the formal curriculum. These developmental factors played a large role in reconstructing the visual arts from formerly classical painting, drawing and sculpture, into a more contemporary context of multiple and mixed medias, allowing budding artists to undertake traditional arts and expand their practices with other input of visual expressions in photography and animation for example.

---

[8]National Arts Council Website, accessed on 27 April 2015: https://www.nac.gov.sg/talent-development/cultural-leadership/overview. The Cultural Medallion preceded administration by the National Arts Council. In 1979, it was administered by the Ministry of Culture; which was later re-organised into various other Ministry portfolios before its current make-up today as the Ministry of Culture, Community and Youth. Today, both the Cultural Medallion and the Young Artist Award are administered by the National Arts Council, but are conferred by the President of the Republic of Singapore.

Since the institution of the Young Artist Award, its visual arts recipients have set the likes of Royston Tan (陈子谦) and Ken Seet (filmmaker and photographer) side by side with Hong Sek Chern (洪雪珍)[9] and Lim Poh Teck (林保德).[10] Sek Chern's work for example draws from the heritage of Chinese ink painting, masters such as Huang Binhong (黄宾虹), yet reinvents her practice to incorporate mathematical precision and architectural form to produce ink painting expressions speaking for contemporary audiences and their experiences. Poh Teck, a painter by training, developed his own work into a new ultra pop style, incorporating local Chinese with mass media derived iconographies into two-dimensional and installation work, exciting the palette of the young and stimulating the old at a threshold of new experiences.

In the last 20 years or so, Singapore has remained a centre of economic exchange, having begun its life as a key trading port under the British. Its development as a nation has hinged on economic prosperity. Side by side with its already established local population, tourists and long-term visitors from all parts of the world have continued to enrich Singapore's sociocultural landscape. This has included cultural practitioners from China, certainly, among other countries. Traditional Chinese painting and modern Chinese painting from the second republic of China (post-1949) show up in Singapore exhibitions and commercial galleries, as well as contemporary art fairs of an international profile. Specific influences from the mainland are no longer isolated to what is culturally bred, but which today is plural and insidious, cross-influencing through channels, East and West, around the world.

The art scene in Singapore is ever evolving. Although change is the only constant, one element that was brought to the shores of Nanyang more than 50 years ago has remained. Visual artists who arrived in Nanyang with influences of both the East and West, and who later set down roots in our society and community, had come in search of cultural dynamics that could invigorate the indigenous and immigrant communities. By identifying themselves with this sojourn and subsequent search for a new artistic style and

---

[9] Tan BT, 2 + 2: The Inaugural Exhibition of Chryse Fine Art: Ler Hock Chuan, Tay Shuh Fung, Chua Say Hua, Hong Sek Chern, 2014.
[10] Kwok, Kian Chow, *Channels & Confluences: A History of Singapore Art.* (Singapore: National Heritage Board/Singapore Art Museum, 1996), Plate 127.

expression unique to the shores of Singapore in Nanyang, that generation's legacy continues, with as much urgency today as ever before.

The world has become more miscible culturally, yet we continue to look for what is uniquely our own. In visual arts, this is no different. If nothing else, the tireless journey into Nanyang has prevailed visually, artistically and culturally. We have drawn from the heritage of the Chinese past, but also taken much inspiration from other similar migrant cultures in India and elsewhere, as well as what was and is located in the region we call Southeast Asia, that is synonymous with Nanyang. Today, the visual arts breach the boundaries not only of convention, but of what is culturally specific. Our language in the arts may be globally articulate and relevant, but strives to reflect the intrepidity of our soul, inherited from our forefathers, *yet always* moving ahead into the future.

Chapter 12

Chinese Calligraphy is Alive and Well in Singapore

WONG Joon Tai

Introduction

Chinese calligraphy is a unique form of Chinese art that is widely practised and revered in the Chinese cultural sphere. In fact, some people view it as a form of Chinese culture rather than just art and craft. For these people, it is a natural thing for Chinese to want to write beautifully.

Scholar Xiong Bing Ming (熊秉明 1922–2002) who spent a major part of his life in France went even further to claim that the core of Chinese culture is its philosophy, and at the centre of this core is Chinese calligraphy.[1]

It is therefore not surprising to observe that where there are Chinese, there will be Chinese calligraphy.

This essay adopts Lasswell's model of communication as the basis for discussing how Chinese calligraphy has developed in Singapore. The model, developed by American political scientist and communication theorist Harold Lasswell, is regarded by many as one of the earliest and most influential communication models. In his 1948 article "The Structure and Function of Communication in Society", Lasswell wrote:

A convenient way to describe an act of communication is to answer the following questions:

Who
says **what**
in **which** channel

---

[1] 熊秉明 (Xiong Bing Ming), "书法和中国文化 (Calligraphy and Chinese Culture)", 香港二十一世纪双月刊, No. 31 (October 1995).

to **whom**
with what effect? [2]

In our discussion on the efforts to spread Chinese calligraphy in Singapore, it is the "who, what, which and whom" elements of the communication that we are mainly concerned with.

Chinese Calligraphy before Singapore's Independence

In its early days, Singapore was an immigrant society whose inhabitants came mainly from the Malay Peninsula, China, the Indian sub-continent and Sri Lanka. When Sir Stamford Raffles first arrived in 1819, Singapore was a small settlement of about 150 people. In 1824, Malays made up nearly three quarters of the population. However, by 1867, with an overwhelming influx of Chinese migrants travelling south in search of better opportunities, the Chinese had firmly established themselves as the majority.[3] I have classified the history of Chinese calligraphy in Singapore into four periods:[4]

1. 19th Century: During the Colonial Years
2. 20th Century: Before Independence
3. 20th Century: After Independence
4. 21st Century: The Singapore Vision of a Renaissance City

One can safely conclude that there was hardly any purposeful spreading of Chinese calligraphy in the 19th century. In the absence of clear elements of "who, what, which and whom" of communication, Chinese calligraphy was probably mainly used to meet specific needs, such as to inscribe business names, as well as names of clan associations and temples.

At the beginning of the 20th century, more Chinese schools were established with the influx of many well-educated immigrants from

---

[2] Harold Lasswell, "The Structure and Function of Communication in Society", The Communication of Ideas. (New York: Institute for Religious and Social Studies, 1948), p. 117.
[3] *Cultures of the World*, (Singapore: Times Books International, 1990), p. 17.
[4] 王运开 (Wong Joon Tai), "新加坡书法历史分期初探 (A Preliminary Study on Historical Periods of Chinese Calligraphy in Singapore)", 《南洋书法半年刊 (*Nanyang Calligraphy*)》, 第一期 (No. 1), (April 2014), p. 6.

China. We now know that in the early 20th century, three calligraphers, Wu Wei Ruo (吴纬若), Tan Heng Fu (谭恒甫) and Xu Yun Zhi (许允之), known as "The Three Calligraphers of Singapore" came from China to make Singapore their home.[5] However, very little else is known about them.

The other first generation calligraphers include Pan Shou (潘受 1911–1999), Tan Keng Cheow (陈景昭 1907–1972), See Hiang To (施香沱 1906–1990), Chan Shou She (张瘦石 1898–1969), Chen Jen Hao (陈人浩 1908–1976), Goh Teck Sian (吴得先 1893–1962) and Tsue Ta Tee (崔大地 1903–1974).

The first modern Chinese school was established in 1905.[6] By 1938, there were 329 Chinese schools with 28,000 students in Singapore.[7] Many of the teachers who came from China were calligraphers who practised the art from a young age. They were also well-versed in literature and poetry. Many students of these Chinese schools became enthusiastic learners of Chinese calligraphy.

The spread of Chinese calligraphy in Singapore in the early years was therefore closely linked to the setting up of the Chinese schools.

The Chinese newspapers also played an important role in promoting Chinese culture and arts. Two major Chinese newspapers were founded in the 1920s, *Nanyang Siang Pau* (南洋商报) in 1923, and *Sin Chew Jit Poh* (星洲日报) in 1929. They provided a valuable and powerful channel to popularise Chinese calligraphy within the community.

20th Century: Economic Survival after Independence

Since its independence in 1965, Singapore has been dramatically transformed from an entrepot centre to a financial and industrial metropolis. Singapore's

---

[5]"星洲早期三大书法家 (Three Calligraphers of Singapore in the Early Years)", 《南洋书法半年刊 (*Nanyang Calligraphy*)》, 第一期 (No. 1), (April 2014), p. 8.

[6]"消失的华校 — 国家永远的资产 (Disappearing Chinese Schools — An Everlasting Part of Singapore's History)" 华校校友会联合会出版 (Singapore: Chinese Schools Alumni Association Publishing, 2014), p. 50.

[7]王运开 (Wong Joon Tai), "新加坡书法历史分期初探 (A Preliminary Study on Historical Periods of Chinese Calligraphy in Singapore)", 《南洋书法半年刊 (Nanyang Calligraphy)》, 第一期 (No. 1), (April 2014), p. 6.

economic achievements are often seen as overshadowing its cultural development. And yet, the arts have always been an integral part of Singapore's national development.[8]

In the case of Chinese calligraphy, we witnessed quite a healthy development in the 20th century. In fact, Singapore's calligraphy standard and activities during this period has been regarded by some overseas observers as the most developed outside China, Japan and Korea.[9] This is attributable to the following factors:

1. Most Chinese schools included Chinese calligraphy as their co-curricular activities.
2. The presence of a large number of first generation calligraphers who came from China.
3. The supportive Chinese news media which either sponsored or reported widely on Chinese calligraphy activities.
4. The founding of many calligraphy and art groups that actively promoted Chinese calligraphy in various ways.
5. Government efforts to provide support for calligraphy activities through agencies such as People's Association (PA) and the National Arts Council (NAC).

Two schools that stood out in their tremendous contributions to the development of Chinese calligraphy are Tuan Mong High School (端蒙中学) and Chung Cheng High School (中正中学). Tuan Mong School, located at Tank Road, was initially set up as a primary school in 1906 by public-spirited Teochew clan leaders. It was renamed Tuan Mong High School when secondary classes were included two years later. Calligraphy was widely popular at Tuan Mong, especially in its early days. The school engaged teachers and principals who were accomplished calligraphers and truly loved the teaching of calligraphy.

Almost all the first generation calligraphers and educators such as Pan Shou, Tan Keng Cheow, See Hiang To and Tsue Ta Tee came from China

---

[8] Renaissance City Plan III — Arts Development Plan, National Arts Council, 2008, p. 7.
[9] 谢光辉与陈玉佩编 (Xie Guanghui and Chen Yupei), "新加坡马来西亚华文书法百年史 (100 Years of Chinese Calligraphy in Singapore-Malaysia", (暨南大学出版社 Jinan University Press, 2013), p. 2.

and eventually made Singapore their home. They had a strong passion for Chinese calligraphy and were generous in imparting and sharing their skills with the younger generation.

Pan Shou[10] is a good example of someone who deeply influenced the local calligraphy and art scene. His calligraphy style was matched by his own poems which were masterful in their own right. In 1934, he became principal of Tao Nan Primary School (道南小学), nurturing it into a premier institution. In 1986, Pan Shou became the first calligrapher to receive the prestigious Cultural Medallion award for achieving artistic excellence in Chinese calligraphy as well as making distinctive contributions to Singapore's arts and cultural landscape. In 1991, then Acting Minister for Information and the Arts George Yeo recognised Pan Shou as a "national treasure"[11] whose works inspired others.

Tan Keng Cheow[12] was principal of Tuan Mong High School for 14 years from 1950 to 1964. Although he did not teach calligraphy while he was in Tuan Mong High School, he created a conducive environment for this Chinese art form. By the time he moved to Chung Cheng High School, he had already cultivated a love for calligraphy which would remain in Tuan Mong and the Teochew community for many years to come.

It was in Chung Cheng High School that he met a group of students who, under his guidance, later became the core members of the second generation of Singaporean calligraphers. The Chinese Calligraphy Society of Singapore (新加坡书法家协会), one of the most important calligraphy organisations in Singapore was founded by his students from Chung Cheng High School.

See Hiang To[13] is remembered as an outstanding art teacher who had trained many second generation artists such as Tan Kee Sek (曾纪策) and Tan Kian Por (陈建坡), two of the founding members of the Siaw-Tao Seal-Carving Calligraphy & Painting Society (啸涛篆刻书画会). A group of his students also founded Molan Art Association (墨澜社) in 1967.

---

[10]《南洋书法半年刊 (Nanyang Calligraphy)》, 第一期 (No. 1), (April 2014).

[11]陈声桂编 (Tan Siah Kwee), "潘受三帖 (Three Articles on Pan Shou)", 2004, p. 8.

[12]"Tan Keng Cheow 陈景昭" Chinese Calligraphy, accessed on 3 May 2015: http://icalligraphy.blogspot.sg/search?q=%E9%99%88%E6%99%AF%E6%98%AD.

[13]"Shi Xiangtuo 施香沱" Chinese Calligraphy, accessed on 3 May 2015: http://icalligraphy.blogspot.sg/2009/07/shi-xiangtuo.html.

Tsue Ta Tee[14] was skilful in many calligraphic styles, such as regular (楷), clerical (隶), cursive (草), official seal (篆), as well as bronze and oracle bone inscriptions. He left China in 1937 to travel around the Southeast Asian countries and came to Singapore in 1946. He later travelled again and spent a few years in Penang before returning to Singapore in 1965 to devote the rest of his life to teaching and promoting Chinese calligraphy. He was the volunteer teacher of the Calligraphy Society of the Hua Yi Secondary School (华义中学). It was during this period that he trained a number of second generation calligraphers such as Yong Cheong Thye (杨昌泰) and Goh Yau Kee (吴耀基), two of the founding members of Shicheng Calligraphy and Seal-Carving Society (狮城书法篆刻会).

The efforts of the first generation calligraphers paid off handsomely as the second generation calligraphers trained by them came of age in the 1980s. Some of these second generation calligraphers are Lim Tze Peng (林子平), Chang Kwang Wee (曾广纬), Tan Siah Kwee (陈声桂), Choo Thiam Siew (朱添寿), Leow Pau Kiang (廖宝强), Khoo Seow Hwa (邱少华), Khoo Seng Kong (丘程光), Ho Ngiap Poh (何业波), Yong Cheong Thye (杨昌泰), Chui Choo Sin (徐祖燊), Goh Yau Kee (吴耀基), Koh Mun Hong (许梦丰), Tan Kee Sek (曾纪策), Chin Soon Tuan (薛振传), Tan Kian Por (陈建坡), Ang Hoon Seng (洪云生), Chang Sow Yam (曾守荫), Anthony Ho (何钰峰), Lim Juay Phing (林锐彬) and Heng Ser Chong (王思宗).

The second generation calligraphers not only worked hard to improve their artistic skills, but also became the backbone of many art groups that were formed during the 1980s and 1990s. Some of these groups are The Chinese Calligraphy Society of Singapore (新加坡书法家协会), Shicheng Calligraphy and Seal-Carving Society (Singapore) (狮城书法篆刻会), Siaw-Tao Seal-Carving Calligraphy & Painting Society (啸涛篆刻书画会), The Senior Citizen Calligraphy and Painting Society (乐龄书画会), Hanshi Calligraphy Society (汉石书艺学会), Xin Hai Calligraphy Society (Singapore) (心海书学会), The Molan Art Association (墨澜社), Singa City Chinese Calligraphy and Painting Society (新城书画学会), and Hua Yuan Calligraphy Club (华苑书法会).

---

[14] "Tsue Ta Tee 崔大地" Chinese Calligraphy, accessed on 3 May 2015: http://icalligraphy.blogspot.sg/2010/03/tsue-ta-tee.html.

The founding of the Chinese Calligraphy Society of Singapore (CCSS)[15] in 1968 has played a crucial role in keeping Chinese calligraphy alive in Singapore. It was founded by seven members of the Chinese Calligraphy Club of Chung Cheng High School at Goodman Road. Most notable among them is Tan Siah Kwee (陈声桂), who continues to manage the Society today.

In the initial years, CCSS focused much of its attention on organising calligraphy classes for the masses. Since the 1980s, the Society has shifted its focus from training to actively holding exhibitions for local and foreign calligraphers. Some of these have been jointly organised with calligraphers and associations from China, Taiwan, Japan, Korea, Malaysia and other ASEAN countries.

In 1988, the International Centre for Chinese Calligraphy (ICCC)[16] Secretariat was set up in Singapore by seven countries/regions, namely China, Hong Kong, Japan, Malaysia, South Korea, Singapore and Taiwan. The Secretariat was managed by CCSS. Two years later in December 1990, ICCC held the first calligraphy exhibition in Singapore. The exhibition was declared open by then Singapore Deputy Prime Minister Ong Teng Cheong. Since the inaugural exhibition, the participating countries/regions have taken turns to organise exhibitions once every two years.

The ICCC Secretariat was moved to China in 2007. This marked the successful completion of the first round of international calligraphy exchanges in the region. It is not an exaggeration to say that Singapore has contributed significantly and decisively in developing and promoting Chinese calligraphy in Asia.

Unlike CCSS and other calligraphy associations that were each formed by students of a particular teacher, the founding members of the Shicheng Calligraphy and Seal-Carving Society (Singapore)[17] came from various backgrounds. Founded in 1994, its main aims are to actively and effectively promote Chinese calligraphy and facilitate international exchanges and

---

[15]《南洋书法半年刊 (*Nanyang Calligraphy*)》, 第一期 (No. 1), (April 2014), p. 12.

[16] "International Centre for Chinese Calligraphy 国际书法发展联络会" Chinese Calligraphy, accessed on 3 May 2015: http://icalligraphy.blogspot.sg/2009/02/international-centre-for-chinese.html.

[17]《南洋书法半年刊 (*Nanyang Calligraphy*)》, 第二期 (No. 2), (October 2014), p. 14.

friendship between calligraphers locally and overseas. It has focused much of its attention on organising its annual exhibition, as well as encouraging its members to participate in overseas exhibitions.

The Shicheng Calligraphy and Seal-Carving Society (Singapore) has become one of the largest calligraphy organisations in Singapore, with about 150 members. Its annual Ink Rhyme of Lion City (狮城墨韵展) is well-participated by local calligraphers.[18]

The People's Association also plays a major role in promoting Chinese calligraphy by encouraging the community clubs (CCs) under its charge to organise calligraphy classes and related activities. Many CCs also form special interest groups for Chinese calligraphy as well as open up their facilities for calligraphy groups to hold their regular gatherings and activities. These include the Hua Yuan Calligraphy Club (华苑书法会) at Serangoon CC, the Bishan Calligraphy Club (碧山书艺会), and Chinese Traditional Arts Centre at Braddell Heights CC (布莱德岭华族传统艺术中心).

Increasingly, more clan associations, school alumni, religious organisations and temples are promoting Chinese calligraphy classes and activities to their members. Many of these groups hold regular exhibitions to showcase the works of their members. One notable example is the Ngee Ann Cultural Centre (义安文化中心)[19] which was established in 1998 as a subsidiary of Ngee Ann Kongsi (义安公司). Its main objectives are to raise Singapore's cultural profile and improve public access to the arts. Its annual large-scale National Day Calligraphy and Painting Exhibition and National Teochew Calligraphy and Painting Exhibition, showcase artworks of different methodologies and disciplines.

The Monthly Calligraphy & Painting Exchange Gathering[20] organised by the Cultural and Educational Committee of the Teochew Poit Ip Huay Kuan (潮州八邑会馆) is another example of an excellent platform for lovers of Chinese calligraphy to exchange views. The first exchange gathering was organised in October 2003 and since then, it is held at 3.00 pm on the last

---

[18] Ibid.

[19] "Ngee Ann Cultural Centre", Ngee Ann Kongsi, accessed on 3 May 2015: http://www.ngeeann.com.sg/en/ngee-ann-cultural-centre/.

[20] "Teochew Poit Ip Huay Kuan: Monthly Calligraphy & Painting Exchange Gathering 新加坡潮州八邑会馆的每月书画交流雅集" Chinese Calligraphy, accessed on 3 May 2015: http://icalligraphy.blogspot.sg/2009/04/teochew-poit-ip-huay-kuan-monthly.html.

Sunday of every month. At each gathering, a famous calligrapher or artist is invited to give a talk on a specific topic. This is followed by an exchange of ideas between the speaker and participants. After the talk, the speaker and participants are invited to write or paint on the spot so that all those who are present can learn from each other.

Exhibitions and competitions have become commonplace in the Singapore calligraphy landscape. Organisations such as CCSS, Shicheng Calligraphy and Seal-Carving Society (Singapore), Siaw-Tao Seal-Carving Calligraphy & Painting Society, the Chinese Societies of Nanyang Technological University and National University of Singapore, CCs of Braddell Heights, Bishan, Sengkang and Yew Tee, have organised regular exhibitions and competitions.

The other major channels for promoting Chinese calligraphy are competitions and on-the-spot writing by calligraphers during special occasions or events such as writing auspicious couplets during Chinese New Year (挥春).

We are seeing more calligraphy competitions organised by various art groups, CCs, universities, and clan associations for various levels of learners. One of the well-established competitions is the Dr Tan Tsze Chor Art Awards organised by the Singapore Art Society. Since 1979, one to three awards have been given to contestants who have achieved high levels of calligraphy. In conjunction with the exhibition for the award winning pieces, 20 to 40 pieces of works by other calligraphers are displayed.

The writing of auspicious messages for display at home has been an age-old tradition for many Chinese families. Various organisations and groups put in effort to organise such activities during the Chinese New Year and give away the calligraphy works free of charge to the residents. The term "Singapore Huichun Festival" (新加坡挥春节) was also coined to mark the importance of such activities in bringing Chinese calligraphy closer to the ordinary folks.[21] As a result of these activities, we are seeing more people practising this tradition now.

In the areas of calligraphy training and teaching, a new generation of trainers has emerged in the past 50 years. Among them are Pang Weng

---

[21]The Singapore Huichun Festival, accessed on 3 May 2015: http://singhuichun. blogspot.sg/.

Khiang (潘永强), Tan Chye Thiam (陈财田), Wong Shuk Wai (黄思伟), Lee See Thong (李士通), Tan Siah Kwee (陈声桂), Chang Kwang Wee (曾广纬), Leow Pau Kiang (廖宝强), and Koh Mun Hong (许梦丰).

The setting up of the National Arts Council (NAC) as a statutory board on 15 October 1991 marked the government's effort to spearhead the development of the arts in Singapore. Among the goals of the NAC is development of artists and art groups, as well as of arts audiences. In furtherance of its objectives, the NAC has provided places and facilities at subsidised rates to calligraphy organisations as well as financial support to hold exhibitions and activities and to publish books on Chinese calligraphy.

The Chinese newspapers and radio stations also play their part in the promotion efforts. For example, the National Huichun (挥春) competitions have been sponsored by the Chinese newspapers since its inception in 1983.[22] Singapore Chinese radio stations have invited calligraphers such as See Hiang To, Tan Siah Kwee and Khoo Seow Hwa to give talks on calligraphy related topics.

It is evident that the development of Chinese calligraphy during the past five decades has been marked by the strong presence of the first and second generations of calligraphers, and mushrooming of art groups in the calligraphy landscape. The channels of communications have been abundantly provided by various organisations in terms of organising exhibitions, competitions, regular calligraphy gatherings, writing auspicious messages and calligraphy training classes.

However, in terms of Lasswell's communication model, are we facing the weakest link of "whom", or the lack of "whom" which art can be effectively and meaningfully spread to? In the case of Chinese calligraphy, this is especially important because its audience need to have a certain level of proficiency in Chinese before they can learn and appreciate the art.

In fact, as early as 1981, *the Straits Times* found it appropriate to give a provocative headline "Dying art?" in its report on Chinese calligraphy and asked three inevitable questions:[23]

"Is Chinese calligraphy a dying art? Should it be taught as a subject in schools? What is its relevance to us in modern living?"

---

[22] Singapore Huichun Festival, accessed on 3 May 2015: http://singhuichun.blogspot.sg/2012/09/blog-post.html.

[23] "Dying art?" *The Straits Times*, 8 September 1981.

21st Century: The Singapore Vision of a Renaissance City

In 2008, NAC published its "Renaissance City Plan III — Arts Development Plan",[24] and in it, it says aptly:

> At the turn of the 21st century, unprecedented advances in information and communication technologies and the rise of the economic giants of China and India starkly transformed the global landscape. Singapore reached a watershed — it needed to make the leap from an industrial to an innovation-driven economy, and to change its image from utilitarian workplace to a vibrant place for work-live-and-play. Arts — with their ability to enhance creativity and add buzz — received new attention for their economic role.

There are a number of reasons to believe that the overall external environment has improved and has become more conducive for the propagation of Chinese calligraphy. Three of them are mentioned here:

1. The rise of China as a world economic power.
2. The presence of Internet as a ubiquitous channel of communication.
3   The efforts of the government to create a more conducive environment to make mother- tongues living languages.

The impact of the peaceful development and the rise of China on Chinese calligraphy is obvious. The world is now paying more attention to things Chinese, its culture and its way of life, of which Chinese calligraphy is an integral part.

At the same time, the Internet has become for many around the world a major channel of communication. Emails, WhatsApp, Facebooks and many other ever-emerging applications are popular tools that provide easy and cost-effective ways to exchange documents and photos, and for asynchronous discussions as well.

Increasingly we see the Internet being used by calligraphers to promote their works. More websites are also being created to promote Chinese calligraphy and its related activities. One example is the websites created by the Nanyang Calligraphy Centre. Its websites impart general knowledge in

---

[24] Renaissance City Plan III — Arts Development Plan, National Arts Council, 2008.

calligraphy and report on Singapore's calligraphy history, activities/events. We also see more people using Facebook for the same purpose. The Singapore Chinese-Calligraphy Facebook group has 540 members as on 2 May 2015.

The continued efforts by the government to fine tune the bilingual education system has seen a number of new programmes introduced since the beginning of the 21st century. Some of these programmes will have a positive impact on the promotion of Chinese calligraphy. Two of these programmes are highlighted here.

In 2005 the Ministry of Education (MOE) implemented the Bicultural Studies Programme (Chinese)[25] in selected SAP schools to ensure that the Chinese language and culture remain vibrant in Singapore. The Programme provides enrichment courses such as the Bicultural Studies Camp and Bicultural Studies Symposium, and most importantly arranges for longer immersion trips to China for these students.

In 2011, as part of its efforts to create an environment conducive to mother tongue usage and learning as a living language, MOE required schools to work with community groups to conceptualise and organise annual Mother-tongue Language Fortnights,[26] camps and structured reading programmes. Many schools have since included a segment to introduce Chinese calligraphy in their programmes.

For the first time, we also see commercial organisations dedicated to the promotion and training of Chinese calligraphy. In 2004, the Singapore Senior Citizen Calligraphy University Centre Pte Ltd (新加坡老年书法大学) was formed by Tan Siah Kwee with the sole aim of offering a three-year course for senior citizens. Nanyang Calligraphy Centre Pte Ltd (南洋书法中心), founded in 2013, focuses mainly on promoting Chinese calligraphy using Internet, and conducting a three-year Chinese Calligraphy Basic Education course. The courses offered by both organisations marked a shift from the old traditional private school (私塾) by introducing standardised syllabi for different levels of attendees.

---

[25] "Nurturing a Core of Students with Advanced Knowledge of Chinese Language and Culture", Singapore Ministry of Education Press Release on 3 September 2004.

[26] "Enhancing the Teaching and Testing of Mother Tongue Languages (MTL) to Nurture Active Learners and Proficient Users — MTL Review Committee Releases Its Recommendations", Singapore Ministry of Education Press Release on 18 January 2011.

In developing the audience of Chinese calligraphy, one must take into consideration the profile of the new generation Singaporean who is likely to be more global in his outlook, less proficient in Chinese as a mother-tongue language (as compared to English), and high reliance on infocomm technologies and smart phones. Hence, we need to have a group of promoters of Chinese calligraphy who are effectively bilingual and familiar with the Internet and its related technologies. This will ensure that the important channels of communication can be fully utilised in order to reach out to as many people as possible.

While there is still much work to be done, it is clear that Chinese calligraphy today is definitely not a "dying art" as pessimistically portrayed in the aforementioned 1981 Straits Times' report.[27]

In conclusion, perhaps it is apt to mention a letter published on 24 April 2015 in the Chinese newspaper *Lianhe Zaobao* (联合早报) entitled "The Joy of Seeing the Flourishing of Chinese Calligraphy" (喜见书法界欣欣向荣).[28] In the letter, the writer noted that, in the last 30 years, there were more exhibitions held every year and that more young people are learning and participating in the exhibitions and competitions. Indeed, there are good reasons for us to have full confidence that this ancient and unique form of Chinese art will continue to develop, flourish and be relevant in our society.

---

[27] "Dying art?" *The Straits Times*, 8 September 1981.
[28] 何清福, "喜见书法界欣欣向荣 (The Joy of Seeing the Flourishing of Chinese Calligraphy)", 交流版, 联合早报 (*Lianhe Zaobao*), 24 April 2015.

CHAPTER 13

The Singapore Chinese Music Soundscape

Terence HO

Prelude

Since the middle of the 19th century, Singapore's immigrant labour has brought a potpourri of new cultures and new art forms into the island. In particular, the rich diversity of performing arts has transformed the music scene into a vibrant soundscape. From classical symphony to traditional Chinese and regional indigenous music, the island state enjoys an exotic fusion of East and West. This chapter will focus on the growth and development of Chinese orchestral music in the country.

The nation's musical journey evolved alongside larger political, social, and economic changes and became more diverse after its independence in 1965.

Since the start of the 20th century there has been significant Chinese orchestral activity due to the initiative and enthusiasm of many amateur Chinese music practitioners. Their investment of time and effort eventually persuaded the government to acknowledge the value of Chinese music as one of the means of projecting Singapore as a first-world nation with a strong economy and rich cultural diversity.

By the mid-1950s, Chinese schools, workers' organisations, and amateur groups had established quite a number of Chinese ensembles. Created for social and recreational purposes, these ensembles brought together people who had a common love for Chinese music. Groups formed during this period included the Ai Tong Alumni Chinese Orchestra (爱同校友会民乐队), the Kangle Music Society (康乐音乐研究会), the Singapore Middle School Arts Society (新加坡中学联合会), and the Chinese High School's Chinese Ensemble (华中校友会民乐队). In 1959, Taorong Music

Association (陶融儒乐社) formed the first full-fledged Chinese orchestra in Singapore with a membership of 47, making it the largest Chinese ensemble in Singapore at that time.

Under the encouragement of Lee Khoon Choy (李炯才), then Minister of State for Culture, the Central Cultural Board Chinese Orchestra (中央文化局华乐队) was formed in 1960. This orchestra was conducted by Lee Yuk Chuan (李煜传), and performed at many official functions. Many of the orchestra's members were later transferred to the government-funded National Theatre Chinese Orchestra (国家剧场华乐团). Set up to consolidate the growing talents in the Chinese music scene, the orchestra exerted a strong impact on the development of Chinese orchestra in Singapore.

Amidst the growth of Chinese orchestras in the 1960s, Radio and Television of Singapore (RTS) (新加坡广播电视台) organised the first Chinese music competition in Singapore in 1968. Response to this was enthusiastic and a second competition was organised in 1979. In view of the overwhelming response to its promotion of Chinese music, RTS took the bold step of forming the first Radio Broadcasting Chinese orchestra (电台华乐团) under the directorship of Tay Teow Kiat (郑朝吉) in 1974. The orchestra was renamed Singapore Broadcasting Corporation Chinese Orchestra (新加坡广播局华乐团). Following the corporate restructuring of SBC, the Chinese orchestra was hived off and renamed City Chinese Orchestra (狮城华乐团). Today, the City Chinese Orchestra is regarded as one of the best non-professional (non-full-time) Chinese orchestras in the region.

After Singapore's independence in 1965, a National Theatre Trust (国家剧院信托局) was established to promote the arts. It launched the National Theatre Arts Troupe (国家剧场艺术团) in May 1968 and the National Theatre Chinese Orchestra (NTCO) (国家剧场华乐团) was formed under its umbrella. NTCO was led by Zhang Zhengquan (张振泉) as its Chairman and Li Xueling (李雪岭) as Vice-Chairman, with Zheng Sisen (郑思森) as conductor.

In the same year, 1968, the People's Association (人民协会) established its own Chinese Orchestra (PACO) — People's Association Chinese Orchestra (人民协会华乐团). Ma Wen (马文) from Hong Kong was appointed as its first conductor. He was succeeded by Li Xueling in 1973.

The existence of two major Chinese orchestras led to intense rivalry and competition for musicians. It was finally decided that NTCO would be dissolved, and the responsibility of promoting Chinese orchestral music would rest with PACO.

In 1974, one of Singapore's most renowned conductors and composers, Ng Tai Kong (吴大江) was hired full-time to lead and conduct PACO. In September Ng recruited six full-time musicians, namely Phoon Yew Tien (潘耀田), Goh Ek Meng (吴奕铭), Yeo Siew Wee (杨秀伟), Xu Li Fang (许荔方), Zhou Bixia (周碧霞), and Lin Yayu (林雅玉). They formed the first professional ensemble outside China.

After Ng Tai Kong's departure, Lim Tiap Guan (林哲源), former conductor of the Singapore Armed Forces Reservists' Association Chinese Orchestra (SAFRACO) (新加坡武装部队后备军人协会华乐团) was appointed PACO's conductor in1977. In 1980, he was succeeded by Ku Lap Man (顾立民), a percussionist and composer. Under the baton of Ku, the orchestra expanded to 32 full-time members in 1984. It made regular public performances and participated frequently in arts festivals. Many of its musicians were also conductors and instructors in schools' and community centres' Chinese orchestras.

In 1992 PACO was renamed the Singapore Chinese Orchestra (SCO) (新加坡华乐团) to reflect its status as Singapore's only professional Chinese orchestra. In 1993 renowned Shanghainese maestro, Qu Chun Quan (瞿春泉) was invited to be the co-conductor of SCO. In 1995, Qu took over as its sole conductor following the retirement of Ku Lap Man. Under the baton of Qu, the SCO took on new initiatives and the standard of the orchestra improved further.

The 1970s and 1980s may be considered as the "boom years" of traditional Chinese music in Singapore. It was a period when the genre of Chinese orchestra became a widely recognised art form among Singaporeans. The performances of the NTCO and PACO, along with other school and amateur Chinese orchestras were well-attended. The number of Chinese orchestral performances also quadrupled in the 1980s from the decade before. The rising popularity of this art form was also reflected in the growing number of community centres offering courses in Chinese music to meet the increased interest in Chinese orchestras.

The National Orchestra — Singapore Chinese Orchestra

As the SCO's reputation grew, it was decided that it should leave the fold of PA and operate as a company limited by guarantee. The Singapore Chinese Orchestra Company Limited (新加坡华乐团有限公司) was inaugurated in 1996 as a non-profit arts organisation. It was an initiative mooted at the highest government level. Proposed by then Prime Minister Goh Chok Tong (吴作栋), the SCO was to be the Republic's second full-fledged professional orchestra. The first, the Singapore Symphony Orchestra (SSO) (新加坡交响乐团), had been set up in 1979 as the national orchestra dedicated to the performance of Western classical music. The government's goal was to enable the SCO to achieve international recognition for outstanding performance of Chinese orchestral music.

As embodied in its vision and mission statement "to be a world renowned Chinese Orchestra with a uniquely Singaporean Character" and "to inspire Singapore and the World with our music", the SCO aspires to be a world class orchestra that people in Singapore and beyond would want to listen to and be inspired by. The SCO staged its inaugural concert in 1997 under maestro Hu Bing Xu (胡炳旭).

Today the 85-musician SCO is Singapore's only professional Chinese orchestra and its patron is Prime Minister Lee Hsien Loong. Since 2002, when Shanghai-born maestro Yeh Tsung (葉聰) took over as music director, the SCO has taken on the twin role of preserving traditional forms and substance and establishing new frontiers through the infusion of Southeast Asian and Western elements.

Since its inception, the SCO has impressed a broadening audience with its blockbuster presentations and it is also establishing a strong reputation among its counterparts around the world. In 2002, it staged a symphonic fantasy *Marco Polo and Princess Blue* as part of the opening festival of Esplanade — Theatres on the Bay. Since then, the SCO has grown from strength to strength. In 2009, the SCO made history by becoming the first Chinese orchestra to perform in the opening week of the Edinburgh Festival, and in 2010, it performed in Paris as part of the Singapour Festivarts.

Well-known for its high calibre and versatility, the SCO has performed at numerous prestigious events such as the World Economic Forum and International Summit of Arts Council (2003), International Monetary Fund Annual Meeting (2006). The orchestra also toured Beijing, Shanghai, Xiamen and Taiwan in 2000, and performed at the Budapest Spring Festival and the Singapore Season in London and Gateshead (1998–2005). Since 2007, the SCO has performed at the Beijing Music Festival, the China Shanghai International Arts Festival, the Macau International Music Festival, the Shanghai Spring International Music Festival and the Singapore-Suzhou Industrial Park's 20th anniversary Concert. These international platforms provide the SCO with opportunities to showcase its talents, propelling it to the forefront of the international music arena.

The Nanyang Musical Voyage

In its relatively short history, the SCO has vigorously promoted the appreciation and understanding of Chinese music. From the beginning, the SCO worked to broaden its audience base beyond the usual Chinese market segment and extend its reach to the non-Chinese speaking communities through innovative programming. The orchestra sought to create an identity which resonated with Singapore's diverse cultural communities and to develop a new "Nanyang style of music" particular to Singapore and the South East Asia region.

The SCO's first multi-ethnic collaboration was presented in 2003. "A Nanyang Musical Journey" was an experimental piece performed by an Indian classical dancer and featuring Balinese, Malay and Chinese songs. In 2004, the SCO collaborated with the Malay community to present "Nanyang Musical Voyage II", or "Pelayaran Muzila", featuring popular local and Indonesian Malay singers and dancers. During the 2005 Singapore Arts Festival, the SCO staged its first full scale performance with a Nanyang flavour — "Zheng He: Admiral of the Seven Seas", a symphonic epic featuring songs, dances, and narration against a scenic backdrop with special lighting effects. In 2006, the SCO launched its inaugural International Competition for Chinese Orchestral Composition (SICCOC) to source for original compositions that would truly evoke the spirit of Nanyang. The competition drew 75 submissions from China, Hong Kong, Malaysia, Singapore and the US.

The second SICCOC was held in 2011. The competitions not only enlarged the talent pool of composers; they also brought new works to the SCO's growing repertoire.

Postlude

As Singapore celebrates its 50th anniversary, the Chinese music landscape is healthy and vibrant. The Republic boasts of some 200 professional and amateur (including school) orchestras which are sustained by musicians, audiences and financial patrons.

The Chinese orchestra scene in Singapore has undergone many stages of development in the past five decades. And even as Singapore moved from Third World to First, its cultural environment has also blossomed. In the Chinese music landscape, we now have an internationally recognised national Chinese orchestra, buttressed by a large corps of budding artistes and smaller orchestras.

According to the SCO's Chairman, Mr Patrick Lee,

> SCO is moving into the new decade with enthusiasm and confidence. The national Chinese orchestra will continue to scale new heights with the support of the Government, sponsors and friends of SCO and our loyal audience.

CHAPTER 14

In Step with Nanyang Dance

Edmond WONG

It is believed that Chinese dance was in existence even before the earliest written Chinese words. A study of Chinese ceramic artefacts indicates that as early as 4000 BC, the people of the Neolithic Yangshao culture were already performing group dances that involved participants locking their arms and stamping their feet while singing to the accompaniment of musical instruments. Until today Chinese dance remains an important element of celebrations, folk rituals and religious ceremonies.

Chinese dances can be broadly categorised as folk dance and classical dance. Over the years, both have developed distinctive styles and characteristics. Today, both folk and classical dances have evolved into intricate and beautiful performance pieces that are choreographed by many Chinese groups worldwide. The keen observer will detect that while the form of dance has changed, its substance continues to be the use of a unique physical vocabulary to express the dancers' thoughts and feelings.

Folk dances depict the lives and stories of people from the 56 tribes in China. While each region or tribe has its own distinct dance traditions they usually share a common physical vocabulary and order of structure.

Classical dances were originally created by the imperial courts. Through intensive training programmes, court ladies acquired precision techniques and consistency in their dances. Such techniques included movements like jumping, flipping or turning the body to portray the dancer's inner expression and artistic connection to the choreographed movements.

In recent years Chinese dance has projected a more dynamic personality by embracing the various cultural influences of our modern times. One such example are the ground-breaking works of the "Cloud Gate Dance Troupe" (云门舞团) of Lin Hwai-Min (林怀民). This Taiwan-based troupe began by establishing a foundation from the Martha Graham School of modern dance, and gradually absorbed elements from traditional Chinese opera, tai chi and martial arts. While it may be heavily influenced by Western dance concepts, there is a growing trend for modern and contemporary Chinese dance to remain distinctly Chinese by incorporating the physical movements and the ethos of its own cultural roots. Very often a typical Chinese dance performance today may infuse elements from ballet, modern dance and Chinese martial arts.

Humble Beginnings in Singapore

Chinese dance activities in Singapore probably started in the 19th century, when they were mainly subsumed under genres like the dragon and lion dances, which were part of religious rituals and Chinese operas; combining dancing with singing, acrobatic movements and martial arts.

It was only during the late 1920s that visiting troupes from China started to introduce Chinese dance as a formal genre to Singapore. In the 1940s, Chinese dance was offered as an extra-curricular activity in the local Chinese schools. During the 1960s, the arrival of Chinese dance doyenne Lee Shu Fen (李淑芬) from Taiwan elevated the interest in and standard of local Chinese dance.

Over the past five decades, several Chinese dance groups have been formed in Singapore. Those which still remain active as Chinese dance practitioners are the Dance Ensemble Singapore (新加坡聚舞坊) (formerly known as the Yan Choon Lian Dance Group) (严众莲舞团), Chinese Dance Artistes' Association (华族舞蹈艺术协会), Tampines Arts Troupe (淡滨尼艺术团) and Theatre Arts Troupe (剧场艺术团). This list excludes schools and clan associations where Chinese dance is also being practiced and performed; such as the Singapore Hokkien Huay Kuan's Dance Theatre (新加坡福建会馆舞蹈剧场).

The Singapore Chinese dance performances also often showcase a wide variety of folk dances from various ethnic Chinese groups such as the Han (汉族), Hui (回族), Yi (彝族) and Miao (苗族).

Developing a People's Culture

As our society transitions rapidly to a modernity that is heavily influenced by Western ideas and cultures, we cannot deny that there is a decline in interest in traditional Chinese dance performances. To remedy the situation, Chinese dance practitioners will have to inject modern forms of expressions within their dance performances, and at the same time, preserve the essence and spirit of their Chinese traditions.

For example, we cannot continue to perform the Lotus Flower dance or Silk Ribbon dance 100 years from now in their original form. While they are beautiful dances, we should attempt to enhance their relevance through innovative choreography that reflect our present lifestyle, culture, and social environment. I am not suggesting a total disregard for traditional culture in our modernising process. What I am proposing is that we need to look at Chinese dance as a concept of time and space that will continually evolve to reflect the social mores of the community and mental outlook of the dancers.

In the past when we were largely an immigrant community we could only absorb and emulate from others in the practice of traditional Chinese dance. Singapore has since become an independent nation and has achieved tremendous progress, both economically and socially. It is now time for us to embark on developing our very own unique self-expressions through dance.

This journey towards a Singapore brand of dance — preserving tradition and, at the same time, incorporating modern trends — requires the support of the government and its various agencies involved in the promotion of the arts. As we move towards merging the traditional and new forms of dance expressions, perhaps the state too needs to adopt a more dynamic and flexible approach in categorising arts practitioners. In a rapidly evolving and vibrant art scene, it is obvious that one size cannot fit all. Those who have the responsibility of nurturing the local art community need to recognise that Singapore has matured and local artistes require encouragement rather than control. Most of all, we should not categorise how the art of dancing ought to be experimented with or exhibited; as the steps of a "people's culture" have to progress and remain relevant with our changing times.

Traditions will always remain relevant as they represent our historical past to be imparted to our future practitioners. What this means is that we ought to continually nurture our next batch of artistes with a strong foundation that is based on our historical developments since independence.

While we have institutions such as NAFA (Nanyang Academy of Fine Arts) (南洋艺术学院), SOTA (School of the Arts) (新加坡艺术学院) and LASALLE (新加坡拉萨尔艺术学院) providing Western and Asian dance foundations, we also need to develop our own unique syllabus to include our local customs and traditions. In our current dance environment, contemporary dance is known to be driving the growth of Singapore's professional dance sector. However, there is a lack of emphasis on developing our unique physical vocabulary in dance through our mainstream arts institutions.

Stepping into Our Nanyang Culture

After Singapore's abrupt separation from Malaysia in 1965, there were many sceptics who doubted the survival of this small island state. But Singaporeans persevered under the leadership of its first and longest serving Prime Minister, Mr Lee Kuan Yew. Fifty years on, Singapore is a thriving global metropolis with per capita GDP of US$55,000. The Republic has done well economically, but how much have we achieved in the cultivation of our local arts scene?

When Prime Minister Lee Hsien Loong said that our "Republic has developed its own Nanyang style of Chinese culture" during his National Day Rally speech in 2014,[1] he marked an important historical moment for Singaporean-Chinese. We are now identified as Southeast Asian Chinese culturally.

The upcoming Singapore Chinese Cultural Centre (新加坡华族文化中心), is one platform that may allow our local arts practitioners to showcase the uniqueness of our Nanyang culture. Moreover, it will allow all practitioners in the local art fraternity — whether they are involved in the literary or performing arts; whether they are artists or calligraphers; whether they are Chinese or from the minority races — to gather and share our rich heritage.

To enable younger Singaporeans to support and appreciate "the steps of our Nanyang culture", I hope our local artistes will produce more

---

[1] Lim Yan Liang, "National Day Rally 2014: New Centre to Promote 'Nanyang' Style Chinese Culture," http://www.straitstimes.com/node/2737364.

original works that are inspired by our Nanyang journey thus far. At the same time, the public will have to continually support and encourage the works of our local art practitioners. Only then will the seedlings bear flowers and fruits.

One example of a small seedling that has grown into a sturdy tree is the Dance Ensemble Singapore (DES). DES started out as a traditional Chinese dance troupe, founded by Mdm Yan Choong Lian in 1993. Supported by the National Art Council (NAC) (新加坡国家艺术理事会), Mdm Yan has always maintained a high standard for traditional Chinese dance as the foundation for all her performing artistes. Although traditional Chinese dance has been the foundation of DES, she has broadened her presentations by experimenting with contemporary movements and martial arts.

One of the main challenges for DES, and most Chinese dance troupes in Singapore, is to find sufficient local performing artistes who are prepared to take on professional Chinese-dancing as a full-time career. In the interim, foreign Chinese dancers are employed to maintain a high standard of professionalism. Most of our efforts have been focussed on providing appropriate training to dance enthusiasts through arts institutions, but it continues to be an uphill climb for local dance troupes to achieve financial sustainability to the extent that they are able to attract full-time local-professional dancers.

Nonetheless, I remain optimistic that the Singapore dance community will continue to scale new heights in the years ahead. This is achievable because we have a government that is pro-actively promoting the development of a vibrant art environment, a growing community of enthusiastic young artistes who are dedicated to their art, and last but not least important, an increasing number of corporate and individual sponsors who support artistic efforts passionately.

Section 4

Interactions with Other Chinese Communities

Chapter 15

Singapore-China People-to-People Exchanges
A Singapore Perspective

LYE Liang Fook and John WONG

Singapore's relations with China today are strong and substantive, and in many ways are unique and special. The two countries interact and cooperate in many fields ranging from politics, economics, business, the arts and culture, to education and the environment.[1] The relationship between the two countries is also manifested at many levels, from government-to-government ties involving the top leaders to people-to-people exchanges of tourists and students.

Reflecting the special relations that exist at the government-to-government level is the Joint Council of Bilateral Cooperation at the Deputy Prime Minister level that meets every year to review the state of bilateral ties. In addition, Singapore has established bilateral cooperation mechanisms with seven Chinese provinces. Another notable feature of bilateral collaboration is the flagship government-to-government projects, namely the Suzhou Industrial Park (苏州工业园) and Tianjin Eco-city (天津生态城), that the two countries embarked on in 1994 and 2008 respectively. The two governments are currently exploring a third project to add value to

---

[1] In 2013, China was Singapore's top trading partner, with total trade amounting to S$115.2 billion. In the same year, Singapore's investments in China reached US$7.23 billion, becoming China's largest investor country. See Singapore's International Enterprise write-up available at the IE Singapore website, accessed on 25 February 2015: http://www.iesingapore. gov.sg/Venture-Overseas/Browse-By-Market/Asia-Pacific/China/Country-Information.

the development of China's inland provinces. The nature of these flagship projects has shifted from the setting up of an industrial park, to creating a quality living environment and to the possibility of promoting the service industry and connectivity among China's inland provinces. Such a shift reflects a continuous effort by the two countries to review areas of cooperation in line with their development needs. To a large extent, they indicate the level of maturity and comfort level that the two countries have attained with each other.

Such a substantive relationship did not occur overnight; it involved a process that has spanned many years. There is a conventional bias that tends to attribute progress in bilateral ties to the start of diplomatic relations between any two countries. Yet, the ties that link two countries normally do not follow such a standard path.

In this essay, we propose to look beyond the usual government-to-government ties by highlighting certain interesting but lesser known aspects of the people-to-people relations between Singapore and China. Such ties did not just start from 3 October 1990 when diplomatic relations were formally established. In fact, as early as the seventh century, there were already informal people-to-people interactions between Singapore and China. Such exchanges were driven by a myriad of factors ranging from geographical proximity, history, economic logic and kinship relations. We will also provide a flavour of the trade and business interactions that took place between Singapore and China when Singapore was part of Malaya as well as after Singapore's independence in 1965. We will focus on the interactions before the first-ever official visit in 1975 by Singapore's Foreign Minister S. Rajaratnam to China at the time, which in our view has received little attention to date.

An interesting but less known aspect of people-to-people relations between Singapore and China lies in the area of sports. In particular, we will try to show that "ping-pong diplomacy", a phrase widely used to refer to the thawing of US-China relations that eventually led to US President Richard Nixon's visit to China in February 1972, was equally applicable to the Singapore-China relationship. The two countries were involved in a number of exchanges of their table tennis teams before Rajaratnam's visit to China in 1975 which in turn laid the groundwork for then Prime Minister Lee Kuan Yew's (李光耀) visit in 1976.

It was China that first used the sport to signal it wanted to improve relations with Singapore. Singapore responded by first sending its table tennis team to China and then agreeing to host a visit by China's table tennis team. In order to temper expectations of the pace of political ties, Singapore made it clear that it was in no hurry to establish diplomatic relations with China until all the other ASEAN countries had done so. Despite this rather cautious stance, such sports exchanges did help to prepare the ground for the eventual exchanges of senior government ministers and leaders on both sides in the mid-1970s.

We will also show how tourism exchanges between Singapore and China have evolved over the years, with particular emphasis on Chinese tourists to Singapore. The statistics show a generally steady and strong increase in the number of Chinese tourists to Singapore since the 1997 Asian financial crisis. Today, Chinese tourists are Singapore's second largest source market after Indonesia. Chinese tourists have become a key pillar in driving the vibrancy of Singapore's tourism sector as well as its economy. The economic contribution of the Chinese tourists is unequivocally positive, but there is a less sanguine aspect to such tourist inflows. Occasionally, reports have surfaced of some Chinese tourists behaving in a loud and brusque manner while travelling overseas. Cognizant of the impact that such incidents may have on China's image overseas, the Chinese authorities have urged their citizens to be more conscious of their actions and behaviour as tourists.

This essay is divided into three sections. The first section will look at the macro people-to-people exchanges between Singapore and China as early as the seventh century. Such exchanges show that well before diplomatic relations was established, people-to-people exchanges were already flourishing and had a natural momentum of their own. The second section will provide an account of the table tennis exchanges between the two countries in the lead-up to the visits by Rajaratnam and Lee Kuan Yew to China in the mid-1970s. The purpose is to show that the impact of such sport exchanges is not necessarily confined to the sporting arena but also has political significance as well. The third section will bring readers to the present day by exploring the evolving nature of Chinese tourist arrivals to Singapore. Such exchanges reveal the growing economic interdependence between Singapore and China, or more precisely, Singapore's greater dependence on China.

Early People-to-People Interactions

Singapore has geographically and historically been an integral part of Southeast Asia. Its interactions with China, in the past and presently, can be viewed not only within a bilateral context but also as part of a wider region. In fact, Singapore-China people-to-people relations go back a long way, well before the establishment of diplomatic relations on 3 October 1990.

Even before the founding of the People's Republic of China (PRC) in 1949, China's relations with Southeast Asia, traditionally called *Nanyang* or South Seas by the Chinese were extensive and deep-rooted on account of history, geography and migration.

Geographically, Singapore was part of the "Pan-Malayan lands". Historically, the trade between China and Pan-Malaya dates back to the seventh century. A fair amount of trade was recorded as early as the Tang Dynasty (618–907). The early trade activities were often mixed with tribute-bearing missions, a peculiar Chinese way of conducting diplomacy with smaller states in *Nanyang*. But regular and steady growth in trade started only after the second part of the 19th century, with the increased influx of Chinese immigrant labour into British Malaya.

In fact, the Chinese had frequented the Malayan peninsula long before the Portuguese conquered Malacca in 1511. In 1349, Wang Dayuan (汪大渊), a Chinese trader from Quanzhou (Fujian province) provided a vivid account of life in Temasek, the name of old Singapore.[2] In 1409, Admiral Zheng He (郑和) led an expedition to Malacca and made it one of China's tributary states.

However, it was not until 1819 when the British East India Company (英国东印度公司) established a settlement in Singapore that sizeable Chinese communities began to grow. In 1826, Penang, Malacca and Singapore were administratively brought together to form the Straits Settlements, under the rule of the British colonial government of Bengal. With this administrative centralisation, the economies of the Straits Settlements started to grow rapidly.

---

[2] Wang Dayuan was a Chinese trader from Quanzhou (Fujian province) who wrote about his overseas travels during the Yuan dynasty (including to Singapore which was then known as Temasek). Wang provided the first foreign eyewitness account of Temasek as well as other localities (that stretched from China to Maluku to East Africa in a publication called Dao Yi Zhi Lue 岛夷志略 in 1349. See John N. Miksic, *Singapore & the Silk Road of the Sea, 1300–1800* (Singapore: NUS Press, 2013), pp. 169–181.

After 1842 when Hong Kong became a British colony, Singapore linked up with it to become an entrepot centre for the expanding trade between China and Southeast Asia. This in turn drew many Chinese immigrants to the Straits Settlements, mainly from Fujian and Guangdong. To a large extent, the growth of Singapore was due to the continuing waves of migration from China. These waves of migration not only helped to augment Singapore's population size but also gave rise to cultural affinity between Singapore and China, especially in terms of language, customs, beliefs and religious practices.

In 1860, ethnic Chinese constituted 60% of Singapore's total population of 82,000, 15% of Malacca's 67,000, and nearly 30% of Penang's 67,000. Most Chinese migrated into Malaya under the contract-labour system. But they soon became traders and craftsman, and they eventually dominated the economic life of the Straits Settlements.

With the birth of the New China in 1949 (following the victory of the Chinese Communist Party over the Kuomintang in China's internal civil war), Sino-Pan-Malayan trade in general continued unabated but China's relations with some Southeast Asian countries such as the Philippines became strained. In 1949, for instance, the Philippine government suspended its trade ties with the mainland because of domestic and regional paranoia of communist expansionism which had penetrated Southeast Asia, including the Philippines.[3]

However, in Pan-Malaya, China was in fact buying a considerable amount of rubber during the Korean War, until the imposition of the UN embargo on China in May 1951 that banned the export of strategic materials including rubber to it.[4] Following the embargo, Malaya did not export a

---

[3]Relations between Manila and Beijing were only normalised when Philippine President Ferdinand Marcos visited China and held talks with Chinese Premier Zhou Enlai in June 1975. Rommel C. Banlaoi, *Security Aspects of Philippines-China Relations: Bilateral Issues and Concerns in the Age of Global Terrorism* (Manila: Rex Book Store, 2007), p. 18. Apart from the Philippines, China's trade with Indonesia and Thailand were either seriously disrupted or banned in the 1950s and 1960s.

[4]In this UN General Assembly Resolution of May 1991, the items that were banned included arms, ammunition and implements of war, atomic energy materials, petroleum, transportation materials of strategic value, and items useful in the production of arms, ammunition and implements of war. See "Additional Measures to be Employed to Meet the Aggression in Korea", 18 May 1951, United Nations General Assembly, accessed on 28 January 2015: http://www.un.org/en/ga/search/view_doc.asp?symbol=A/ RES/500(V).

single ton of rubber to China in 1952 compared with 22,700 tons in 1951.[5] Even though exports from Singapore to China were almost halted in 1952, Singapore continued to import from China that same year. Thus, trade between Singapore and China was not disrupted completely.[6]

Following its success at industrialisation under the first Five-Year Plan (1953–1957), China started to produce a wide range of manufactured products for export to industrially less sophisticated markets. Thus Southeast Asia became the natural destination of China's first major export drive, with Singapore spearheading this development on account of its strategic location and entrepot tradition.

In February 1956, the Singapore branch of the Bank of China (中国银行) (China's de facto embassy in the absence of diplomatic relations) staged a "China Products Exhibition" at its showroom at Battery Road. This was apparently the first exhibition of its kind to be organised in Malaya by a communist country. On show were reportedly more than 1,000 different items including bicycles, sewing machines, electrical appliances, textiles, porcelain, silk, tea, medicine, food products and products of some cottage industries. According to the Chinese dealers of these products in Singapore, the prices of most commodities were reasonable and competitive.[7]

Apart from the opening of this exhibition at the Bank of China, other "China Products Exhibitions" were subsequently held at other venues such as the Great World Amusement Park.[8] In one such exhibition held there in August 1956, it was reported that "Hami melons" (a type of muskmelon from Hami, Xinjiang) were brought into Singapore for the first time.

---

[5] "Rubber exports drop last year", *The Straits Times*, 11 January 1953, p. 3.

[6] John Wong, "The Role of China in Singapore and Southeast Asian Trade", *Southeast Asian Journal of Social Science*, Vol. 3, No. 1 (1975), p. 51.

[7] "Peking woos overseas Chinese through trade", *The Straits Times*, 3 February 1956, p. 8 and "Peking eyes on our market: Singapore exhibition soon", *The Singapore Free Press*, 9 January 1956, p. 1.

[8] The Great World Amusement Park or Great World was a popular location in Singapore in the 1950s and 1960s, and even the 1970s. It was a place where residents headed to enjoy various opera and revue shows, carnival rides and good food. For further details, please see "Great World Amusement Park" by the Singapore National Library Board, accessed on 30 January 2015: http://eresources.nlb.gov.sg/infopedia/articles/SIP_1046_2006-06-09.html.

With the lifting of the UN embargo in June 1956, Chinese buyers returned to the Singapore rubber market.[9] Not long after, in September 1956, the first Singapore Trade Mission (albeit an unofficial one) led by Yap Pheng Geck (叶平玉) visited Beijing to explore the expansion of business ties between the two countries. Yap was an English-educated Chinese who was a prominent banker and committee member of the Singapore Chinese Chamber of Commerce at that time.[10] The delegation of over 60 members comprised largely representatives from the Chinese Chamber of Commerce and businesses related to rubber, timber, shipping, textiles, foodstuffs, sundry goods, copra, wine and spirits, spray painting, paper and Chinese drugs. In a deliberate effort to show that this was not a trade delegation comprising entirely of Chinese representatives, Yap reportedly included some Indian, European and even Malay business representatives.[11]

The huge size of the Singapore delegation apparently came under some criticism at that time. Responding to such criticism, Mr Yap explained that the delegation was large because "we are not only going to promote trade but will be prepared to buy and sell on the spot".[12]

Trade relations between Singapore and China were not all that smooth sailing in the 1950s. China's successful industrialisation led to a large influx of labour-intensive manufactured goods (particularly cotton textiles) into Pan-Malaya, which resulted in a serious trade dispute between the two sides

---

[9] John Wong, "The Role of China in Singapore and Southeast Asian Trade", p. 51.

[10] Yap Pheng Geck was born in Johore in 1901. He was educated at the Anglo-Chinese School in Singapore and obtained a degree from the University of Hong Kong. He started his career as a teacher at his alma mater where he taught until 1931. He served as a volunteer in the Straits Settlement Volunteer Corps (SSVF), a military reserve force under the British, from 1925. In 1932, he was commissioned as an officer and commanded the "E" Chinese Company of the 2nd Battalion of the SSVF until the fall of Singapore. After the war, he joined the Sze Hai Tong Banking and Insurance Company (that was merged with the Overseas Banking Chinese Corporation in 1998) as manager and became chairman of the Central Board of Pineapple Packers of Malaya. See "Leaders of business in Malaya", *The Straits Times*, 23 January 1953, p. 10. See also Yao Pheng Geck, *Scholar, Banker, Gentleman Soldier*. (Singapore: Institute of Southeast Asian Studies, 1982.)

[11] "Singapore plans to outbid Hong Kong in business talks with China", *The Straits Times*, 12 July 1956, p. 6.

[12] "China traders: mission must be big for on-the-spot deals — Yap", *The Straits Times*, 15 July 1956, p. 4.

and prompted the Kuala Lumpur government to impose a partial trade ban on imports from China. The formation of Malaysia in 1963 (through a merger of Singapore, Malaya, Sabah and Sarawak) caused a further deterioration in Sino-Malaysian relations as China supported Indonesia's confrontation against Malaysia. Sino-Malaysian relations reached its lowest ebb when the Federal government took measures to close the Penang and Singapore branches of the Bank of China. In reality, the closure order on the Singapore branch was never implemented, as Singapore repealed it immediately after its separation from Malaysia in August 1965.

After independence, Singapore was able to pursue a more open trade policy with China that was relatively free from political and ideological hangovers. One instance of this was the Republic's first 19-member trade mission to China in October 1971 led by Wee Cho Yaw (黄祖耀), President of the Singapore Chinese Chamber of Commerce & Industry (SCCCI) at the time.[13] The purpose of the mission was to further strengthen trade between the two countries and to study China's industrial development.[14] Another objective was to request China to consider providing additional ships to ply between Singapore and Europe to help break the near monopoly of the Far East Freight Conference (FEFC). Before the trade mission, Singapore shippers, especially those in the rubber and timber business, were extremely unhappy with the FEFC for announcing an impending increase in freight charges in February 1972 on top of an earlier increase in January 1971.[15] In their view, the substantial increase in freight charges would seriously affect their business as they were already being hit by

---

[13] Accompanying the 19-member mission were three journalists: Leslie Fong of *The Straits Times*, Pang Cheng Lian of the *New Nation*, and William Lee of *Sin Chew Jit Poh*. The delegation's visit was hence well covered in the local media.

[14] At that time, Wee Cho Yaw reportedly said that the quality of Chinese goods was "excellent" and the prices were "cheap", and that they were "especially suited to the needs of Singaporeans". He also commended China for not only being able to "meet the needs of its 700 million people but also to earn foreign exchange by exporting its goods". See "Two targets of the mission to China", *The Straits Times*, 8 October 1971, p. 18.

[15] At that time, the Far East Freight Conference (FEFC) had a near monopoly on shipping lines in and out of Singapore. It had announced an increase of freight charges by 10% in February 1971 and made a further announcement in September 1971 (a month before the first trade mission led by Wee Cho Yaw to China) to raise freight charges by another 20% in January 1972.

falling prices of the commodities they handled. In the event, the trade mission managed to secure China's in-principle agreement to help Singapore break away from the contract system operated by the FEFC.[16]

In the 1970s, as individual ASEAN countries started to normalise relations with China, Singapore also went ahead to improve ties with China although it decided to establish formal ties only after all the other ASEAN states had done so.[17] Singapore-China relations improved with the first ever visit by Singapore Foreign Minister Rajaratnam to China in March 1975. Among the highlights of the visit was a meeting with Chinese Premier Zhou Enlai (周恩来).[18] This paved the way for the visit by Singapore Prime Minister Lee Kuan Yew to China in May 1976 where Lee met with Chairman Mao Zedong (毛泽东).[19] Although the meeting with Chairman Mao did not constitute a "substantive conversation", Lee was of the view that the Chinese side had extended a courtesy to the Singapore delegation through such a meeting to signal that China considered Singapore important enough.[20]

On the basis of these political milestones, the two countries took a step further to establish more formal trade ties. In December 1979, Singapore and China signed a trade agreement that provided a broad framework for increased trade and economic cooperation.[21] This was followed a few

---

[16] "China's aid package", *The Straits Times*, 21 October 1971, p. 1.

[17] The ASEAN countries that normalised relations with China in the 1970s were Malaysia (on 31 May 1974), the Philippines (on 9 June 1975) and Thailand (on 1 July 1975). Indonesia, which had severed ties with China in April 1967, only normalised ties with China on 8 August 1990. Singapore was the last among the ASEAN countries to establish diplomatic ties with China on 3 October 1990.

[18] On this trip, Minister Rajaratnam was companied by Lee Khoon Choy, then Senior Minister of State of Foreign Affairs, three officials (Joseph Koh, Foreign Ministry Desk Officer and Secretary of the Delegation; Howe Yoon Chong, Port of Singapore Authority and Development Bank of Singapore Chairman; and I.F. Tang, Economic Development Board Deputy Chairman) and five Singapore newsmen. See "Raja sees the sights in Canton after train journey", *The Straits Times*, 13 March 1975 and "It all began at a dinner in New York...", *The Straits Times*, 14 March 1975, p. 1.

[19] Lee Kuan Yew could not meet Zhou Enlai during his visit in May 1976 as the latter had passed away in January that year.

[20] "Lee Kuan Yew, *From Third World to First: The Singapore Story, 1965–2000*. (New York: HarperCollins Publishers Inc., 2000), p. 582.

[21] This trade accord was signed by Singapore's Finance Minister Hon Sui Sen and Chinese Foreign Trade Minister Li Qiang in a ceremony attended by Senior Vice-Premier Deng

months later in June 1980 with a bilateral agreement to set up commercial representative offices in each other's country.[22] Singapore went on to set up a Trade Office in Beijing in September 1981, shortly after China set up a similar office in Singapore in the same month.[23] Diplomatic ties were formalised in October 1990.

Apart from the commendable work carried out by the SCCCI in promoting commercial ties with China, another organisation that deserves a mention here is the Singapore China Business Association (SCBA) (新加坡中国商会) formed in 1970 to promote trading activities between the two countries. Its role, like that of the Singapore Chinese Chamber of Commerce, was particularly important in the days before the government played an active role in facilitating business interest in China. Since then, it has remained a valuable platform for businesses from both sides to interact, explore market opportunities and find valuable partners. The scope of SCBA's activities has expanded beyond merchandise trade to include businesses in the manufacturing and transportation sectors, as well as the services industry, amongst others.

More platforms have been formed over the years to promote business and people-to-people relations between Singapore and China. In 1993, a group of 10 Singaporeans formed the Singapore China Friendship Association (新加坡–中国友好协会) with the objective of deepening the friendship and mutual understanding between the peoples of the two countries through exchange of visits and cultural activities. In 2007, Singapore launched Business China (通商中国) to nurture a bi-cultural group of Singaporeans comfortable with interacting in both English- and Chinese-speaking environments. It seeks to promote extensive use of the Chinese language as a medium of communication not only to sustain Singapore's multicultural heritage but also to build various forms of linkages (including economic, business, social, cultural and educational) with China. Over the

---

Xiaoping. See "Hon signs trade accord with Beijing", *The Sunday Times*, 30 December 1979, p. 1.

[22] This agreement was signed between the Chinese Vice Minister for Foreign Trade Wang Runsheng and the Permanent Secretary of Singapore's Ministry of Trade and Industry Ngiam Tong Dow. See "Boost in Trade Ties with China", *The Business Times*, 16 June 1980, p. 1.

[23] The first Singapore Trade Representative to China was Tan Song Chuan, then Deputy Trade Director of Trade Development.

years, Singapore youth, businessmen and professionals have benefitted from the programmes and activities sponsored by Business China.

Ping Pong Diplomacy

When "ping-pong diplomacy" is mentioned, one would normally associate this phrase with the American ping pong team that was invited to China in April 1971 for a series of friendly table tennis matches with their Chinese counterparts.[24] This exchange, involving the first group of Americans allowed into China since the Chinese Communist Party assumed power in 1949, is widely regarded to have helped pave the way for détente between the United States and China. What is less known is that ping pong diplomacy was also at work in the Singapore-China relationship.

In fact, when China decided to improve its relations with Singapore (as part of an overall shift in its foreign policy orientation) in the 1970s, the first contact came through "ping pong diplomacy" in 1971.[25]

To be exact, the exchange of table tennis teams between Singapore and China did not begin only in 1971. After the PRC was formed in October 1949, the first group of sportsmen from China visited Singapore in September 1950.[26] They were described as a "crack" table tennis team from Shanghai. This team partnered with a team from Hong Kong to compete in a triangular table tennis meet involving Hong Kong, Malaya and India.[27] As expected, the combined Shanghai-Hong Kong team trounced their Malayan and Indian counterparts.[28]

---

[24] On 14 April 1971, Premier Zhou Enlai received the visiting table tennis teams from the United States, Canada, Colombia and Nigeria at the Great Hall of the People in Beijing. The table tennis teams from Britain and Australia also subsequently visited China in the same month of April 1971.

[25] Lee Kuan Yew, *From Third World to First*, p. 575.

[26] "First sportsmen from red China", *The Straits Times*, 8 September 1950, p. 12.

[27] "China team meets Malaya tonight", *The Straits Times*, 20 September 1950, p. 12. The matches were held at the Happy World Stadium. Happy World Stadium was another famous location in Singapore (apart from Great World mentioned earlier) with entertainment outlets including cabaret, operas, movies, gaming, sports matches, and shopping. For further details, please see "Gay World (Happy World)" by the Singapore National Library Board, accessed on 3 February 2015: http://eresources.nlb.gov.sg/infopedia/articles/SIP_1044_2006-06-01.html.

[28] "Wing Sun beat Indians 4-1", *The Straits Times*, 25 September 1950, p. 12.

When Singapore was preparing to host the first Asian Table Tennis Championship in November 1952,[29] it had to grapple with the issue of accepting the participation of a team from China. Unlike the 1950 game when Shanghai partnered Hong Kong, China would now be sending a team entirely on its own and on a much larger and more important platform.

A month before the Asian Table Tennis Championship, China made public its intention to send a table tennis team to Singapore to participate in the event.[30] This announcement apparently caught the Singapore organising committee by surprise as they had not extended an invitation to China to participate. In the end the British colonial government considered it "inadvisable" to allow the Chinese team to enter Singapore in view of the existing state of emergency that was still in force.[31]

The Cultural Revolution that began in 1966 marked the lowest point in China's table tennis history.[32] Thus, when Singapore hosted the Eighth Asian Table Tennis Championship in August 1967, China did not indicate its intention to send a team.[33] This event was the first international meet hosted by Singapore since its independence in 1965.

---

[29] The Asian Table Tennis Championship was organised by the Table Tennis Federation of Asia (TTFA) from 1952–1972. The TTFA was founded as a supplementary organisation to the International Table Tennis Federation (that administers the World Table Tennis Championships) in promoting the game in Asia.

[30] "Red China team for Singapore", *The Straits Times*, 16 October 1952, p. 1.

[31] "Red China barred", *The Straits Times*, 10 November 1952, p. 12. The state of emergency was declared by the British colonial government of Malaya (of which Singapore was a part of) in 1948 and lifted in 1960. The emergency sanctioned measures to be taken against the Malayan Communist Party that mounted a guerrilla campaign to oppose the formation of the Federation of Malaya in 1948.

[32] Before the Cultural Revolution, China had already made a name for itself in the international table tennis circuit when it won multiple World Championship titles from 1959 to 1965. In 1967 and 1969, China did not participate at the World Table Tennis Championship due to the Cultural Revolution. Several Chinese players and coaches were persecuted during this period. See Mayumi Itoh, "Mr Goto goes to Beijing: The Origin of Ping-pong Diplomacy", *Sino-Japanese Studies*, Vol. 18 (2011), p. 22, accessed 3 February 2015: http://chinajapan.org/articles/index.php/sjs/article/viewFile/25/29.

[33] Those that participated included teams from Singapore, South Korea, Hong Kong, India, Indonesia, Iran, Japan, Malaysia, the Philippines, South Vietnam and Formosa (Taiwan). See "Let's help each other to improve, says Othman Wok", *The Straits Times*, 11 August 1967, p. 20.

China started to signal its return to the table tennis world when it sent a team to participate in the World Table Tennis Championship in Nagoya from March to April 1971 after an absence of six years.[34] It took a step further by inviting teams from 51 countries when it hosted the First Afro-Asian Table Tennis Invitational Tournament in Beijing in November 1971. It was in this context that the China Table Tennis Association (中国乒乓球协会) extended an invitation to the Singapore Table Tennis Association (STTA) (新加坡乒乓球协会). Singapore responded by sending a 14-member team.

The decision to participate was announced by Lim Kim San (林金山), then President of the STTA and Minister of Education, at a dinner to celebrate the 41st anniversary of STTA in October 1971. It was also an occasion to mark the sending off of the Singapore team to Beijing.[35] In announcing the decision, Lim reportedly said that table tennis had helped to "make friends and build bridges across frontiers".[36]

This was the first time that Beijing had extended an official invitation to Singapore sportsmen to visit the country. More importantly, it indicated Beijing's desire to improve relations with Singapore which it had previously vociferously vilified. In a highly symbolic gesture, Premier Zhou Enlai attended the closing ceremony of the tournament on 14 November 1971 and even met with all the participating teams the following day (Singapore included).[37]

The tempo of the exchanges between Singapore and China increased after the Afro-Asian Table Tennis Friendship Games. A few months later, in May 1972, Singapore sent a delegation to participate at the inaugural meeting of the Asian Table Tennis Union (ATTU) hosted by Beijing.[38] The ATTU was formed with the intention to replace the Table Tennis Federation of

---

[34] The last World Table Tennis Championship Title that China won was in 1965 in Ljubljana (Slovenia).

[35] "S'pore ping-pong team to play in Peking", *The Straits Times*, 24 October 1971, p. 1. The STTA was established in 1931.

[36] "Chou to meet ping-pong team", *The Straits Times*, 25 October 1971, p. 1.

[37] Fan Hong and Lu Zhouxiang, "Sport in the Great Proletarian Cultural Revolution (1966–1976)", *The International Journal of the History of Sport*, Vol. 29, No. 1 (January 2012), p. 57.

[38] There were 16 countries represented at this inaugural meeting. They were Singapore, Cambodia, China, North Korea, Iran, Iraq, Japan, Kuwait, Lebanon, Malaysia, Nepal, Pakistan, Palestine, Sri Lanka, Syria and Vietnam. Singapore and Malaysia were the only two countries from ASEAN that were present.

Asia where Taiwan was a member and China was not.[39] Chinese Premier Zhou Enlai, who had pushed for the formation of the ATTU, met with the visiting delegates.[40] At the same meeting, the Singapore representatives reportedly invited China to send its table tennis team to play in Singapore.[41]

The Chinese table tennis team comprising 21 members arrived in Singapore in July 1972 for an eight-day visit. Over a few nights, they played against their Singapore counterparts and also held exhibition matches among themselves that thrilled capacity crowds at the Gay World Stadium.[42]

Reflecting the importance Singapore attached to the visiting Chinese delegation, Lim Kim San, the President of STTA, hosted a reception for the delegation at the Istana.[43] In his memoirs, Lee Kuan Yew disclosed that before the arrival of the Chinese table tennis team, Singapore had turned down two earlier requests for visiting delegations from China. One was a troupe of acrobats while the other was a Beijing trade mission.[44]

Riding on the momentum generated by the visiting Chinese table tennis team in July 1972, Singapore sent a 15-member team to participate in the Asian Table Tennis Championship in Beijing in September 1972. This was the first Asian Table Tennis Championship hosted by China since the ATTU was formed in May 1972. Singapore continued to send teams to participate in major table tennis events hosted by China such as the First Asian-African-Latin American Table Tennis Invitational Tournament in Beijing from August to September 1973. This tournament is an enlarged version of the Afro-Asian Table Tennis Invitational Tournament that includes teams from Latin America in addition to those from Asia and Africa.

It is difficult to ascertain the contribution of the Singapore-China ping-pong diplomacy to the improvement in bilateral ties. But what can reasonably be concluded is that China embarked on people-to people diplomacy via ping-pong and other sports to improve relations with countries which it

---

[39] The ATTU was officially recognised by the International Table Tennis Federation as its subordinate organisation representing Asia at its 33rd Congress in Calcutta in April 1975.

[40] "Peking to stage 'new' Tourney", *The Straits Times*, 9 May 1972, p. 27.

[41] "China T.T. team to tour Singapore", *The Straits Times*, 18 May 1972, p. 22.

[42] "Scintillating show by China", *The Straits Times*, 9 July 1972, p. 28; "China power their way to 3-0 win", *The Straits Times*, 10 July 1972, p. 28; "Chinese 'lose' two matches to Singapore", *The Straits Times*, 11 July 1972, p. 27.

[43] "Kim San plays host to China table tennis team", *The Straits Times*, 15 July 1972, p. 1.

[44] Lee Kuan Yew, *From Third World to First*, p. 576.

had previously vilified, Singapore included. Singapore was also ready, although it displayed more caution and a preference for a gradual pace, to engage in people-to-people exchange with China. It is reasonable to argue that such exchanges did help in some way to "sweeten the ground" before Singapore and China initiated official contacts in the mid-1970s. At the very least, it helped to make the official contacts appear less abrupt.

Today, the fact that Singapore has successfully inducted talented Chinese paddlers to join the national table tennis team is a sign of how far people-to-people relations has progressed. This infusion of new citizens has helped raise the standard of the game and brought glory to Singapore. In 2007, Li Jiawei (李佳薇) and Wang Yuegu (王月古) emerged third in the women's doubles at the World Table Tennis Championship. This was the first world championship medal won by Singapore.

In 2008, Feng Tianwei (冯天薇), Li Jiawei and Wang Yuegu clinched a Silver medal in the women's team event at the Beijing Olympics, ending the Republic's 48-year wait for an Olympic medal. In 2012, Feng Tianwei clinched Singapore's first individual Olympic medal in 52 years when she took the Bronze in the women's singles. Feng Tianwei, Li Jiawei and Wang Yuegu went on to secure a second Bronze medal for Singapore in the women's team event.[45]

Tourism Exchanges

Apart from sports exchanges, tourism flows is another important dimension of people-to-people relations between Singapore and China. This section will focus on how the flow of Chinese tourists to Singapore has changed over the years, the distinguishing features of Chinese travellers to Singapore and some local perceptions of these Chinese visitors.

Before we look at the inflow of Chinese travellers, a few words about Singapore travellers to China is in order. The number of Singapore visitors (including repeat travellers) to China has stayed around 1 million annually between 2010 and 2012. In 1995, this figure stood around 260,000. By 2010,

---

[45] In addition, in 2010, the Singapore Table Tennis National Women's Team made history by upsetting defending champion China at the World Table Tennis Championship in Moscow. See Singapore Table Tennis Association website, accessed on 5 March 2015: http://www.stta.org.sg/about-us/important-milestones.

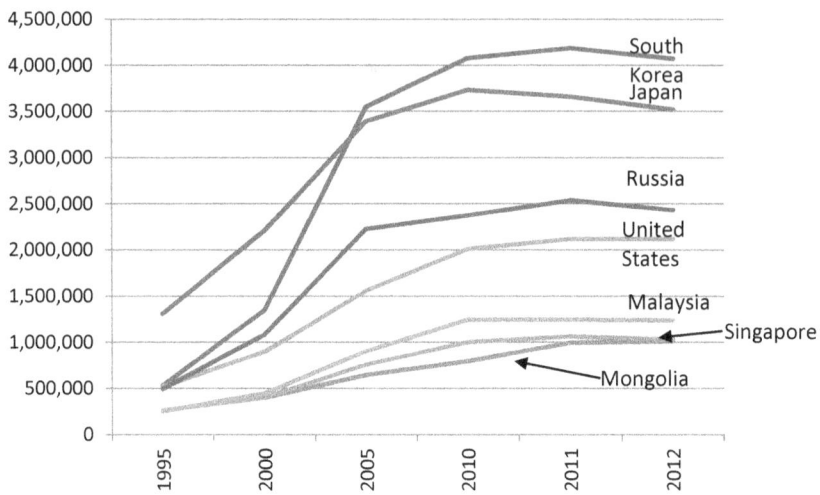

Figure 1. Top visitor-generating markets for China (1995–2012).

Source: China Statistical Yearbook (2013).

this figure had risen to 1 million (an almost fourfold increase) and has stayed relatively constant since (see Figure 1). To a large extent, this relatively stable figure of 1 million should not come as a surprise in view of Singapore's small population size. There is therefore a limit to how much Singapore visitors to China can grow.

The top few source markets for China in 2012 in terms of visitor arrivals are South Korea (4.06 million), followed by Japan (3.5 million), Russia (2.4 million), United States (2.1 million) and Malaysia (1.2 million). Singapore was ranked sixth with 1 million visitors to China, a commendable ranking given its small population size. Singapore was ahead of other countries such as Mongolia, India, Indonesia, United Kingdom, Germany, France, Canada and Australia. However, the Singapore figure of 1 million has to be set in context as it represents only 3.8% of the total number of foreign visitors to China.

On the other side of the coin, the number of Chinese visitors to Singapore has grown at a much faster rate and has far greater potential for further growth. Japan and Taiwan were the two most important tourism source markets for Singapore in 1995, but their importance has declined over the years and reached a low point around the period of 2008 to 2009.[46]

---

[46] In 1995, the number of Japanese and Taiwanese visitors to Singapore stood at 1.18 million and 0.56 million respectively. By 2009, the number of Japanese and Taiwanese visitors to

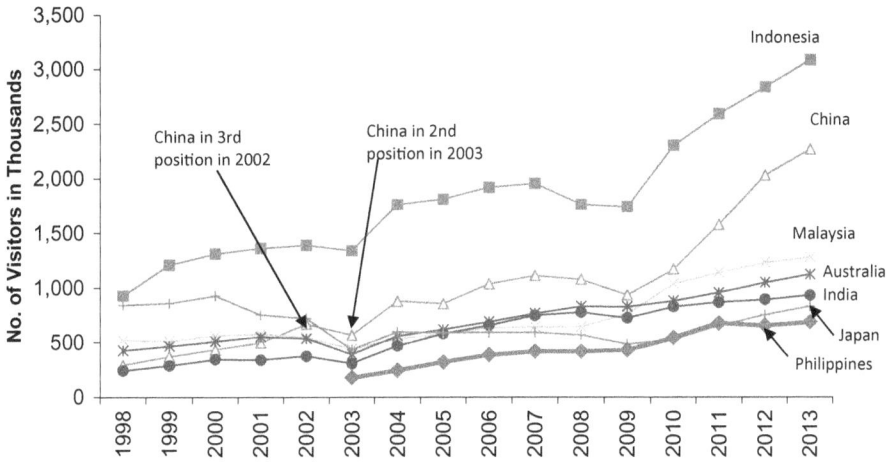

Figure 2. Top visitor-generating markets for Singapore (1998–2013).

Source: Singapore Tourism Board Statistics (various years).

Note: The countries highlighted above are the top seven visitor generating markets for Singapore in 2013.

The decline in the number of Japanese and Taiwanese tourists has been offset by increases in tourist arrivals from other countries such as China, India and Australia. Among these countries, the growth in Chinese visitor arrivals to Singapore has been most significant.

In 1995, the number of Chinese visitors to Singapore stood at a modest figure of 200,000.[47] Over the years, the number of China tourists has shown strong and steady growth. Chinese visitors to Singapore crept into the 10th position (at 0.24 million) for the first time in 1997, rising to 8th position in 1998 (0.29 million), 3rd position in 2002 (at 0.67 million after over-taking Malaysia and Australia) and 2nd position in 2003 (at 0.57 million after over-taking Japan, see Figure 2). It is worth mentioning that the tourist arrival figures for Chinese travellers to Singapore only started to appear in the 2004 issue of the *Yearbook of Statistics Singapore*. This in itself is an indication of the growing importance of Chinese travellers to Singapore.

The number of Chinese travellers to Singapore has remained in second position since 2003. Nevertheless, in terms of the absolute figure, the

---

Singapore had declined to 0.49 million and 0.16 million respectively. See Chiang Min-hua, "Tourism in China-Singapore Economic Relations", *EAI Background Brief* (unpublished), No. 664 (7 October 2011), p. 9 and *Yearbook of Statistics Singapore* (various issues).

[47] *Yearbook of Statistics Singapore 2006* by Singapore Department of Statistics.

number has quadrupled from 0.57 million (in 2003) to 2.3 million (in 2013). Perhaps more significant is the increase in the proportion of Chinese visitors to Singapore. In 2003, Chinese travellers comprised 9.3% of the total number of visitors to Singapore. Ten years later, in 2013, this proportion has risen to 14.6%.

Another indication of the growing importance of Chinese travellers can be gleaned from their contribution to Singapore's tourism receipts. In 2008, China overtook India to become the second top Total Expenditure of Visitors (TEV) generator. In 2013, China took the top spot from Indonesia to become Singapore's biggest tourism receipt market.

In 2013, China, Indonesia and India in that order were the top 3 tourism receipts generating markets, accounting for 40% of Singapore's total tourism receipts.[48] Visitors from China spent a total of $2,981 million (an 18.5% increase from 2012), followed by Indonesia at $2,978 (a 5.2% decline from 2012) and India at $1,224 million (a 9% growth from 2012). In percentage terms, Chinese travellers contributed almost 17% of Singapore's total tourism receipts.[49]

In terms of tourism receipts per capita expenditure in 2013, Chinese visitors took the second spot, an improvement from their fifth ranking in 2012. Each Chinese traveller spent an average of $1,313, compared to their Indian and Indonesian counterparts of $1,311 and $964 respectively.[50] Surprisingly, the only foreign traveller that spent more than the Chinese in 2013 was the Vietnamese at $1,618.

Another important characteristic of a Chinese traveller is that he or she tends to spend a disproportionate amount of expenses on shopping. In 2013, 47% of tourism receipts of Chinese travellers was derived from shopping, representing an increase of 9.3% from 2012. In contrast, the

---

[48] This excludes expenditure on sightseeing, entertainment and gaming. See *Annual Report on Tourism Statistics 2013* by Singapore Tourism Board.

[49] The proportion for Indonesian travellers is also almost at 17% followed by Indian travellers at 6.8%.

[50] In 2012, the tourism receipts per expenditure of a Chinese traveller was ranked fifth at S$1,237, behind the US traveller (at $1,375), the Thai traveller (at $1,302), the Indian traveller (at $1,255) and Japanese traveller (at $1,254). See *Annual Report on Tourism Statistics 2012* by Singapore Tourism Board.

proportion of expenditure by other foreign travellers on shopping ranged from 9% to 31%.[51]

The economic benefits to Singapore of Chinese visitors are obvious based on the data cited above. There is also the intangible benefit of promoting better understanding and linkages when Chinese travellers interact with the locals in Singapore. However, there is also a negative dimension in the form of some Chinese tourists behaving in a loud and brusque manner while travelling overseas.[52] Furthermore, reports about the unscrupulous behaviour of some Chinese residing in Singapore have served to reinforce negative perceptions of the Chinese.[53]

The tourism exchanges between Singapore and China, especially from China to Singapore, is expected to increase further due to China's large population, greater affluence and better connectivity.[54] To be sure, the negative reports about Chinese travellers need to be put in perspective as the benefits do appear to far outweigh the downsides. Nevertheless, there may be a need to generate greater awareness among Chinese travellers of the importance of being sensitive to the cultures and values of the countries they are visiting as each of them is an "Ambassador" of China in his or her travel overseas.

---

[51] American travellers spent 9% of their tourism receipts on shopping while the figure for the Indonesian travellers was 31%.

[52] "Chinese Tourists: Mind Your Manners", *The Economist*, 6 November 2013, accessed on 5 February 2015: http://www.economist.com/blogs/analects/2013/11/chinese-tourists.

[53] "Yang Yin charged for misappropriating money from wealthy widow", *Channel NewsAsia*, 18 December 2014. Yang Yin, a former tour guide from China, had befriended a wealthy Singapore widow when the latter was travelling in China. Yang later moved in to stay with the widow in her Singapore home.

[54] This is expected to be the general trend. In the short run, however, there could be disruptions. Already, in the first 11 months of 2014, Singapore Tourism Board figures indicate that the total number of Chinese travellers to Singapore had dipped to 1.3 million. It was reported that the factors contributing to this decline included a tourism law implemented by China in October 2013 that tightened regulations on overseas travel, the disappearance of Malaysian flight MH370 (in March 2014), the abduction of Chinese visitors in Sabah (in April and May 2014), and the ensuing political unrest in Thailand. A large proportion of Chinese tourists usually visit Singapore, Malaysia and Thailand as part of a multi-destination tour involving these countries. See "Decline in Chinese tourists hits Singapore visitor arrivals", *AFP*, 15 October 2014, accessed on 5 February 2015: http://news.asiaone.com/news/travel/decline-chinese-tourists-hits-singapore-visitor-arrivals.

Concluding Remarks

This essay has looked at three aspects of people-to-people relations between Singapore and China. The first is a historical overview of the interactions between Singapore and China that began in the seventh century. It also highlights the exchanges among traders and working level officials in Singapore with their counterparts in China in the 1950s and 1960s before Minister Rajaratnam's visit to China in 1975. The second part focuses on the role that ping-pong diplomacy played in the relationship between the two countries. We contend that the exchanges of table tennis teams from both sides especially in the early 1970s helped to make it easier for the two countries to improve relations in the mid-1970s.

The third part of the essay seeks to bring readers to more present developments by looking at how the tourism relationship, involving ordinary folks from both sides, has developed and progressed over the years. This interaction shows how asymmetric the relationship between Singapore and China is. For China, Singapore travellers hardly make an impact on its tourism sector. But for Singapore, Chinese travellers form a key pillar of not only the Singapore tourism sector but also the Singapore economy as a whole given their absolute numbers and contribution to its tourism receipts. Singapore depends much more on tourist arrivals from China. This dependence is likely to increase in the years ahead as there is much potential for more Chinese to travel to Singapore.

This essay does not pretend to be exhaustive in describing the people-to-people relations between Singapore and China. Instead, what it has done is to selectively highlight elements of the people-to-people relationship that is less well-known. In doing so, it seeks to draw readers' attention to what has taken place and is taking place beyond the high-brow official and diplomatic exchanges between the two countries. Hopefully, readers' interests will be piqued and they will be interested to find out more about the people-to-people exchanges that exist between Singapore and China. There is no denying that any bilateral relationship between nations can only grow stronger and be more enduring if it encompasses broad and deep engagement in various fields and at many levels. This calls for more people-to-people interactions.

CHAPTER 16

Singapore as a Centre of Southeast Asian Chinese
Some Reflections

Leo SURYADINATA

When Sir Stamford Raffles "discovered" the small island sandwiched between the Malayan peninsula and the Indonesian archipelago in 1819 he envisaged that Singapore's strategic location would make it the centre for maritime Southeast Asia and beyond. What he did not foresee was the huge influx of Chinese immigrants who not only built Singapore into a trading centre but also transformed it into a socio-cultural centre for the Chinese in the region.

As Singapore celebrates its 50th anniversary of nationhood, it continues to be a centre for maritime Southeast Asia, and for the Chinese community in the region. This essay seeks to show the social and cultural networks that link Singapore's Chinese community to the Chinese communities in the region. Over the years, these intricate ties have contributed towards Singapore's economy and its role as the regional hub for education and for Chinese culture and literature.

Beginning in the 16th century, European powers competed for footholds and colonies in Southeast Asia. They started dividing up the region arbitrarily, resulting in British Malaya, the Dutch East Indies, Spanish Philippines, French Indochina, British Burma and an independent but shrinking Siam/Thailand. The colonial boundaries, however, were not rigidly fixed and interactions among local people continued to ignore them. This was also the case for the Chinese communities scattered throughout the region.

Soon after the landing of Raffles and the establishment of British rule over Singapore and the Malayan peninsula, traders, labourers, artisans, carpenters, adventurers, writers, and colonial officials followed suit. Singapore soon became a multi-ethnic city and business centre. The immigrant Chinese became the largest and dominant group as economic prosperity attracted newcomers to work and stay in the island.

Shipping

In fact, long before the arrival of the Western powers, the Chinese were already present in Southeast Asia, and some Western scholars such as Leonard Blusse called the 18th century the "Chinese Century".[1] The maritime trade was dominated by Chinese traders. It was only in the 19th century that the Europeans began to gradually dominate the scene.

By the end of the 19th century and the beginning of the 20th century, Southeast Asia's maritime trade was transformed as sailing junks gave way to steamships. The Singapore River was transformed into the centre for Chinese shipping from all over the region as intra-regional trade grew. Local Chinese shipping companies were established, and neighbouring Chinese shipping companies also set up branches, and some even headquarters, in Singapore.

The first Southeast Asian multinational company, the Oei Tiong Ham Concern (黄仲涵总公司) (formerly known as Kian Gwan 建源), though based in Semarang, Indonesia, established a branch office in Singapore in 1914. When the Tan Kim Tian Steamship Co went into liquidation in 1911, Oei Tiong Ham (黄仲涵) bought five ships from the liquidated company and in 1912 formed a company called Heap Eng Moh (协荣茂) Steamship Co.[2] Oei Tiong Ham himself later moved to Singapore with his family and died in Singapore in 1924.

After World War II, more Indonesian Chinese shipping firms set up offices in Singapore. Most well-known are Tong Djoe (唐裕) and Adil Nurimba alias Lim Eng Hway (林英怀). Tong Djoe (1922–), a Sumatran-born Chinese who belongs to the Ann Kway clan group, was educated in

---

[1] Leonard Blusse, "Chinese Century: The Eighteenth Century in the China Sea Region", *Archipel* 58 (1999), Volume III, pp. 107–129.
[2] Charles Coppel, "Oei Tiong Ham", in Leo Suryadinata, ed., *Southeast Asian Personalities of Chinese Descent: A Biographical Dictionary*. (Singapore: Institute of Southeast Asian Studies, 2012), pp. 797–798.

a Chinese school in Singapore. In 1943 he joined a small shipping firm owned by his brother, and during the Indonesian independence movement, he supplied rice, medicine and military equipment to the Indonesian Republican Army. It was during this period that he became acquainted with Indonesian nationalists who later became leaders after Indonesia's independence (such as A. K. Gani and Ibnu Sutowo).[3]

Tong and his brother were invited by A. K. Gani (1905–1968), then the Governor of South Sumatra and during 1946–1948 Minister of Economic Affairs and Vice-Prime Minister, to help establish the Indonesian National Shipping Company (PELNI) in 1949. In 1953 Tong himself formed a shipping company. Towards the end of the 1950s he became the overseas representative of Pertamina (the Indonesian state oil company) and its agent in Singapore. The chief of Pertamina was Ibnu Sutowo (1914–2001). In 1961 Tong Djoe established the Tunas company in Singapore, which was involved in shipping and import-export trade. Later it was developed into the Tunas Group, with business extending to Indonesia and Hong Kong. The Group continued to engage in shipping, travel and tourism industries. In the 1990s his business started to decline partly due to over expansion. Although Tong still keeps his Indonesian citizenship, he has served as the President of the Singapore Ship Owners' Association and Singapore Ann Kway Association (安溪会馆 *Anxi Huiguan*).

Another Chinese shipping giant who had close connections with Singapore was Lim Eng Hway (1922–2006). He was born in Sumatra but was educated at Chung Ling School (钟灵中学) in Penang. In 1958 he moved to Jakarta and in 1963 he established PT Gesuri Lloyd. Prior to his success he used to make three trips a week across the Melaka Straits to transport goods to and from North Sumatra to Malaya and Singapore.

In recent years, the biggest Indonesian Chinese owned shipping company involved in bulk shipping is Berlian Laju Tanker. It was founded by Hadi Surya alias Ong King Kie (王庆基 1936–) of Surabaya, from the Daya Sakti Group. It began with two oil tankers chartered to Pertamina and grew rapidly in the 1990s. It is listed on both the Jakarta and Singapore stock exchanges.

---

[3] Liu Hong, "Tong Djoe", in Leo Suryadinata, ed., *Southeast Asian Personalities of Chinese Descent*, pp. 1201–1204.

Other Businesses

Singapore not only attracted the Chinese shipping companies of the region. Businessmen of Chinese descent who were involved in trading activities in other Southeast Asian countries also made their way to the thriving city. Among them were the Aw brothers (胡氏兄弟) of Burma/Myanmar, Boon Haw (文虎) and Boon Par (文豹), who moved their well-known Tiger Balm to Singapore and from here it spread to the region. Aw Boon Haw later became a leader of the Hakka community in Singapore.

Other Chinese enterprises which moved into Singapore after World War II included Koh Leong Hin (高隆兴) owned by Koh Teck Kin (高德根), the Metro Group (美罗集团) by Ong Tjoe Kim (王梓琴), the O.G. Company by Tay Tee Peng (郑智炳), Zhongqiao Department Store (中侨百货) and Zongyi Organisation (综艺机构) by Lin Rishun (林日顺) and Tat Lee Bank by Goh Tjoei Kok (吴水阁).

Koh Teck Kin (1911–1966) is probably the most interesting. He was a Hokkien from Long Xi (龙溪) who migrated to Palembang (Sumatra), Indonesia, when he was young and worked in his father's store, Koh Leong Hin. Soon after World War II, Koh Teck Kin established a branch in Singapore, dealing with agricultural products, shipping and remittances. Later he was also involved in the rubber business. In the 1950s he established Ho Chiang (和昌) Shipping with four ships to ply between Indonesian and Malaysian harbours. He eventually became a Singaporean. In 1954 he was elected as the President of Singapore Chinese Chamber of Commerce and served for nine years. In 1964 he was elected as the Chairman of the Nanyang University Council and after Singapore's separation, Koh served as Singapore's first High Commissioner to Malaysia. He died in the following year.

After World War II, and especially in the 1950s, many Chinese trading firms from Malaya/Malaysia and Indonesia came to Singapore to establish new footholds. For instance, Robert Kuok (Kuok Hock Hien 郭鹤年 1923–, Johor) first moved his shipping business to Singapore in 1948. In the following year he established Kuok Brothers Sdn Berhad in Malaya and began to engage in sugar and other agricultural products. In the 1970s he moved into real estate, finance and hotel industry. He later moved his headquarters to Hong Kong. Today the Kuok Brothers' businesses extend across Malaysia, Singapore and Hong Kong.

The Hong Leong Group's story is just the opposite. China-born Kwek Hong Png (郭芳枫 1913–1994), the founder of the Hong Leong Group (丰隆集团), came to Singapore in 1928. He set up Hong Leong Co in 1941 together with his three brothers. The company started out in construction and trading, later moving to finance and also expanded to Malaysia. Hong Leong Singapore is now headed by his son Kwek Leng Beng (郭令明 1941–), while Hong Leong Malaysia is led by his nephew Quek Leng Chan (郭令灿 1941–). It is said that the "the Quek family of Malaysia (Quek Leng Chan) and Kweks of Singapore (Kwek Leng Beng) hold significant proportions in a complex interlocking shareholding structure".[4]

Another example was Goh Tjoei Kok (吴水阁 1905–1994), a China-born migrant to Indonesia at the age of 15. His first business in the garment industry was not successful, but his subsequent move to rubber changed his fortune dramatically. After World War II he moved to Singapore and established the Tat Lee Company (达利公司) which dealt in steel. In 1973, with a capital of $36 million, he established the Tat Lee Bank (达利银行). Unfortunately after his demise the bank's business was affected by the 1997 financial crisis. In 1998 it merged with Keppel Bank and became KeppelTatLee Bank (吉宝达利银行). The bank was eventually purchased by OCBC Bank (华侨银行) in 2001.[5]

After Singapore achieved independence in 1965, major ethnic Chinese companies in the region began expanding their businesses to the new Republic. For instance, the largest business group in Indonesia during the Suharto era, the Salim Group founded by Liem Sioe Liong (林绍良 alias Sudono Salim, 1917–2012), and the Lippo Group (力宝集团) founded by Li Wenzheng (李文正 alias Mochtar Riady, 1929–) shifted a large part of their operations to the island state. Another Indonesian tycoon Oei Hong Leong (黄鸿年 1941–), a son of the Sinar Mas Group's boss Oei Ek Tjhong (黄奕聪 alias Eka Tjipta Widjaja 1923–) moved to Singapore to start his own business after spending many years in China. He established the United Industrial Corporation (UIC) (联合工业有限公司). As many Indonesian

---

[4] Beh Loo See, "Quek Leng Chan", in Leo Suryadinata, ed., *Southeast Asian Personalities*, p. 914.

[5] "吴水阁 (Goh Tjoei Kok)", 百度百科, baike.baidu.com/view/8371273.htm; see also "A Brief History of Keppel TatLee Bank", www.keppelbank.com.sg/history/.

Chinese businessmen are also members and even leaders of some Singapore clan associations it is pertinent to discuss the interactions among the regional clan associations briefly.

Chinese Clan Associations

Clan associations (会馆 *huiguan*) began as mutual help organisations established by the Chinese overseas to help their fellow clan members when they moved to countries outside China. Hence, in the many enclaves of Chinese communities in Southeast Asia, one can find clan associations based on geographical or kinship ties. Singapore, with its predominant Chinese population has about 300 registered *huiguan*.

As many of the traditional welfare services provided by the Singapore clan associations have been taken over by the government, the *huiguan* have initiated new roles to ensure their continued relevance. Besides the promotion and preservation of the Chinese heritage, many of these clan associations have begun creating regional and global networks based on kinship ties. Singapore's associations have played host to a myriad of international clan meetings. A World Fujian Conference held in 2012 drew more than 4,000 attendees from Singapore and overseas.

Singapore's recent development as a hub for global clansmen meetings has been boosted by the strong business links with the Chinese in Southeast Asia. Take, for example, the Singapore Futsing Association (新加坡福清会馆) and its successful establishment of the International Federation of Futsing Clan Convention in 1988.

That year the *huiguan* of Futsing clansmen from Fujian province held a triple celebration — the Association's 78th anniversary, its Poi Ching (培青) School's 68th anniversary and the official opening of the Futsing Building in Allenby Road.[6] The celebration attracted more than 300 overseas Futsing clansmen from nearby Indonesia and Malaysia, and distant countries like the US and Europe. The completion of the building and the grand celebration owed much to the fact that it was supported by people like Liem Sioe Liong and Mochtar Riady. Arising from the forum

---

[6] 王田 (Wang Tian), "新加坡福清会馆三庆纪念 (Singapore Futsing Association Triple Anniversaries Celebration)", 《融情 (*Futsing News*)》, 创刊号 1988, p. 4.

discussion held in conjunction with the triple celebration, the International Federation of Futsing Clan Convention (世界福清同乡联谊会) was created, with Liem as its President and the Singapore Futsing Association as its secretariat.

Speaking as Honorary Chairman of the Singapore Futsing Clan Association at the grand celebration, Liem revealed that the world convention had chosen Singapore as its venue because "Singapore's communications are very well-developed with modern facilities, it is the most convenient place for the Futsing people to assemble and exchange views."[7]

Another clan association that went global with the support of Indonesian clansmen is the Singapore Ann Kway Association. In 1977, the *huiguan* celebrated its 55th anniversary with Dr Goh Keng Swee (吴庆瑞), then Deputy Prime Minister, as guest of honour. About 2,000 participants attended the function. Tong Djoe, an Indonesian Chinese as previously mentioned, was elected as President and held the position until 1992. In the last year of his term which coincided with the 70th anniversary of the association, Tong Djoe initiated the establishment of the World Ann Kway Convention (世界安溪同乡联谊会). The Convention's secretariat is based in Singapore while the bi-annual meetings are rotated among member countries.

Chinese Educational and Cultural Hub

Chinese education in Singapore was initially started by the community during the British colonial days. At the beginning of the 20th century more Chinese schools teaching in Mandarin and the first Chinese high school (华侨中学 Hwa Chong) was established. Many Chinese students from neighbouring countries came to Singapore to receive Chinese education, especially after World War II.

The first Chinese medium university in Southeast Asia, Nanyang University (南洋大学) (Nantah 南大) was established in Singapore in 1955. Proposed by the Chairman of the Singapore Hokkien Huay Kuan (福建会馆), Tan Lark Sye (陈六使) who personally pledged $5 million to the university fund, Nantah was built on land donated by the Huay Kuan in Jurong.

---

[7] "世界福清同乡联谊会成立 (Establishment of the International Federation of Futsing Clan Convention)", 《融情 (Futsing News)》, 创刊号 1988, p. 16.

The Chinese university was meant to provide tertiary education for Southeast Asian Chinese school graduates. Due to political and economic reasons, many Southeast Asian Chinese school graduates were unable or unwilling to go to mainland China and Taiwan for their tertiary education; the emergence of Nantah fulfilled the dream of these students. Hence the university's fundraising drives received tremendous support from the region's Chinese communities.

Nantah was officially opened in 1955 and began to accept Chinese high school graduates from Southeast Asia. When it first started, the majority of the students was from Singapore (325 students, 55.65%), with 41.61% (243 students) from Malaya, 1.54% (9 students) from northern Borneo, and only 0.34% (2 students) from Indonesia, the rest 0.56% (5 students) from other areas.[8] However, five years later, the number of Singapore students decreased to 721 (38.74%) while non-Singapore students increased to 1,140 (61.26%), of which 54.81% (1,020 students) came from Malaya, 3.28% (61 students) from north Borneo, 1.45% (27 students) from Indonesia and 1.72% (32 students) from other countries. In 1965, the 10-year old Nantah continued to attract more non-Singaporeans. More than half of Nantah undergraduates (60.01%) were from outside Singapore.[9]

In its first 10 years Nantah attracted some of the best talents from the Chinese schools in the region. The Nantah graduates, then numbering around 3,000,[10] worked and contributed towards the economies of Singapore and its neighbouring countries. Their contributions were especially notable in Singapore and Malaysia where the largest number of Nantah graduates was distributed. They were found in every field and occupied significant positions in education, journalism, commerce, banking, and the academic world. However, as Nantah degrees were generally not recognised by the regional governments, many graduates went into business and became wealthy businessmen. Many others also pursued further studies in the West and became outstanding academics in the region and beyond.

---

[8] "历年南洋大学依国籍分类学生人数分配表 (Distribution of Students by Nationality)", 《南洋大学创校十周年纪念特刊 1956–1966 (*Nanyang University 10th Anniversary Book*)》. (Singapore: Nanyang University, 1967), p. 317.

[9] Ibid.

[10] The actual number was 2,890, ibid., p. 319.

After Singapore became an independent state in 1965 Nantah gradually became a Singapore rather than a regional university. It underwent a series of reforms and the number of non-Singapore students started to be reduced. Nantah was eventually merged with the University of Singapore to form the National University of Singapore (NUS) (新加坡国立大学). In 1992 the Nanyang Technological University (NTU) (南洋理工大学) was founded at Nantah's old campus in Jurong. Both NUS and NTU keep about 20% of its annual enrolment for international students, and many of these are Southeast Asians of Chinese descent.

It should be pointed out that Nantah graduates played important roles in teaching and spreading Chinese culture and literature. After Singapore attained independence, many Nantah graduates who became writers founded the Singapore Writers' Association (新加坡作家协会). This association had greater interactions with writers from Taiwan and mainland China.

In 1980, another Chinese literary association, the Singapore Literature Society (新加坡文艺研究会) was established. It was first led by Yang Songnian (杨松年), a Nantah graduate. He was succeeded by Luo Ming (骆明) whose real name is Ye Kuncan (叶昆灿), also a Nantah graduate in 1990. The Singapore Literature Society has been active in collaborating with the Southeast Asian Chinese writers through ASEAN Literary Camps (亚细安文艺营). Its members include writers' associations in Singapore, Thailand, the Philippines, Indonesia and Brunei. It was first formed in 1988 and a literary camp was held in member countries every two years.

In addition to literary camps, the Singapore Literature Society also initiated the ASEAN Chinese Literature Awards (亚细安华文文学奖), which were given to outstanding Chinese writers in ASEAN. Much later, the Confucius Institute (孔子学院) at NTU initiated the Nanyang Chinese Literature Awards (南洋华文文学奖), which have been given only to Singaporeans. However, in 2014 a special award was given to a veteran Indonesian Chinese writer Oei Tong Pin (黄东平) to recognise his contributions to Chinese literature in Indonesia and beyond. The Chinese language was banned during the Suharto era and many Indonesian writers, including Oei, published their Chinese writings in Singapore.

Singapore has also been the hub for the propagation of Chinese textbooks in the region. From 1938 Chinese book stores and publishers based in

Singapore such as the World Book Company (世界书局), Shanghai Book Company (上海书局), Nanyang Book Company (南洋书局), Zhonghua Book Company (中华书局) and Commercial Book Company (商务书局) supplied Chinese textbooks to Chinese-medium schools in other Southeast Asian countries. This business became more active after World War II.[11] The last four book companies even combined to form a joint publishing firm (联营出版社) to publish textbooks for Chinese medium schools in the region. Although the collaboration was short-lived, the World Book Company and Shanghai Book Company continued to be active. The Shanghai Book company even published different editions of Chinese textbooks for the different countries in Southeast Asia, such as the Singapore-Malaya edition, Indonesian edition, Philippine edition, Thai edition, and Cambodian edition.[12]

Although there were no more Chinese medium school in Singapore after 1987, Chinese continues to be important as the "mother tongue" of the Chinese. Singapore's "Chinese as a Second Language" textbooks have been very popular in neighbouring countries. In Indonesia for instance, during the Suharto period (1966–1998) all Chinese schools were closed down. Even the teaching of the Chinese language was prohibited. As a result, there were many private tutors teaching Chinese at home. Many tutors used Singapore Chinese textbooks to teach Indonesian Chinese children. After the fall of Suharto, Chinese was allowed to be taught again. Some trilingual schools and Chinese language centres have adopted Singapore Chinese language textbooks. According to a report in *Lianhe Zaobao* (联合早报), Singapore Chinese textbooks since 2000 have been used in schools in the Philippines, Vietnam, Thailand and the United States.[13]

After 1965 many Chinese from neighbouring countries continued to send their children to Singapore, initially for Chinese education and later for bilingual education. Many come from Malaysia and Indonesia while smaller numbers come from other Southeast Asian countries. After the

[11] 林恩和 (Lin En He), "新加坡华文出版的峥嵘岁月: 1945–1965 新加坡华文出版的观察 (The Peak Years of Chinese Publishing in Singapore: 1945–1965 Observations on Chinese Publishing in Singapore)", 《亚洲文化 (*Asian Culture*)》No. 38, August 2014, pp. 107–116.
[12] Ibid., p. 110.
[13] 陈端能 (Chen Duan Neng), "本地的华文课本近年海外受落 (Local Chinese Textbooks Entering Overseas Markets in Recent Years)", 《联合早报 (*Lianhe Zaobao*)》, 10 February 2014.

1980s, Chinese from mainland China and Taiwan have also begun to send their children to study in Singapore, making Singapore a new hub of bilingual education for ethnic Chinese in the Asian region.

As early as the end of the 19th century, Chinese language newspapers were published in Singapore. The first Chinese language newspaper, *Lat Pau* (叻报) (1881–1932), was published in Singapore in 1881. The major Chinese newspapers such as *Nanyang Shang Pau* (南洋商报) and *Sin Chew Jit Poh* (星洲日报) came into being only in the second decade of the 20th century and they were read by Chinese readers beyond Singapore.[14]

Nanyang Siang Pau was established in 1923 by Tan Kah Kee (陈嘉庚),[15] a migrant from China's southern province who later became the leader of the Chinese community in Singapore, while *Sin Chew Jit Poh* was set up in 1929 by the Tiger Balm King, Aw Boon Haw, from Burma (Myanmar) who also had many newspapers outside Singapore. Both newspapers, though published in Singapore, had Malayan editions, but were controlled by the companies in Singapore. However, after Malaya and later Singapore achieved independence, both the Malayan *Nanyang Shang Pau* and *Sin Chew Jit Poh* were separated from their Singapore head offices. Singapore's *Nanyang* and *Sin Chew* papers eventually merged under Singapore Press Holdings (SPH) (新加坡报业控股) and the combined paper is known today as *Lianhe Zaobao*. In Malaysia the two papers remain separate.

Lianhe Zaobao is not only a major paper in Singapore; its electronic edition is widely read in Southeast Asia and China. Apparently, many Chinese find the reports on China and the region interesting and are not carried in many Chinese newspapers both in the region and China.

Peranakan Chinese

The Chinese in Singapore are not a homogenous group. Culturally they can be divided into the Peranakan Chinese (土生华人) and migrant Chinese (known as *sinkeh* 新客, a Hokkien term meaning "new guest") and their

---

[14]The information on Southeast Asian Chinese newspapers has been derived from 崔贵强 (Cui Gui Qiang),《东南亚华文日报现状之研究 (*A Study of Current Chinese Dailies in Southeast Asia*)》, 新加坡华裔馆, 南洋学会 (Singapore CHC and South Seas Society), 2002.

[15]Ibid., pp. 53–54.

descendants. The latter were called *totok* in Indonesia. The former have settled in this area much longer and are culturally more identified with the local population. Peranakans often use Malay, mixed with Hokkien and English or other European language as their medium of communication. The *sinkeh* who mostly arrived in the 20th century usually communicated in Chinese dialects or Mandarin.[16]

In the past, Peranakan Chinese in Singapore had connections with those in peninsular Malaya and the Dutch East Indies (Indonesia). Medan and Penang Peranakans interacted most often, while Singapore Peranakans interacted most frequently with their counterparts in Melaka (Malacca) and Batavia (Jakarta, Java). The rise of the Confucian movement in Singapore for instance, also affected Java. At the turn of the 20th century, some Peranakan Confucianists in Java came to Singapore to meet Lim Boon Keng (林文庆 1869–1957), who was then the leader of the Straits Chinese community in Singapore. Lim Boon Keng also visited Java to meet Chinese Peranakan leaders who supported Confucianism. He became adviser of the Batavia-based Tiong Hoa Hwee Koan (THHK) (中华会馆), a pan-Chinese organisation established in 1900, which initially aimed to promote the teachings of Confucius.[17] It should be noted, however, the medium of communication among the Peranakan leaders was either Malay or English.

As time passed, the THHK was transformed into an educational institution that promoted Chinese-medium schools and its leadership was gradually taken over by the *sinkeh* (*totok*) Chinese. As the Straits Settlements received more new Chinese immigrants, the interactions between the Chinese in Java and Singapore began to be conducted in Chinese. Peranakan Chinese in Java became more inward-looking and culturally became more Indonesian. During the Suharto era the Chinese were encouraged to be

---

[16] For a good discussion on the Peranakan Chinese and totok Chinese, see Leo Surydinata, "Peranakan Chinese Identities in Singapore and Malaysia: A Re-examination", in Leo Suryadinata, ed., *Ethnic Chinese in Singapore and Malaysia: A dialogue between Tradition and Modernity*. (Singapore: Times Academic Press, 2002), pp. 69–84.

[17] For a study of the rise of Confucianism in Indonesia, see 廖建裕 (Liao Jian Yu),《印尼孔教初探 (Preliminary Explorations into Confucianism in Indonesia)》, 新加坡华裔馆 (Singapore Chinese Heritage Centre), 2010; on the THHK, see *Riwajat Tiong Hoa Hwee Koan 40 Tahon* (Batavia, 1940).

assimilated into the indigenous Indonesian community. Both *sinkeh* and Peranakan associations were suppressed. The Peranakan identity was only revived after the fall of Suharto and the end of the New Order (1966–1998). After World War II, The Peranakan organisations in Singapore and Malaya were not developed either and few contacts were made between the Singapore and Indonesian Chinese Peranakans. Instead interactions among clan associations in the region increased.

Concluding Remarks

Long before its independence, strategically located Singapore had already been the centre for Southeast Asian Chinese. The region's shipping industry was well-developed in the late 19th and early 20th centuries and Singapore was the shipping and trading centre of the Chinese in the area. Singapore also became the Chinese educational hub in Southeast Asia, symbolised by the establishment of Nanyang University in 1955.

After Singapore's independence, the Republic has become a modern business hub as well as a global financial centre. The country's economic success also owes much to the strong people-to-people relations between the Singapore Chinese community and the rest of Southeast Asia. As this essay has shown, the Singapore Chinese have developed an intricate network of kinship, social and economic links in the region over the years. So long as it maintains its prosperity and stability, Singapore will continue to be a focal point of the Chinese in Southeast Asia.

Acknowledgements

Besides the 17 essayists who have provided invaluable insights of the Chinese community in Singapore, many unseen hands have helped in the publication of this book.

In particular, the editor would like to thank the secretariats of the Singapore Chinese Chamber of Commerce & Industry, the Singapore Federation of Chinese Clan Associations, the Chinese Development Assistance Council, Chinese Heritage Council, and Ee Hoe Hean for their assistance and provision of photos.

Thanks must also go to Dr Ho Yi Kai, who helped kick-start the project, and the editorial team led by Ms Dong Lixi at World Scientific.

www.ingramcontent.com/pod-product-compliance
Lightning Source LLC
Chambersburg PA
CBHW080130270326
41926CB00021B/4419